Multiplayer

I0004446

In the past decade, digital games have become a widely accepted form of media entertainment, moving from the traditional "core gamer" community into the mainstream media market.

With millions of people now enjoying gaming as interactive entertainment there has been a huge increase in interest in social multiplayer gaming activities. However, despite the explosive growth in the field over the past decade, many aspects of social gaming still remain unexplored, especially from a media and communication studies perspective.

Multiplayer: The Social Aspects of Digital Gaming is the first edited volume of its kind that takes a closer look at the various forms of human interaction in and around digital games, providing an overview of debates, past and present.

The book is divided into five parts that explore the following areas:

- Social Aspects of Digital Gaming
- Social Interaction in Virtual Worlds
- Online Gaming
- Co-Located and Console Gaming
- Risks and Challenges of Social Gaming.

This engaging interdisciplinary book will appeal to upper-level students, postgraduates and researchers in games research, specifically those focusing on new media and digital games, as well as researchers in media studies and mass communication.

Thorsten Quandt is a Professor of Communication Studies at the University of Münster. He is the founding chair of ECREA's Temporary Working Group "Digital Games Research." His research and teaching fields include online communication, media innovation research, digital games and online journalism.

Sonja Kröger (MA in Education, Media Studies and German Literature) works as a junior lecturer at the Institute of Communication Studies at the University of Hohenheim. Her research and teaching fields include media education, young children and media, and digital games with a focus on advertising.

Routledge Studies in European Communication Research and Education

Edited by Nico Carpentier, *Vrije Universiteit Brussel, Belgium and Charles University, Czech Republic* and
François Heinderyckx, *Université Libre de Bruxelles, Belgium*
Series Advisory Board: Denis McQuail, Robert Picard and Jan Servaes

ECREA

http://www.ecrea.eu

Published in association with the European Communication Research and Education Association (ECREA), books in the series make a major contribution to the theory, research, practice and/or policy literature. They are European in scope and represent a diversity of perspectives. Book proposals are refereed.

Multiplayer
The Social Aspects of Digital Gaming

Edited by
Thorsten Quandt and Sonja Kröger

Routledge
Taylor & Francis Group

LONDON AND NEW YORK

First published 2014
by Routledge
2 Park Square, Milton Park, Abingdon, Oxon OX14 4RN

and by Routledge
711 Third Avenue, New York, NY 10017

Routledge is an imprint of the Taylor & Francis Group, an informa business

© 2014 Thorsten Quandt and Sonja Kröger for selection and editorial
matter; individual contributions, the contributors

British Library Cataloguing in Publication Data
A catalogue record for this book is available from the British Library

Library of Congress Cataloging in Publication Data
Multiplayer: The Social Aspects of Digital Gaming / Edited by Thorsten
Quandt and Sonja Kröger.
   pages cm. -- (Routledge studies in European Communication Research
   and Education)
   Includes bibliographical references and index.
   1. Internet games--Social aspects. 2. Shared virtual environments.
   I. Quandt, Thorsten, editor of compilation.
   GV1469.17.S63M85 2013   794.8--dc23
   2013016477

ISBN: 978-0-415-82885-7 (hbk)
ISBN: 978-0-415-82886-4 (pbk)
ISBN: 978-0-203-62748-8 (ebk)

Typeset in Sabon
by Bookcraft Limited, Stroud, Gloucestershire

Contents

List of Figures

List of Tables

Acknowledgments

Editing the volume *Multiplayer: The Social Aspects of Digital Gaming* required exceptional effort by many people. Special thanks go to Katharina Wohlgemuth for going above and beyond the call of duty when formatting chapters and solving all APA style challenges. Furthermore, we would like to thank all the authors for their superb submissions, their commitment, and their patience with the editors, even when they asked for revisions and last-minute changes. It was a pleasure to work with you on this project!

Thorsten Quandt and Sonja Kröger,
April 2013

List of Contributors

Dr Judith Ackermann is a lecturer in media studies at the University of Siegen (Germany). 2012/13 she was visiting professor of digital media culture at the University of Film and Television in Potsdam (Germany). She is a coordinator of the Digital Games section of Gesellschaft für Medienwissenschaft (German association of media studies). Research interests: game studies, social media, media communication.

Dr Richard A. Bartle is Professor of Computer Game Design at the University of Essex (UK). He is best known for having co-written the first virtual world, MUD, in 1978 and for his 1996 Player Types model, which has seen widespread adoption by the MMO industry. His 2003 book, *Designing Virtual Worlds*, is the standard text on the subject.

Johannes Breuer graduated in media studies and is a PhD candidate at the University of Cologne. He works as a research associate in the ERC-funded project SOFOGA at the University of Münster (Germany). His research interests include digital games and aggression, learning with digital games, and media entertainment.

Steve Bromley is a video game user researcher and recently completed an MSc at the University of Sussex (UK) on measuring social interaction in co-located gaming. He has worked on projects with companies such as Sony and Relentless, and writes regular blog posts about games user research on his website.

Dr Vivian Hsueh-Hua Chen, PhD in Communication, is an assistant professor at Nanyang Technological University (Singapore). Her research focuses on the sociocultural impact of new media on society and children, intercultural and interpersonal communication, and specifically video games.

Cédric Courtois is a researcher at the research group for Media and ICT (iMinds-MICT) at Ghent University (Belgium), where he conducts research into media consumption in a converging media landscape, youth and new media, and online prosuming.

Melanie De Vocht is researcher at the research group for Media and ICT (iMinds-MICT) at Ghent University (Belgium), where she conducts research into risk communication as part of the interdisciplinary European project Veg-i-Trade.

Emese Domahidi (MA in Communication Studies, Philosophy and German Literature) is a PhD candidate at the University of Münster (Germany). She works as a research associate in the ERC-funded project SOFOGA. Her research and teaching fields include community-building processes in online social network sites and digital games, as well as social network analysis.

Dr Lina Eklund is a researcher in sociology at Stockholm University (Sweden). Her research includes different aspects of digital gaming and ICT use, such as: relational sociology, social life, identity, and gender structures. Her PhD dissertation concerns social digital gaming from a mixed-methods perspective.

Malte Elson graduated in psychology, and is pursuing his PhD on frustrating experiences in digital games. Currently he works as a research associate in the ERC-funded project SOFOGA at the University of Münster (Germany). His research interests include digital games and aggression, media effects research methods, and social aspects of co-playing.

Aníbal Gonçalves has a bachelor's degree in Sociology from the University of Minho (Portugal). Recently, he finished his master's degree on Organizations and Work at UM, about virtual communities in video games contexts, entitled "Videogames Online as a Sociological Phenomenon." He is a member of the Portuguese Society of Videogame Sciences and editor at the Portuguese version of the *Eurogamer* magazine.

Dr Mark D. Griffiths is a chartered psychologist and Director of the International Gaming Research Unit at Nottingham Trent University (UK). He has published over 400 refereed papers, three books, 70 book chapters and over 1000 other articles (mainly in the area of behavioral addiction). He has won thirteen national and international awards for his work on gambling and gaming.

Dr Magnus Johansson is a researcher at the department of computer and systems sciences at Stockholm University (Sweden). His research interests are directed at digital games with a focus on the social fabrics of player groups, the development of believable non-player characters and how social believability in NPCs may affect immersion. His PhD thesis concerns how the social believability in NPCs can be studied.

Rachel Kowert (MA in Counseling Psychology from Santa Clara University) is in the final stages of completing her PhD from the University of York, where her research focuses on the relationships between social competence and online video game involvement. She is currently an associate researcher at the University of Münster working on the ERC-funded project SOFOGA.

Sonja Kröger (MA in Education, Media Studies and German Literature) is a PhD candidate at the University of Paderborn (Germany). She works as a junior lecturer at the Institute of Communication Studies at the University of Hohenheim (Germany). Her research and teaching fields include media education, young children and media, as well as digital games with a focus on advertising.

Benny Liebold is a junior lecturer at the Institute of Media Research at Chemnitz University of Technology (Germany). His field of research includes emotion and media effects on emotion, human-computer interaction with special focus on emotional virtual agents, as well as media psychological aspects of computer game studies.

Dr Frans Mäyrä is Professor of Information Studies and Interactive Media at the University of Tampere (Finland). There, he is heading the Game Research Lab, and has taught and studied digital culture and games from the early 1990s. His research interests include game cultures, meaning making through playful interaction, online social play, identity, as well as transmedial fantasy and science fiction.

Dr Graham McAllister is the founder of Player Research, a playtesting and user research studio that provides insights into players and gameplay. He was previously an academic in the areas of video games user experience and accessibility. He has published over 50 peer reviewed papers and is a regular speaker at video game conferences in the US and UK.

Pejman Mirza-Babaei is a video games user researcher at the University of Sussex (UK). His research focuses on triangulation of physiological measurements with other user research methodologies to gain a better understanding of user experience in games. He has created a technique for affective evaluations of player experience to suit the game development cycle towards providing formative feedback for game developers.

Dr Torill Elvira Mortensen is associate professor at IT University of Copenhagen (Denmark). She has been studying digital multiplayer games since 1995, and has a PhD discussing early text-based multiplayer games. The main focus of her research is game culture and Internet culture, and she studies social media and the relationship between text and user both in games and on the internet.

Jonathan Napier is a project manager at Relentless Software, one of the leading UK independent developers. Having delivered several games across the *Buzz* and *Blue Toad Murder Files* franchises, Jonathan is currently managing the development of the ground-breaking *Kinect Nat Geo TV* title for the Xbox 360.

Dr Peter Ohler is Professor at Chemnitz University of Technology (Germany) and Director of the Institute of Media Research and owner of the chair of Media Psychology/Media Sociology. His research interests include cognitive media psychology, emotional and cognitive effects of media, laboratory experimental methods for media research, computer game studies, and children and the media.

Dr Julian A. Oldmeadow is Lecturer in Social Psychology at the University of York (UK). His research interests center on social cognition and social perception, with a focus on the formation and function of stereotypes.

Daniel Pietschmann is a junior lecturer at the Institute of Media Research at Chemnitz University of Technology (Germany). His research focuses on media effects of computer games, especially in terms of entertainment, immersion, and storytelling. Other research fields include television studies and transmedia storytelling.

Dr Thorsten Quandt is a Professor of Communication Studies at the University of Münster (Germany). He is the founding chair of ECREA's Temporary Working Group "Digital Games Research." His research and teaching fields include online communication, media innovation research, digital games and online journalism.

Dr Tim M. Schoenmakers works as a research manager at the IVO Addiction Research Institute and its Center for Behavioral Internet Science (The Netherlands). He supervises different applied research projects and PhD projects on alcohol addiction, tobacco use and Internet-related addictions. He has a PhD in alcohol addiction and a master's degree in commercial and health communication.

Dr Christina Schumann is a research assistant at the Department of Media Research and Political Communication, Institute of Media and Communication Science, Ilmenau University of Technology (Germany). Her general research interest is in reception and audience studies, computer-mediated communication, and empirical methods. In particular she concentrates on the reception and effects of video games.

Björn Stråät has an MSc degree in computer and systems sciences and is a PhD student at his alma mater—the Department of Computer and Systems Sciences at Stockholm University (Sweden). His research interests currently include human–computer interaction in computer games and game agents.

Georg Valtin is a lecturer at the Institute of Media Research at Chemnitz University of Technology (Germany). His research interests include computer game studies, film studies, and research methods in the field of media studies.

Dr Dike van de Mheen is Director of Research and Education at the Addiction Research Institute Rotterdam (The Netherlands). She has extended experience in research (both quantitative and qualitative) on addiction and risky behavior. She is Professor of "Addiction Research" at the Erasmus University in Rotterdam and professor of "Care and Prevention of Risky Behaviour and Addiction" at Maastricht University.

Dr Regina J. J. M. van den Eijnden, PhD in Social Psychology, works as an Assistant Professor at the Department of Interdisciplinary Social Science at the University of Utrecht (The Netherlands). Her research focus is on the development of substance (ab)use and (behavioral) addictions (e.g., compulsive Internet use, compulsive gaming), and on the relationship between media use and sexual development during adolescence.

Dr Jan Van Looy is Professor and Senior Researcher at the research group for Media and ICT (iMinds-MICT) at Ghent University (Belgium), where he conducts research into various aspects of digital gaming.

Dr Antonius J. van Rooij defended his PhD thesis on Online Video Game Addiction in 2011 at the Erasmus MC. He is employed as a senior researcher at the IVO Addiction Research Institute. He currently focuses on the translation of findings to practical interventions and continues to study behavioral addictions.

Dr Harko Verhagen (MSc in Sociology, PhD in Computer and Systems Sciences) is currently employed as an Associate Professor at Stockholm University (Sweden). His research has focused on simulation of organizational behavior, simulation as a scientific method, the use of sociological theories in multiagent systems research, and more in particular theories on norms and autonomy.

Lotte Vermeulen is a researcher at the research group for Media and ICT (iMinds-MICT) at Ghent University (Belgium). She is currently doing a PhD on identity formation of female players and the role that digital games play in their everyday lives.

Dr Ad A. Vermulst was a senior researcher at the department of Developmental Psychopathology of the Behavioural Science Institute of the Radboud University Nijmegen (The Netherlands). His expertise is in statistics, methodology, and social scientific research.

Henrik Warpefelt has an MSc in computer and systems sciences, and is a PhD student at his alma mater—the Department of Computer and Systems Sciences at Stockholm University (Sweden). His research interests currently include the classification of NPCs and the development of more believable game agents.

Dr Jeffrey Wimmer is assistant professor for digital games at the Ilmenau University of Technology (Germany). His main research fields are sociology of media communication; especially digital games and the public sphere. He is also speaker of the ECREA-section "communication and democracy."

Dr Nelson Zagalo is Assistant Professor at the University of Minho (Portugal). He got his PhD on Communication Technology; working on new interaction paradigms in virtual environments. He is Director of the Master's on Interactive Media, co-chairs the research group engageLab, and is founder of the Portuguese Society of Videogames Sciences.

Part I

Social Aspects of Digital Gaming

1 Introduction

Multiplayer Gaming as Social Media Entertainment

Thorsten Quandt and Sonja Kröger

For many years, digital gaming has been portrayed as being on the fringes of media and communication studies. While there were always some more or less diverse forms of digital games research, even in the early days of digital gaming, most of it was only loosely connected to traditional media and communication research. The existing social-scientific research has arguably focused on problematic uses and stereotypical user groups. The interest in problematic aspects of new media is not uncommon, and it follows the logic of protecting society from the harmful effects of yet unknown (media) influences.

However, in the past decade, digital games have become a widely accepted form of media entertainment, even outside the traditional *core gamer* segment. In tandem with this shift into the mainstream media market, we have seen an increasing interest in *social* multiplayer gaming activities from three directions: the gaming industry, the audience, and academia.

Indeed, the gaming industry itself has been flourishing rapidly in terms of economic relevance in comparison with other sectors of the creative industries, and has become a central part of the global entertainment industry in recent years. Since the first appearance of digital games for the public in the early 1970s, there has been a dramatic change in the hardware and software technological innovations for digital games. In the context of technology convergence, digital game manufactures currently develop digital games for different platforms, such as PCs and consoles, or for mobile devices, such as smartphones or tablet PCs. The emergence of new technologies and the development of new digital game types, such as social network games (e.g., *Farmerama*), serious games for (school) learning environments, or even digital games for health education, promote new ways for consumers to use digital games. Consequently, the audience for digital games has increased, and besides the traditional young male core gamer, new user groups, such as seniors and women, have been captured by the digital game industry.

Likewise, these economic developments and socio-cultural changes based on the emergence of digital games are of great academic interest. As is so often the case when researchers analyze the complex interdependencies of new technologies and social changes, filling in the blanks takes time. Ongoing research from different research disciplines helps to uncover multiple aspects of these phenomena to understand the role and impact of digital games in people's everyday lives. Studies have been initiated to investigate the social foundations of virtual worlds, massively multiplayer online role-playing games (MMORPGs), multiplayer shooters, e-sports, and social cooperation in party-oriented console gaming, yet digital games research remains a relatively new field. Despite an explosive growth in the field over the past decade, many aspects of social gaming still remain largely unexplored. For that reason, this edited volume will take a closer look at the various forms of social interaction in and around digital (multiplayer) games to fill in the blind spots on the digital games research map.

About This Book

This volume is loosely based on an international conference, with a focus on the social side of gaming, that was organized by the European Communication Research and Education Association (ECREA) Temporary Working Group on Digital Games Research, held at the University of Hohenheim (Stuttgart, Germany) in July 2011.

Coming from a social-scientific perspective, the objective of the volume is to provide a platform for the latest research findings in the field of digital games studies, alongside an overview of the discussion in the field. However, the book is not intended to be a simple "proceedings" volume, but a more general introduction to the field. Therefore, we added well-known games researchers as authors to widen the focus of the book, and to give an overview of past and present debates regarding the topic. With its 19 key articles, the book is unique in its intention to bridge the gap between digital games research and social-scientific communication research.

The aim of this edited volume is to present theoretical and methodological approaches to contemporary digital game studies with a focus on the social aspects of digital multiplayer gaming. The volume brings together articles from many countries, and the authors come from different backgrounds, such as media and communication studies, educational science, psychology, and game design.

Structure of the Volume

In this volume, we distinguish between five different perspectives on multiplayer gaming. Each part of the book consists of between three and five selected articles.

Part I, Social Aspects of Digital Gaming, provides a starting point for readers and lays out the challenges for science and research. This part of the book focuses on both online-multiplayer gaming with co-players in virtual life, such as MMRPGs, and offline-multiplayer gaming with co-present fellow gamers in real life, such as party console games. The first part of the book strives to explain why a deeper understanding of the social aspects of online gaming and virtual worlds is needed.

Following this introductory text by the two editors, unique cross-national research is presented in the chapter by Thorsten Quandt, Vivian Chen, Frans Mäyrä, and Jan Van Looy. The authors offer data from large-scale surveys to allow for a comparative view of digital gaming between countries, which reveals striking differences between various world regions, and some obvious research gaps that need to be addressed in future studies.

The chapter by Richard A. Bartle—co-author of the first virtual gaming world, *MUD*, and considered by many as a key thinker in game design—discusses the principles of designing multiplayer games. He also draws on his theories on multiplayer gaming in general, including the Bartle typology of gamer types in MUDs.

Part II, Social Interaction in Virtual Worlds, takes a closer look at the social structures in virtual environments. Computer gaming is not a hobby for isolated persons. Gamers share their thoughts and experiences with others, both in game-related communities (either off- or online) and in their "other" everyday communities. Clans and guilds are just one type of game community, but there are also gaming boards, electronic sports leagues, specific game-related subcultures, and so on. Thus, this part of the book focuses on questions regarding the emergence of such groups, their social order and interaction rules, as well as how they are embedded into real-life contexts.

From the perspective of media psychology, the research group of Georg Valtin, Daniel Pietschmann, Benny Liebold, and Peter Ohler reports on exemplary research on the role of avatar attractiveness in prosocial behavior using *in situ* experiments. In doing so, the authors give insights into the use of experimental methods in virtual environments from both the methodological and the practical points of view.

Lotte Vermeulen and Jan Van Looy explore how social interactions as a motivator differ across genders. The study is a significant contribution to the ongoing debate as to whether gender plays an important role in this context. In contrast to the stereotypical view, the results suggest that female gamers are less attracted to social communication features and interaction during digital game play.

Based on the theory of subjective quality assessments, Christina Schumann investigates a mixed-method research design to give a better understanding of how social interaction with non-player characters (NPCs) should be designed to enhance the game experience of players. Her research gives fruitful hints for scholars and practitioners as to how NPCs should be designed in the future.

Another approach to social interactions between players and NPCs is presented by Magnus Johansson, Björn Strååt, Henrik Warpefelt, and Harko Verhagen. Applying an experimental design, and based on the assumptions of different rational agency models, the authors present a conceptual model of agency for NPCs with the addition of social dynamics.

Part III, Online Gaming, is concerned with the experience of online gamers in real-world and game-world environments. Thus, chapters included in this part of the book deal with (primarily PC-based) digital online games—where thousands, and in some cases even millions of people interact—as a new type of social environment in which people meet and socialize. In contrast to single-player games, online games are much more (socially) complex, as they usually include some modes of communication and human interaction. However, players cannot only exchange items and thoughts—they can also interfere with the actions of others, leading to complex action–reaction patterns.

This part of the book starts with the chapter by Rachel Kowert and Julian A. Oldmeadow, who take a closer look at the stereotype of the socially inept (online) gamer. Focusing on the social skills approach to social competence, their chapter examines the current state of empirical understanding of the relationship between social competence and online gaming. The overview illustrates promising but also inconsistent findings in this field, and shows that further research is needed to help uncover the exact nature of the relationship between social competence and online gaming.

Jeffrey Wimmer is interested in gamers of the fast-growing online gaming networks such as Steam, Xbox LIVE, and the PlayStation Network, and how these systems support social interaction among their users. Wimmer chooses a quantitative approach and takes Oldenburg's concept of so-called third places into account. In line with Oldenburg's assumptions, the author understands online gaming platforms as social meeting points, creating new socio-culturally and politically relevant spaces for interaction. The analysis concludes that, to a limited extent, several characteristics of real-world third places can also be found in the virtual space of these gaming networks.

Based on participant observation, Torill E. Mortensen analyzes the use of phasing in the massively multiplayer online game (MMO) *World of Warcraft (WoW)* (Blizzard Entertainment, 2004). By taking *time* as an example, the author explores what impact phasing can have on the continuity of the gaming environment. Her contribution gives insights into how MMOs pose serious problems for game designers, and how the implementation of phasing can lead to various forms of togetherness and parallel play.

Nelson Zagalo and Aníbal Gonçalves also probe the question of game design, but by drawing the concept of social interdependency, they take a broader perspective on the design of MMOs. They discuss how game designers implement game mechanics that support and also control social interactions during gameplay. Additionally, to figure out how designers control the experience in MMOs, and how they keep gamers attached to the game, the authors present a study on persuasion techniques used in the design of social game mechanics.

Part IV, Co-Located and Console Gaming, discusses empirical research results regarding the potential for collaborative activities in and around games. Chapters within this part of the book focus on console game systems, such as Nintendo's Wii, Microsoft's Xbox 360, and Sony's PlayStation 3. They typically facilitate multiplayer games with co-present fellow gamers, which can be regarded not only as digital games, but also as social events. The presence of fellow gamers requires forms of cooperation and competition different from the ones encouraged by online games (with more or less *invisible* co-players). This mixture of *real-life* and *in-game* interaction has hardly been researched yet, so this part of the book aims to provide explanations as to what co-presence adds to the interaction of players, how it changes the players' perception, and whether the effects of games are modified by co-present players.

In the first chapter of this part of the book, Sonja Kröger and Thorsten Quandt collect and structure the work that has been done on console gaming so far. Their literature review illustrates that research in this field provides important insights into six key subjects: health, social interaction, communication, family, motivation, and game mechanics. However, the overview of console gaming also uncovered research gaps, especially in the social sciences, and the authors conclude that a deeper understanding of the special features of console gaming is required.

Lina Eklund is interested in how console playing is embedded in the social context of the family. To study sociality and family gaming, and inspired by a phenomenological approach, she presents the results of a qualitative study that focuses on the participants' own experiences. The author points out that gaming with the family is not performed instead of other activities, but rather that it complements them. Therefore, she concludes that gaming shares many of the same functions that other (non-mediated) leisure activities do.

A practical methodology for measuring social interaction during co-located gaming comes from the research group of Steve Bromley, Pejman Mirza-Babaei, Graham McAllister, and Jonathan Napier. To become aware of the complex adaption of theoretical approaches into practical guidelines, the presented concept was created in collaboration with a games development company. Based on Richard A. Bartle's player typology (see Chapter 2) and categories of social interaction behavior suggested by Voida and colleagues, the authors evaluate an approach to understand how forms of social interaction resonate with specific player types. The results show a correlation between the interactions and biometric results emerging among players who share categories. By combing both theoretical assumptions and practical methods, the results of this chapter might provide the industry with a deeper understanding of social interaction in their games.

The next chapter also addresses social interaction in digital game playing, but Judith Ackermann focuses on communication between gamers participating in local-area network (LAN) events. To highlight the way in which community gaming is accompanied by direct talk, the author presents the results of three LAN parties in a (mostly) natural context. The article gives an insight into the multi-dimensional group communication that occurs during and around computer gaming in a co-located group. From her findings, she is able to refute the widespread stereotype of the silent game player who is not able to communicate.

Part V, Risks and Challenges of Social Gaming, concentrates on the reasons for excessive use and forms of addiction in digital multiplayer games, as well as on the relation between games and aggression. Even if this volume's intention is to emphasize the social aspects of digital gaming, problematic uses of digital games need to be included. This is not only a necessity because some aspects of the public debate around digital games (and many research efforts) have focused on the detrimental effects of aggressive or supposedly addictive game content, but because many negative aspects are also directly linked to the effects of social interaction in virtual worlds in general, and MMOs in particular.

Mark D. Griffiths opens the discussion and gives a brief overview of the risks and challenges of multiplayer gaming based on a multitude of studies and empirical evidence. From these studies, he can identify specific features of gaming addiction; however, he also notes that the phenomenon of gaming addiction might not be as widespread as some voices in the public discussion might imply.

Coming from a sociological perspective, the initial point of the research by Emese Domahidi and Thorsten Quandt concerns the lives and gaming behaviors of so-called extreme gamers. Applying a qualitative approach, the basis of the study involves biographical interviews with extreme gamers differing in social background, education, age, life, and work situation. The authors identify different ways of integrating excessive gaming into everyday life, and recurring patterns of interaction with other persons, both within the real world and the virtual world. Their contribution helps in understanding the complex phenomenon of excessive gaming with respect to its social foundations.

The Dutch research group of Antonius J. van Rooij, Tim M. Schoenmakers, Regina J. J. M. van den Eijnden, Ad A. Vermulst, and Dike van de Mheen provide another perspective on game addiction and adolescent psychosocial well-being. The chapter focuses on the moderating role of friendship quality in the relationship between online activity and psychosocial well-being, based on a large-sample survey in secondary schools. The findings of the quantitative analysis reveal that the relationship between addiction and psychosocial problems can be positively moderated by the quality of both online and real-life friendships.

The chapter by Malte Elson und Johannes Breuer addresses the shortcomings in the field of *digital games and aggression* research to provide suggestions on how to overcome the lack of social realism in this area. The authors report methodological differences in experimental studies on the effects of digital multiplayer games, such as the research design, the way the studies are carried out, and the data analysis, which lead to ambiguous results. The authors argue that the application of the frustration–aggression hypothesis could be a fruitful approach for research on digital games and aggression. Additionally, they suggest that future experimental studies in this field should attempt to systematically vary features of the game and the social context, while rigorously controlling other features.

Jan Van Looy, Cédric Curtois, and Melanie De Vocht close the last part of the volume with another analysis of the moderating effects of avatar identification and pathological gaming in MMOs. Taking the MMO *WoW* as an example, the research group analyzes the theory of self-discrepancy (introduced by Higgins in 1987) to determine if gamers with high avatar identification have a character that is closer to their ideal self in terms of several factors.

Games Cited

Blizzard Entertainment (2004), *World of Warcraft*, Vivendi Activision Blizzard.

2 Design Principles

Use and Misuse

Richard A. Bartle

Introduction

Wouldn't it be great if we knew *why* people played social games?

To some degree, obviously we do know: people are social animals, therefore its merely being social makes a game attractive. Unfortunately, this only tells us why people might prefer a social game over a non-social game, not why they may prefer one social game over another social game. Those who design or study social games are therefore more interested in learning which particular feature sets of social games are liked by which particular groups of players. If we knew that, we could create better games – and understand what "better" meant.

At the moment, the designers of social games are using a strongly metrics-based approach to assessing which features of a social game are the most significant (Donham and Koster, 2010). This typically involves making incremental or competing changes to a live game and presenting those changes to distinct subsets of the player base. If the performance in some key metric is improved, the changes are adopted wholesale; otherwise, they are dropped. For example, the change might involve a single adjustment to the user interface, with an increase in "time/money spent playing" being used to judge success. It's a form of A/B testing, and although it has been used with great success by major developers on platforms such as Facebook, it has its limits. Essentially, it's a hill-climbing algorithm through the space of metrics: it can find a local maximum, but not necessarily a global maximum.

Designers of social games are therefore looking beyond metrics for other ways to improve social games. Likewise, those who study player-related phenomena are seeking ways to get a handle on what's going on here. The most obvious approach is that of using tried-and-trusted abstract design principles, which have met with success elsewhere. There are several candidate models and typographies available (Farmer, 1994; Lazzarro, 2004, 2009; Bateman and Boon, 2006; Radoff, 2011), but by far the most popular is Player Type theory (Bartle, 1996). The subject of this chapter is the use and misuse of such design principles; Player Type theory is selected as the primary exemplar because of its widespread adoption in social games, but the points raised do apply to the use of design principles in general.

Social Games

It would indeed be great if we knew why people played social games. At present, however, there isn't even a commonly accepted definition of what a "social game" actually is. It's typically used as a label for a particular group of games that share some similar properties, chief among which is the fact that they are played on social networks (hence, their name). There are two important things to bear in mind here: firstly, they barely qualify as being social (interactions are intermittent and do not occur on the main field of play); secondly, they barely qualify as being games (you can't win, lose or draw in them). It is thus important in this context that words such as "social" and "game" are not taken at face value. Just because the word "social" normally comes loaded with a set of particular implications to do with groups, communities, societies and cultures, this does not mean that any of these necessarily follow in the case of "social games". In fact, "social" operates on something of a sliding scale. Depending on what aspects of it you are interested in, it could apply to any game which has:

- more than one player
- more than Dunbar's number (Dunbar, 1992) of players
- a massive number of players
- a community of players
- players exhibiting anti-social behavior
- an effect on how individual players think about other people
- an effect on wider society.

Indeed, it could be argued that *all* games – even single-player games – are at least in *some* way social, because the people who play them are framed by the society in which they live. Subjectively, though, certain types of game are "more social" than others because they involve more people interacting more often in more ways.

On this basis, massively multiplayer online (MMO) role-playing games and other virtual worlds are far, far more social than are genre social games. Because of this, they are the natural first port of call for anyone wishing to learn how to make a more social social game. There is also a much larger and more established body of work concerning MMOs than there is for other types of online game, as they have been around in one form or another since 1978 (Bartle, 2003).

Now as it happens, for MMOs there is also an existing theory to explain why people play them: Player Type theory. It has been used routinely in MMO design since *Ultima Online* (Origin Systems, 1997) and is still cited as a major influence in new AAA[1] MMO designs, such as that of *WildStar* (Carbine Studios, forthcoming). Over 700,000 people have taken the online Bartle Test of Gamer Psychology (Andreasen and Downey, 1996), a questionnaire, which aims to determine the respondent's player type.

Player Type theory is very familiar not only to those who research or design virtual worlds, but even to a good many players.

Because of this, Player Type theory has been used and is being used as a design principle for new (non-MMO) social games.

The question is: *should* it be so used?

Player Types

Player Type theory is commonly known as *the Bartle types*, after the person who formulated it. Being Bartle, I'm something of an authority on the subject. However, I'm not quite arrogant enough to believe it's universally known, so present here a brief overview.

The basic model purports to identify four different types of people who play virtual worlds (that is, those multiplayer worlds that are either social- or game-oriented – I don't just mean social worlds) for fun. It does this by locating their interests along two continuous dimensions. One dimension represents whether they are more interested in *acting on* or *interacting with* things. The other dimension represents whether they are more interested in the virtual *world* itself or in the *players* whom they encounter in the virtual world.

The dimensions can be charted as a two-dimensional graph, giving four quadrants. Players whose interests fall within the same quadrant broadly find the same things fun. See Figure 2.1.

Those in the upper-right quadrant are trying to bend the game world to their will, usually so they can "beat" it. We call these people *achievers*. Those in the bottom-right quadrant like interacting with the world so as to understand it, to unearth its secrets. We call these people *explorers*. Those

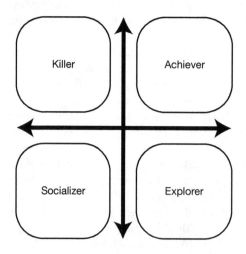

Figure 2.1 Player Types Interest Graph.

in the bottom-left quadrant like interacting with other players, to learn more about them and about themselves. We call these people *socializers*. Finally, in the top-left corner are players who find enjoyment in acting on other players, trying to dominate them so as to assert their own self-worth. We call these people *killers*.

The basic theory has a noun (players, world) and a verb (acting, interacting). The full theory (Bartle, 2003; Bartle, 2005) adds an adverb (*implicitly* or *explicitly*) in the form of a third dimension. This doubles the number of types to eight. In so doing, it solves a number of issues with the four-type model, in particular it:

• differentiates between two observed sub-types of killer: the *politician* (go-getting organizers) and the *griefer* (mischief-makers)
• explains how and why people move between types
• ties into wider theories of identity, in particular the *monomyth* (Campbell, 1949).

Despite, or perhaps because of this extra complexity, Player Type theory is almost invariably used in its four-type form. When the eight-type model is mentioned at all, it's in the context of offering deeper theoretical support for the four-type model. For this reason, I shall not go into further detail about the workings of the eight-type model here.

One of the main features of Player Type theory is that although its name suggests the contrary, it's not a categorization: it's a model. This means that not only can players be associated with particular types, but their relationships with players of other (or the same) types can be ascertained and the consequences played out. As a model, it can be "run" predictively. Excellent categorizations do exist (Yee, 2005), but they only address the *what*, not the *why*. For our purposes, we need the *why*.

Another important feature of Player Types is that it is exhaustive. It claims to account for everyone who plays virtual worlds for fun, with no gaps in its coverage. Extra dimensions can be added for refinement, but there is no room for anything extra-dimensional. Because a single counter-example could collapse the whole edifice, this means that it has been subjected to fairly rigorous scrutiny. As yet it has withstood such attacks, which has given it a certain level of credibility (although of course it yet remains potentially falsifiable at any moment).

A final notable point is that the theory was primarily created for the use of virtual world designers. In the early days of virtual worlds most designers created worlds that they, personally, wanted to play. Player Type theory was published in the hope that it would encourage designers to create worlds that *people* want to play. It showed that there were several valid ways for players to look at virtual worlds, which may or may not match the designer's own playing preferences; furthermore, it posited that these contrasting views were inter-dependent and that without a balance between them among the player base, the health of the virtual world as a whole would suffer. In this regard, Player Type theory has actually achieved its goal, to the extent that it's now quite hard to believe that designers ever thought there was only one kind of fun important to virtual worlds.

As an example of the efficacy of Player Type theory in action, consider the case of *GoPets* (Symbiosis Games, 2004). *GoPets* was a loosely coupled *Tamagotchi*-like environment in which players raised their own virtual pets that were allowed to travel to other players' parts of the world. In the words of the designer, it "carpet-bombed" the socializer quadrant, on the grounds that this was the most populous and would guarantee the most users (Bethke, 2007). *GoPets* did OK using this approach, but some achiever content did nevertheless slip in: a player character could stand beneath a tree without moving for an hour, whereupon a nut would fall from the tree, which they could then pick up. The developers noticed that some players were indeed standing beneath trees without moving for an hour, simply to be one of the few people who owned a nut. They correctly identified this as achiever behavior, so added a few more achiever-friendly elements. As a result, the revenue from *GoPets* doubled within seven days. It turned out that although there were not many achievers around in a game designed to attract socializers, each was 44 times more profitable than a socializer; later enhancements revealed that individual explorers were 64 times more profitable than individual socializers. Even among socializers, overall playing activity rose because the community became more vibrant. Player Type theory predicts that for a virtual world to be a success you need *all* player types to be present in sufficient numbers, rather than have one type swamp all the others. *GoPets* was enough of a virtual world for the theory to apply.[2]

Player Types and Social Games

It is important to mention the point that *GoPets* did have (tenuous, but still present) virtual world elements. This is because the metaphorical warranty on Player Type theory is only good for describing *people who play virtual worlds for fun*. If the theory does apply elsewhere, that's all well and good – it's just that there is no explanation as to *why* it would apply elsewhere. It would be like using psychoanalysis on plants on the basis that it works on people: if it does work on plants, well that's wonderful news but … why *would* it work?

The basis of Player Type theory (which derives from the eight-type model that subsumes the four-type model) is all to do with identity: being and becoming yourself. People typically play MMOs for two to four hours most evenings (Williams, Yee, and Caplan, 2008); if they don't quit in the first six months, they'll play for two years before they ease off (UnSub, 2004). Even the most diehard *FarmVille* player is not going to do that while remaining sane; the reason players can do it for MMOs is because there they are undertaking Campbell's *hero's journey*; this assertion is the underpinning of the whole of Player Type theory.

For Player Type theory to work, players must therefore visit a persistent, automated, real-time, shared "other world" using a conduit object that is "in" that world (their *character*, or *avatar* as it is often known). If they don't do that, then the theory doesn't hold up. Unfortunately, in social games, the "shared world" criterion is absent. The "character" is also usually absent, and sometimes even the world itself is absent. The preconditions for applying Player Type theory are not satisfied in the case of social worlds.

Social interaction in games with no shared immersive space (such as genre social games) can only occur through mechanisms external to the game world. Such games can *invite* social contact, but they can't *effect* social presence: you can *communicate* with people in them but you can't *be* with people in them. For Player Types to hold up theoretically you need to have the latter; the former isn't a strong enough condition.

Nevertheless, social game designers and researchers do apply Player Type theory to social games, regardless of whether this is incorrect or inappropriate. They do the same with other design principles, of course, not just Player Types – that's just our working example.

So, let's take a look at some of the most common mistakes made.

Mistake 1: Means to an End

Some designers apply the theory to get results. They don't care why the theory works, only that it does work (or at least that it works better than having no theory at all). To them, it's like a magic formula: you mutter the right incantation, throw the chicken bones in the correct manner, then mysterious, arcane sorcery does the rest. You don't understand why, but then you don't *need* to understand why. Few people who take a pill to cure a headache feel the need to know *why* it works, so long as it works.[3]

Naturally, people who adopt this black-box approach do need some assurance that it has indeed worked and that their effort has not been wasted. They will therefore often construct questionnaires for their players to find out what types they are. They analyse the results statistically, invariably discovering that they do have a good mix of players from all types who do interact with one another as expected. Job done!

Except, well, *of course* their players fit the types exactly! The game was designed to herd the players into those categories. For all we know, there could be half a dozen other categories of player, but these stopped playing because the game has nothing for them. If a design filters for four types, you're going to get those four types – it's a self-fulfilling prophecy.

Mistake 2: Beyond Limits

Some people knowingly apply Player Type theory beyond its limits. They understand that it doesn't have anything to say in their application domain, but they see an analogy between what they're doing and what the theory says. Analogies can be very useful in many situations: for example the basics of how electric circuits works can be understood by looking at how water flows through pipes – the "electronic–hydraulic" analogy. It's perfectly reasonable for someone acquainted with Player Type theory to be looking at a group of people and think, "hey, these folk seem to think a bit like achievers, hmm … ".

Sometimes, this does seem to be effective. For example, Player Type theory has been successfully applied this way across a range of domains, from the relatively proximate, such as educational games (Liu and Liu, 2005), through more distant but still digital domains, such as website design (Kim, 2000), all the way to outliers such as neuro-linguistic programming (Burgess, 2011).

Assuming the analogy isn't a bad one, it's not a mistake simply to use it. The mistake comes should you treat the analogy as if it were identity. This would be the equivalent of thinking that electricity would flow out of a broken wire in the same way that water would flow out of a broken pipe because electricity "is" just a different kind of water rather than working analogously to it. Likewise in a Player Types context, if you start treating your achiever-analogues as if they were actual achievers, you may find yourself drifting away from your application in the direction of virtual worlds. You may try to present opportunities for behaviors that make sense in virtual worlds but that don't make sense for your users. Just because virtual worlds benefit from a small number of killers, for example, that doesn't mean your online store will.

Mistake 3: Bandwagon

Some people make no effort to understand the theory. They read little beyond a superficial, bullet-point explanation of its fundamentals, which they then espouse because everyone else is espousing it. They see a theoretical bandwagon and jump on it, reasoning that if it works and they hadn't jumped on it, they'd regret it. Then they buy some piece of middleware that offers an off-the-shelf, generic solution and try it out. If it works, they retire rich; if it doesn't, they blame the theory for being wrong and move on to the next bandwagon.

For Player Type theory, we see this effect with new ideas such as *gamification*. Gamification involves the use of game design patterns for non-game purposes.[4] It works reasonably well when trying to encourage people to do things they already want to do (such as lose weight) and it also succeeds when it's basically a bribe (as is the case with loyalty card points); bespoke, creative solutions to individual problems can also produce good results (Richardson, 2009).

Gamification is an area in which Player Type theory has been successfully applied (Zichermann and Linder, 2010), as an analogy more than as a hard-and-fast rule. This is fair enough: treat it as a guideline and you're fine. However, although those who originally advocated use of the theory had a grasp of what it says, those who now enthusiastically apply it from the bandwagon often don't. One common mistake is to try to encourage explorers by giving them points whenever they discover something new. That would be sensible if explorers valued points, but they don't: points are an achiever thing. Explorers eschew points. It would be like trying to attract more vegetarian diners to your restaurant by giving them a free steak for every ten salads they ordered. Yes, it's a basic error – but it's one that happens time and time again.

"People play MMOs for these different reasons, so perhaps the same kind of thing happens in gamification?" is a reasonable analogy to make. Completely ignoring the implications of the analogy is not so reasonable.

Mistake 4: Inapplicable Disproof

For every theory, there will be people who want to break it. This is generally a good thing: if a theory breaks, we can find out why and get a better theory as a result. For Player Types, the fact that one counter-example would kill it has led to many research papers and articles on the subject; I shan't list them here out of professional courtesy, but they do keep coming.

It's a source of disappointment to me that Player Type theory has yet to be broken and superseded, because I really *want* to see better virtual worlds. From my perspective, its job was done when designers stopped thinking about what they themselves would like to play and started to think about what the people who were going to play what they were designing would like to play. I was hoping we'd have a much more developed theory by now, but sadly that is not the case. I therefore welcome attacks on the theory, because ultimately it only takes one bullet to find its mark and we can progress beyond it.

Unfortunately, most of the pot shots at Player Type theory are taken by people with very poor aim. Here (paraphrased) are the top three misses that I keep seeing whistling past it:

- "Your theory doesn't account for merchants! Or leaders! Or gold-farmers!"
  Well, yes it does. True, it doesn't have a "merchant" player type, but you have to ask yourself *why* someone is playing as a merchant. Are they doing it to make money in a goal-driven fashion? Then they're achievers. Are they doing it because they want to figure out how the economy works? Then they're explorers. Are they doing it because they like trading with people? Then they're socializers. Are they doing it so as to build up trust so that suddenly they can run away with all their clients' money, laughing maniacally as they do so? Then they're killers. That's not to say that regarding players as merchants or as non-merchants isn't for some purposes superior to regarding them as one of the four types; however, it is to say that regarding them that way doesn't break Player Type theory. As for leaders, well you could use a similar analysis for those but there's no need: "leader" is pretty well the same

as "politician", one of the sub-types of killer in the eight-type version of the theory. Such labelling differences for the same basic types arise fairly frequently. Finally, gold-farmers don't even need to be considered as possible counter-examples because they're not playing for fun, so the theory doesn't apply to them anyway. So far, all the proposed theory-breaking player types I've seen have either been orthogonal to the Player Types categorization ("you don't account for male/female players!"), map onto it ("you don't have discoverers!") or are excluded anyway ("you don't have MMO designers!").

- "You don't have a player type for people who like immersion."
  That's correct. Immersion is one of those concepts that frequently gets mentioned when you ask MMO players why they play, so on the face of it shouldn't it be a player type? None of the category errors outlined in the previous point apply: it doesn't yield to deeper analysis (that is, people don't get immersed in order to "achieve" more or whatever); it doesn't map onto an existing type; it most certainly applies to people who play for fun. A full, eight-type reading of Player Type theory does explain it, however: what players find fun (reflected by their player type) is determined by how far they are along the road to immersion. Immersion is their goal state; they gradually change type over time as they get closer and closer to becoming fully immersed. All players who are playing for fun are (usually subconsciously) aiming to become immersed – that's ultimately what "fun" means in MMOs. So the theory *does* explain immersion: "people who like immersion" is a description that can be applied at least to some degree to anyone who plays MMOs for fun.
- "My survey says otherwise."
  The first possibility is that you're testing the wrong thing. Watching what players do doesn't mean you know why they're doing it. For example, killers will often present as another player type – sometimes for months! – so as to make their planned, treacherous assault more shocking and exquisite (Bartle, 2009). The second possibility is that your survey doesn't have enough respondents. I've seen this "my survey says otherwise" argument presented at conferences based on questionnaires and interviews with as few as 12 players. Surveys with 16 to 20 respondents are more popular but still laughably low. Yet if Nick Yee's structured analysis (Yee, 2002) of 6,700 MMO players showed up no explorers, and it took him a more nuanced and detailed study of 3,200 further respondents (Yee, 2005) to tease them out, what chance does a survey of even a whopping 32 people have of being representative? Also, and I apologize for stating the obvious here, but if you interview griefers, don't assume that they will constrain their griefing to virtual worlds. Some of them may grief you by making up their answers ...

Player Type theory has been around for long enough that its demise is not likely to be because you found that it didn't work. It's more likely to be that you found something that worked better. If you want to join two pieces of wood together using a screw, a hammer will do a better job of it than would beating the screw in with your fist, but really you want a screwdriver. For MMOs, we have Player Type theory as the hammer, but we're still looking for someone to invent a screwdriver.

Mistake 5: Meta-Theory

The final mistake I see quite often with the use of Player Types concerns not the theory's application but its relation to other theories. There are several theories that come with attractive categorizations that look temptingly as if they might equate to player types. The classic example is Myers-Briggs (Myers and Briggs, 1943), which has been linked unpersuasively to Player Type theory on a number of occasions; this lack of success is perhaps not entirely surprising, as the two have completely incompatible underlying theories and won't align unless subjected to brutal force (Bateman and Boon, 2006). It's not that either is wrong, it's as if one is a road and one is a railway: they serve similar purposes and head in similar directions but they're dissimilar themselves and you have to be very careful where they cross.

This isn't to say that all meta-theories are mistaken. Some can be genuinely useful and exciting tools. For example Rademacher's (Rademacher, 2011) marrying up of Player Type theory to Callois' structures (Callois, 1961) allows for games and game genres to be "fingerprinted" so that it's possible to determine in advance if a given player is likely to prefer one game over another. Meta-theories that attempt to reconcile several disparate theories into one universal theory are less likely to be feasible, but practically anything is possible if you reinterpret enough (Stewart, 2011).

Volte Face

From the above, it can be seen that applying Player Type theory outside of its defined parameters at best leads to a positive outcome lacking an explanation and at worst leads to a negative outcome that can be explained all too well. We know why the theory works for virtual worlds; if it works for anything else, well that's splendid but there's no real way we can build on it as a theory. To build on it we need to know *why* it works, but all we know is why it *shouldn't* work.

So, in 2009 I attended a conference in Magdeburg, Germany, at which a young researcher, Monica Mayer, outlined the results of her recent work (Mayer, 2009). She had come at games from the direction of psychology, and analysed players using a wants/needs analysis. From this, she developed a dynamic model explaining how players play to satisfy their needs. When she ran this model, she found that it had four stable configurations of player wants/needs. In other words, when a person plays games for fun, that person will satisfy their wants/needs in a feedback-oriented way that leads to one of these four steady states. Those states map directly onto the types of Player Type theory.

Importantly, because she had designed her research from the perspective of psychology, she *hadn't come across Player Type theory* when she made her findings. The fact that they mapped onto Player Type theory's types was only pointed out to her afterwards. Had she published 15 years earlier, designers would be talking about *the Mayer types*, not the Bartle types.

Mayer's work does offer a theoretical explanation as to why players fall into the types they do, but it's purely in terms of what they want and need. It doesn't say where these desires originate, just that these are what they are and what they mean. As such, her work is not incompatible with Player Type theory, but neither does it support it. It simply reaches the same conclusions. At the moment, these are two theories that describe observed phenomena in two related but separate fields, producing identical results but for no apparent reason.

It does seem remarkable, though, that the same four player types could be derived from two radically different approaches. Although I am always careful not to make applicability claims for Player Type theory that I can't justify, that doesn't mean they are intrinsically unjustifiable. It could be that Player Type theory is one footprint of a larger theory for which Mayer's work is another. Perhaps some of the success-using-analogy applications of Player Type theory work not because the analogy is good, but because they too are footprints of some larger theory?

Whatever, it's clear that there is more to Player Type theory than we currently know.

Conclusion

The example used throughout this chapter has been Player Type theory, but the same could be said for any theory: "there is more to it than we currently know".

Time to own up: I haven't been writing about the use of Player Type theory here, I've been writing about theory use *in general*. This book is multi-disciplinary: the whole point of it is for you to come across ideas that are new to you but which are accepted as canon elsewhere. You may be tempted to enforce, extend, apply, break or subsume those ideas for your own subject area – and that's good! However, it's only good if you *understand* the ideas first.

For any theory or model or typography, to use it you should understand it. You need to know why it's *supposed* to work, even if it doesn't seem to work that way. Otherwise, if you find holes in it you have no way of knowing that they *are* holes. If you do understand it, you can seek to fill those holes. Filling them will lead to a more robust or more widely applicable theory.

I don't mind if people apply Player Type theory out of its comfort zone, so long as they understand what the theory is saying. If they break it or extend it, that's great! It's great, because then, we get a better theory.

Then, we get better games.

In the end, that's all I ever wanted from any of this: better games.

Notes

1 Pronounced "triple-A", it means the ones with the biggest budgets.
2 *GoPets* was bought by Zynga in November 2009 and closed down almost immediately. Zynga's *Petville* launched days later.
3 I've never had a headache myself, but am assured by people I know who have had headaches that this is the case.
4 Originally, it meant making something that isn't a game a game. Now it means making something that is a game not a game.

References

Andreasen, E., and Downey, B. (1996). *The Bartle Test of Gamer Psychology.* Retrieved from http://www.gamerdna.com/quizzes/bartle-test-of-gamer-psychology.

Bartle, R. (1996). Hearts, clubs, diamonds, spades: Players who suit MUDs. *Journal of MUD Research, 1*(1), 19.

Bartle, R. (2003). *Designing virtual worlds.* Indianapolis, IN: New Riders.

Bartle, R. (2005). Virtual worlds: Why people play. In A. Thor (Ed.), *Massively multiplayer game development 2* (pp. 3–18). Hingham, MA: Charles River Media.

Bartle, R. (2009). Understanding the limits of theory. In C. Bateman (Ed.), *Beyond game design: Nine steps toward creating better videogames* (pp. 117–133). Boston, MA: Cengage Learning.

Bateman, C., and Boon, R. (2006). *21st century game design.* Hingham, MA: Charles River Media.

Bethke, E. (2007). Proceedings of the Austin Game Developers Conference 2007: *MMO goal structures as a panacea.* Austin, TX.

Burgess, F. (2011). *The NLP cookbook.* Carmarthen, Wales: Crown House.

Callois, R. (1961). trans. Barash, M.: *Man, play and games.* Glencoe, IL: Free Press. From: Callois, R. (1958) *Les jeux et les hommes* Paris: Librairie Gallimard.

Campbell, J. (1949). *The hero with a thousand faces.* New York City, NY: Pantheon Press.

Donham, J., and Koster, R. (2010). Proceedings of the Austin Game Developers Conference 2010: *AAA to social games, making the leap.* Austin, TX. Retrieved from http://twvideo01.ubm-us.net/o1/vault/gdconline10/slides/11524-AAA_To_SocialGames.pdf.

Dunbar, R. (1992). Neocortex size as a constraint on group size in primates. *Journal of Human Evolution, 22*(6), 469–493.

Farmer, F. R. (1994). Social dimensions of habitat's citizenry. In C. E. Loeffler and T. Anderson (Eds.), *The virtual reality casebook* (pp. 87–95). New York City, NY: Van Nostrand Reinhold.

Kim, A. J. (2000). *Community building on the web: Secret strategies for successful online communities.* Berkeley, CA: Peachpit.

Lazzaro, N. (2004). *Why we play games: Four keys to more emotion without story.* Retrieved from http://xeodesign.com/xeodesign_whyweplaygames.pdf.

Lazzaro, N. (2009). Understand emotions. In C. Bateman (Ed.), *Beyond game design: Nine steps toward creating better videogames* (pp. 1–48). Boston, MA: Cengage Learning.

Liu, Z., and Liu, Z. (2005). Proceedings of the 12th International Conference on artificial intelligence in education: *Building an intelligent pedagogical agent with competition mechanism to improve the effectiveness of an educational game*. Amsterdam, The Netherlands.

Mayer, M. (2009). Proceedings of the Game Cultures: *Why playing games is better than living lives: Motivation, emotion and cognition based on digital games*. Otto von Guericke University, Magdeburg.

Myers, I., and Briggs, K. (1943). *The Myers-Briggs assessment*. Mountain View, CA: CPP.

Rademacher, R. (2011). Assessing serious games using the E/E grid. In L. Annetta and S. Bronack (Eds.), *Serious educational game assessment: Practical methods and models for educational games, simulations and virtual worlds* (pp. 95–118). Amsterdam, The Netherlands: Sense.

Radoff, J. (2011). *Game on: Energize your business with social media games* (pp. 27–29). Indianapolis, IN: Wiley Publishing.

Richardson, K. (2009). *The speed camera lottery: Fun theory*. Retrieved from http://www.thefuntheory.com/2009/11/12/fun-theory-award-winner-speed-camera-lottery.

Stewart, B. (2011). *Personality and play styles: A unified model*. Retrieved from http://www.gamasutra.com/view/feature/6474/personality_and_play_styles_a_.php.

UnSub (Ed.). (2004). *"This SuXX0rz; I quit!!11!": An examination of player exit motivations in massively multiplayer online games (MMOGs)*. Retrieved from http://www.thebeholder.org/research/mmogexit.htm.

Williams, D., Yee, N., and Caplan, S. (2008). Who plays, how much and why? Debunking the stereotypical gamer profile. *Journal of Computer-Mediated Communication*, 13(4), 993–1018.

Yee, N. (2002). *Facets: 5 motivation factors for why people play MMORPG's*. Retrieved from http://www.nickyee.com/facets/home.html.

Yee, N. (2005). *Motivations of play in MMORPGs: Results from a factor analytic approach*. Retrieved from http://www.nickyee.com/daedalus/motivations.pdf.

Zichermann, G., and Linder, J. (2010). *Game-based marketing: Inspire customer loyalty through rewards, challenges, and contests*. Hoboken, NJ: John Wiley.

Games Cited

Carbine Studios (forthcoming). *WildStar*. Aliso Viejo, CA: NCSoft.
Origin Systems (1997). *Ultima Online*. Austin, TX: Electronic Arts.
Symbiosis Games (2004). *GoPets*. Seoul, South Korea: Symbiosis Games.
Zynga (2009). *FarmVille*. San Francisco, CA: Zynga.

3 (Multiplayer) Gaming Around the Globe?

A Comparison of Gamer Surveys in Four Countries

Thorsten Quandt, Vivian Chen, Frans Mäyrä, and Jan Van Looy

Uncharted Territory: Open Questions on Digital Games Research

Digital gaming has become a major global entertainment sector. The games industry itself claims that gaming has surpassed the film sector in terms of financial turnaround in recent years,[1] and the interest in games is rising as games have penetrated mainstream society. The traditional stereotype of the male, adolescent player (Griffiths, Davies, and Chappell, 2003) obviously no longer represents the majority of gamers, as gaming has developed into an adult hobby, and now includes groups that have previously not been involved in gaming.

However, most of these observations are based on very scant data. Surprisingly—given the importance of the field—it is extremely difficult to obtain any dependable and precise information on the diffusion rates, gaming habits, and other "standard" use data on a representative basis. Additionally, it is even more difficult to obtain comparable data from more than one country, and on specific gaming modes, such as multiplayer gaming. This is a serious gap in current games research: For other media, communication scholars and media research companies have detailed use data at their disposal, following comparable patterns in most countries around the globe. Such data are needed as a reference point for many other studies. Before analyzing the media effects in very specific groups, or identifying the types of gamers, or examining the everyday use of games by some of these groups, one needs to know who the gamers really are, how many of them there are, how much they play, and what the composition of the overall group is. If such base information is missing then many studies will lack context, and their societal relevance will rely on overly broad assumptions.

What we do know from the scattered scientific data (to be discussed in more detail in the next section), industry studies, and anecdotal press articles is that millions of people play together via the Internet or in co-located situations in front of their TV screens, every single second of every day. However, the diffusion rates and the general acceptance of gaming vary between countries. There is some evidence that there are countries and regions that are more open to technological advancement and gaming in particular. For example, some Asian countries—such as South Korea (Chee, 2005; Hjorth and Chan, 2009)—supposedly welcome digital games as a part of their accepted societal entertainment. Multiplayer game matches are shown on television, and some of the best players are regarded as sports stars, with avid fan bases and substantial incomes. In other countries, gaming is largely regarded as being problematic, or even as a threat to the young, prohibiting a larger diffusion of gaming. In some European nations, there is an ongoing, heated debate on the negative effects of aggressive or addictive games, especially in relation to adolescent players. For example, Germany implemented a very strict age-rating system to protect young players from harmful games, handled by the Unterhaltungssoftware Selbstkontrolle or USK (the Entertainment Software Self-regulation Body), in addition to the existing EU rating system of PEGI (Pan European Gaming Information), and there is also a supervision body for online games designed to protect underage players (Kommission für Jugendmedienschutz, KJM, translated as the Commission for the Protection of Minors in the Media).

Comparative research on the spread of gaming and gamer demographics from independent sources is scarce, but as the area of games research matures, this type of data has become crucial for understanding the wider context of gaming in different societies and nations, and the potential influence of culture, policies, and of the available infrastructure on the use of digital games. Multiplayer gaming, as discussed in this volume, is particularly sensitive to country and culture specifics: It involves human player interactions, and, as such, is much more dependent on social context, and on specific cultural and national influences than solo gaming, where individuals experience (mostly) the same game with the same AI-controlled, non-player characters and enemies, no matter where they are located.[2]

This article certainly cannot solve the problem of missing cross-national research; however, it is one of the first attempts at presenting several large-scale surveys in a comparative manner. The countries under analysis include Finland, Belgium, Germany, and Singapore, offering insights into varying types of societies and markets, and their adoption of gaming. The studies include data both on adolescent and adult gamers, based on large-scale samples with hundreds or even thousands of respondents in each country. Methodologically, the studies are based on computer-assisted telephone interview (CATI) surveys (Singapore, Germany), computer-assisted personal interview (CAPI) surveys (Belgium), and controlled mail surveys (Finland). The combination of studies allows for the first comparative view on computer gaming, which reveals stark differences between the countries under analysis. Reasons for these differences are debated based on cultural aspects as well as market conditions. However, it must be noted that the selection of countries is neither systematic nor representative for larger world regions—it is obviously based on the availability of data, and, as such, also reflects some of the problems with the current status quo of the research. Therefore, we will also discuss theoretical and methodological difficulties, not only of the studies presented here, but also of games studies as a whole. Despite these pitfalls of comparative survey research, it needs to be pointed out that it also offers many possibilities, and that it is necessary for the further development of the field.

Identifying the Gamer: Status Quo and Challenges of Digital Games Surveys

As mentioned above, representative surveys on digital games are scarce. That does not mean that there are no data on game use and gamers: Rather, the data are scattered across various sources and types of research. Finding those data is not easy, however, and their focus and aims, their samples and methods, and their analyses differ vastly. While it is nearly impossible to sum up all of this information (which is also not the aim of this article), one can still identify a number of general types of data sources.

Some *general collections of studies*—mostly united through edited books—focus on gaming in general, while some others look at specific aspects of gaming. The volumes by Fromme and Unger (2012), Vorderer and Bryant (2006), or Quandt, Wimmer, and Wolling (2009) are just some examples of books with various chapters on gaming in general. They offer some base information on game use, gaming motives, gamer groups, as well as on the effects and consequences of games. The respective studies have a broad range of samples, approaches, methods, and topics, as they do not follow one common principle. There are other, more *specific collections* that are united through a common theme. They focus on specific aspects of gaming, such as questions of gender (Cassell and Jenkins, 1998), or selected types of games, such as serious games (Ritterfeld, Cody, and Vorderer, 2009), to name just two of these focal areas. While the studies are more coherent, they are still from different sources and present different aims, approaches, and methods.

Meta-analyses of studies follow a different route: They unify various studies on the same topic under one roof, and incorporate secondary analyses of data following a structured approach with comparability in mind. In digital games research, these meta-analyses primarily focused on violent content and aggressive behavior based on dozens of studies on the topic. Meta-analyses by Anderson and Bushman (2001), Ferguson (2007), Hartmann (2006), Sherry (2001), and others serve as useful overviews of that type of research, and they offer some information on game use. Naturally, as the sources of the meta-analyses are mostly concerned with short-term effects under lab conditions, with typical samples of experimental studies, and as they are fairly US-centric, their applicability for general use research is limited. Obviously, this is a limitation in principle, but it is still important to point this out again, as in the public discussion, such studies are often quoted as if they are explaining gaming per se, or as if they are applicable to all games and players.[3]

The above-mentioned data sources do not form a closed body of material that follows a joint organizational principle, and in many aspects, the use data from such sources do not represent larger formations of society or societies. In many cases, the data are also very limited in terms of size and applicability. Larger-scale samples focusing on use data primarily come from the games industry itself. One example of such *industry use studies* is the annual household survey by the Entertainment Software Association (ESA, 2013). It gathered data from more than 2,000 US households in 2012 where a games console or a gaming PC was present. Another example is a German study by the Bundesverband interaktiver Unterhaltungssoftware (BIU, translated as the Federal Association of Interactive Entertainment Software). The survey (BIU, 2013), conducted by a market research institute on 25,000 Germans, is meant to offer representative data on gaming behavior and the national games market. From such industry-driven studies, we learn primarily about diffusion rates in individual countries, the volume and frequency of use, the preferences of the users regarding games, and some use habits. The data usually focus on aspects of gaming that are deemed to be interesting for a wider (media) audience and that depict gaming as a successful entertainment market. For scientific use, the information from industry sources poses many problems. While the data might be gathered by a third party, such as in the German case (where the claim is that the data come from an "independent" market research institute), there is an obvious conflict of interest here—one cannot expect the data to be independent from the interests of the contracting party. There might be a bias in the selection and reporting of the data and the data might even be beautified—obviously, the industry would not publish information that draws a negative picture of their market and business. Furthermore, one cannot expect those data to emanate from a process that follows scientific principles of empirical research, and usually, one cannot check the quality of the data. Consequently, the industry data need to be taken with a grain of salt and interpreted with caution. For example, diffusion rates might be exaggerated, and the negative effects of gaming might be downplayed, for obvious reasons.

Finally, there are some—more or less representative—*independent use studies* out there, most of them coming from an academic context. There are only a few examples from various countries. In the USA, there is the PEW Internet and American Life Project that produced some gaming data based on a representative, telephone-based survey with more than 2,000 adults (Lenhart, Jones, and Macgill, 2008) and more than 1,000 teen respondents (Lenhart, 2008). In Germany, there is the LFM (Landesanstalt für Medien Nordrhein-Westfalen) study (Fritz, Lampert, Schmidt, and Witting, 2011), based on a combination of quantitative survey methods, which offers data from a study with 600 respondents, and the annual GameStat study (which is partially covered in this article). For Flanders, see the annual Digimeter study (iMinds-iLab.o, 2012), a combination of online and live surveys reaching over 1,400 respondents. In Finland, there is the three-year Finnish Player Barometer study with an overall total of 3,335 respondents (Karvinen and Mäyrä, 2011). This list is not complete, and there are certainly several examples from other countries, but overall, there is not a vast number of studies available.

In many ways, the independent use studies can be seen as having the opposite problems to those of the industry studies: The samples are usually relatively small, often due to limited funding (while industry studies tend to have comparably large samples to appear as impressive), and the aims—and therefore the questions—of these studies differ from those of industry-driven studies (with industry-driven studies usually offering fairly similar information, especially concerning diffusion rates, use frequency, and use volume). Furthermore, such independent studies are usually not produced on a regular basis, as most of them are single projects funded by a research grant or even in-house funding. On the other hand, the studies with an academic background follow the rules of scientific enquiry, and, in general, not only report their findings (many industry sources only report selected aspects), but also their methods and theoretical bases.

To sum up, the current situation is difficult, as regular, independent, and representative data on the use of digital games is missing. The few existing data sources have various limitations. Some of the information suffers from sampling problems, from conflicts of interest and bias, some of the research is rather anecdotal, and in many cases, outliers and special groups are presented as typical cases. Regular, longitudinal data are virtually nonexistent, and more specific fields, such as multiplayer gaming, are only marginally touched upon (via some questions on online game use).

Therefore, some simple but crucial questions remain unanswered, at least on a reliable basis that fulfills expectations regarding systematic, scientific research: What are the most relevant gamer groups? What is the composition of the overall group of gamers? How do gamers play games? What are their preferences? Have we moved beyond the "stereotypical" gamer presented in early research (Griffiths, Davies, and Chappell, 2003)? If so, who is the "new" gamer? Is the situation the same—everywhere? And what about more specific uses, such as multiplayer gaming?

Naturally, not all of these questions can be answered in this article. However, we will present academic studies from four countries aiming to fill some of the gaps mentioned above. By comparing these studies, we will identify the opportunities, but also the obvious challenges of survey research, and we will see what needs to be done to finally reach the desired level of comparability of data across nations and time.

Selected Studies from Europe and Asia: The Surveys

In this section, we will present the four individual studies and their respective national context. The basic outline of the studies, including the sample, the aims of the research, and the methodology will be briefly discussed.

Belgium/Flanders

Country context

Flanders is a Dutch-speaking region with approximately 6.3 million inhabitants in Belgium in Western Europe. There was little public interest in gaming until the topic of bullying surfaced due to the announcement of the game *Bully*, later released as *Canis Canem Edit* (Rockstar, 2006). As a reaction to the moral panic following a highly mediatized shooting in Antwerp, the Flemish Parliament commissioned a study into "Youngsters and gaming" (De Pauw, Pleysier, Van Looy, and Soetaert, 2008), and from then on, there was a rising societal and scientific interest in games as a pastime, serious gaming, and online gaming (also as a field of interaction where bullying might happen).

Study

The data gathered are part of a larger, annual study, Digimeter, which aims to map the media ownership, usage, and behavior of Flemish citizens on an annual basis. Digimeter is an initiative of iMinds, which is an independent institution aiming to support demand-driven, interdisciplinary research in collaboration with technology suppliers and users. The instrument is an extensive survey that takes ownership of 44 technologies as a starting point. Subsections include television, telephony, computers, the Internet, gaming, and other media and ICT. Recruitment takes place offline and online. Offline survey respondents are recruited through quota sampling, using quotas for gender, age, and provinces. The offline survey participants take part in the study by using the CAPI methodology with trained interviewers. Online recruitment happens via the Digimeter website (www.digimeter.be). A weighting coefficient is used for online respondents. The sample is representative for Flanders. In total, 1,403 participants took part in the study, of which 628 respondents were recruited offline via the CAPI method, 291 were recruited online, but had taken part in a previous Digimeter study using the CAPI method, and 484 were recruited exclusively online. The respondents' ages ranged from 15 to 85 years, with a mean of 48. The data were gathered between August and November 2010.

Finland

Country context

Finland is a (post-)industrialized north European country, with a population of approximately 5.4 million. Traditional games have long been part of the folk culture, but it was particularly during the 1980s when digital games started gaining popularity. The Commodore 64 gained a particularly enthusiastic following in Finland. Illegal copying and cracking (of copy protection) stimulated the growth of *demoskene* (a computer art subculture). Some of the key persons in the Finnish game industry have their background in demoskene. The game industry in Finland is large and vibrant compared to the size of the country, with the developers of best-selling games (such as the *Max Payne* series by Remedy Entertainment, 2001; the *Alan Wake* series by Remedy Entertainment, 2010; or the *Angry Birds* series by Rovio Entertainment, 2009) coming from the country.

Study

The Player Barometer is a mail survey study about how various kinds of games (digital as well as non-digital) are played in Finland. The study has been initiated as a part of the Creation of Game Cultures: The Case of Finland research project, which was a joint effort by the universities of Tampere, Jyväskylä, and Turku from 2009–2012. The Barometer was conceived as a longitudinal, annual survey of game playing in Finland. Questions primarily included items on the frequency of play in both traditional, digital entertainment, and gambling games. The survey form was sent to a representative sample of 4,000 people aged between 10 and 75. A similar survey was conducted over three successive years in 2009, 2010, and 2011. The data from 2009 and 2011 were collected from May–June, and the data from 2010 from June–August. The final numbers of respondents were 1,169, 1,087, and 1,079, respectively, the response rates being 29%, 27%, and 27%. As the response rates were relatively low, the data sets were weighted by gender and age group. Compared to the age/gender distribution in the Finnish population (aged 10–75), respondents aged from 50–70 were clearly overrepresented, and young male adults were especially underrepresented. The use of the weight variable should balance these issues. In this article, we will present some data from the 2011 study.

Germany

Country context

Germany, with its 82 million inhabitants, forms the second biggest games market in Europe after Great Britain (which, despite having a smaller population, is still the leading European games market), and it is among the biggest games markets in the world (for current industry data, see http://www.biu-online.de). Despite its economic importance, and some successful games companies based in Germany (such as Crytek, Bigpoint, and Gameforge, among others), there is an ongoing discussion about the positioning and value of games in society. The public debate was heavily influenced by two school shootings (Erfurt, 2002; Winnenden, 2009), where a link to the perpetrators' use of first-person shooter games was made. Unsurprisingly, the public debate and some parts of the research have primarily focused on the effects of the violent content in games (for a general overview of the research, see Quandt, 2010), and, more recently, on the addictive effects of games (see Festl, Scharkow, and Quandt, 2013). Use research is underrepresented—there are still only a few independent studies that offer base data on the use of digital games (Fritz et al., 2011; Quandt, Scharkow, and Festl, 2010; Quandt, Festl, and Scharkow, 2011).

Study

The German survey GameStat is part of a larger project funded by the European Research Council ("The social fabric of virtual life"; see Acknowledgments). To identify gamers and to achieve reliable information on the diffusion of gaming throughout society, 50,012 persons aged 14 and older were interviewed regarding their use of games (CATI, carried out by a professional market research institute). The bus[4] sample was randomly selected and is representative of the German-speaking population in the respective age range. Out of the gamers in the bus sample, 4,506 respondents were randomly selected for a 3-wave panel[5] study to be repeated annually from 2011 to 2013. An additional 500 non-gamers were randomly selected for comparison, and were interviewed in parallel to the gamers. The panel study focused much more on the details of game use (with an interview length of approximately 20 minutes), while the bus study examined diffusion rates. Additional calibration samples (with approximately 1,000 persons) were also incorporated annually to check for changes in the diffusion rates using the same items as the initial bus study.

Singapore

Country context

Singapore is a Southeast Asian country with roughly 5.5 million inhabitants. The density of the population is high, as the territory of Singapore is just slightly over 700 km². The country is technologically and economically advanced, with trade and the financial sector being essential for the country's economy. Singapore is one of the most networked societies in the world, with 99% of households and businesses connected to a nationwide network (Lee and Willnat, 2009). The video game industry and market in Singapore is vibrant. Japanese game titles have been some of the more popular video game products in Singapore, with games such as the *Final Fantasy* series (Square Enix, 1987–2013) and *Dragon Quest* series (Armor Project, 1986–2012) enjoying popular followings. There are approximately 40 to 45 game companies in Singapore, most of which include development teams (Toyad, 2011). Big players in the industry such as LucasArts have also set up offices in Singapore to tap into the burgeoning pool of talent in the country, and to create games that blend Western animation with Japanese anime, which caters to the expanding Asian video game market. Singapore's online game market revenue is estimated to have hit $31.5 million in 2012, and is predicted to grow at a double-digit rate through 2014. Although the general concern about the negative impacts of video gaming is present, many efforts have been made to make video games useful for human life.

Study

The data presented here comes from the national CATI survey for adults aged 21 and above carried out in 2011. Out of the 2,049 respondents, 843 were gamers and 1,205 were non-gamers. Singapore is a multi-ethnic country, so this was checked as well: 80.4% of the respondents were of Chinese origin, 8.8% were Malay, 8.3% Indian, with 2.6% of others.

(Multiplayer) Gaming Everywhere? Some Initial Findings

The studies discussed here come from different countries and they follow different methodological routes. Despite the variations, the aims and some of the data are roughly comparable: They include findings on diffusion rates and base data on gaming according to standard socio-demographic features (age groups, such as adolescent gamers versus adults, gender, and so on), gamer types, and genres.

Online or multiplayer gaming, as discussed in this volume, is not directly part of most surveys. However, genre preferences and some items in some countries reveal details about the basis of multiplayer gaming.

In this section, we will present an overview of the survey data in a comparative fashion, highlighting some interesting similarities and differences between the individual countries under analysis. Naturally, as the background and the context of these studies differ, the findings need to be carefully interpreted and seen in their specific context of origin. The presentation in one table should not lead to the conclusion that the data are directly comparable; it is rather a way to give a condensed overview of what is available. In some cases, this is also helpful in visualizing the general differences, not only in the data, but also in terms of the very basis of the respective studies; thus, supporting the notion that more standardized and unified approaches are required.

Overview Data

The four studies (partially) presented here use different approaches to reach a similar goal: getting dependable information on the gamer population in the respective countries. Two studies (Germany, Singapore) use CATIs, while the Finnish study is based on a controlled mail survey, and the study from Flanders relies on CAPIs. The sample size varies between 1,000 and 50,000 people.

These varying approaches already explain some similarities and differences that will be observed later on. However, there is one difference that is probably much more relevant: The definition of what defines a "gamer" is not the same in all cases. While all studies use *activity* as the base criterion, the threshold that defines a person as an active gamer varies. Some studies rely on the frequency or the last time of use, others primarily ask whether the respondents play games in general. Some consider the use time to be relevant, others do not. It is obvious that data variation is inevitable if the base definition is not exactly the same—and it is difficult to identify the factor influencing the outcome (is it the definition or is it an actual country-specific, alternative factor?).

Despite these difficulties, the studies already offer some interesting insights. The diffusion rates of gaming in the respective countries show striking differences (see Table 3.1). The case of Germany is especially surprising: While the study applies a fairly wide criterion of what a gamer is (simply: a person that plays digital games, without any further defini-tional restriction), the diffusion rates are very low. This becomes even more obvious when compared to the data in Flanders in which the same criterion was applied. Obviously, the specific discussion in Germany (see above) has

Table 3.1 Base Data and Diffusion Rates

	Finland	*Flanders*	*Germany*	*Singapore*
Survey type/data collection	Controlled mail survey	CAPI	CATI (bus + panel)	CATI
N	1,079	1,403	Bus: 50,012; panel: 5,000 (4,500 gamers + 500 non-gamers)	843
Definition of gamer/filter criterion	At least once a month + use time in study	Active gamer (play digital games) Use time in study	Active gamer (play digital games) Frequency and use time in panel	Active gamer (played video games in past six months)
Active gamers (% of respective group)				
Female	42.9	39.4	20.9	48.0
Male	57.6	43.0	30.1	53.0
Age groups				
15–19	90.5	77.0	63.1	–
20–29	73.5	57.0	48.7	81.8
30–39	55.0	47.3	35.0	56.0
40–49	38.5	44.3	24.9	39.4
50–59	33.7	37.5	17.7	17.9
60–64	27.1	26.3	14.8	13.2
65+	22.0	25.5	9.7	3.3
Overall	50.2	41.2	25.2	41.1

a dampening effect on the diffusion rate, in addition to other effects (such as the higher average age in the German population). The other diffusion rates are much more similar, with Finland leading for the male respondents, and Singapore leading for the female respondents. For females, we find a diffusion of approximately 40–50%, and for males, of approximately 45–60%.

Thus, in principle, there is still a gender imbalance in all countries under analysis, but it is surprisingly small in the case of Flanders and Singapore— which contradicts the stereotype of the male gamer. The diffusion across age groups shows a similar pattern in all countries under analysis: Gaming is very much a young people's hobby. Again, the diffusion rates vary greatly between countries, with Flanders and Germany showing much lower numbers for the younger groups, despite having a wider definition of a "gamer." This could be attributed to a more critical central-European approach toward gaming—but given the differences in definition, this is just one possible explanation.

The use time was available for all four countries (see Table 3.2). The actual playing time of gamers is quite low for Finland and Germany, and much below other forms of media use (for example, TV viewing). It has to be noted that these are the numbers for the gamers, so the actual use time for the whole population would be even lower. The data from Flanders implies a much higher use time. However, this might be due to the way in which this was calculated: While in Finland and Germany the survey included a specific item on game use, the playing duration in Flanders was per device (PC, console, mobile) on an average day during the week and at the weekend. The addition of data from per-device questions might lead to an overreporting (or vice versa, the question regarding "overall gaming time" might lead to underreporting). The data for Singapore lies in between, probably due to the more positive approach to digital gaming in the country (when compared to Finland and Germany).

Gaming frequency was reported in two countries (see Table 3.3), with varying categories. Despite slight differences in the wording, the results are very similar.[6] The core gamer who plays games on a daily basis seems to be a minority: About one-fifth of the gamers reported playing every day. Nearly half of the gamers belong to the *casual gamer* category with a low gaming frequency—these people play a few times or once a month, or even more rarely.

Table 3.2 Game Use (All Gamers)

	Finland	Flanders	Germany	Singapore
Duration (minutes/day)	37.5	105	49.8	65.2

Table 3.3 Gaming Frequency (All Gamers)

	Finland		Germany
Daily	22.1	Daily	22.3
Weekly	35.7	Several times a week	32.8
About once a month	18.2	Several times a month	19.8
Seldom	24.0	Seldom	25.1

Genre

The base data above already revealed some interesting trends, the problems with varying methods, definitions, and instruments notwithstanding. An important question beyond the general diffusion of gaming concerns the genres: What types of games are played in the countries under analysis? This question is already interesting in terms of the topic of this volume (multiplayer and social gaming), as some genres are more likely to be played together with others (for example, adventure games are more geared toward single-player modes, whereas music and party games are usually played in groups, as they are mostly dependent on player interaction).

Genre information was available for three countries, again with differing questions and genres. The genres were re-grouped and partially collapsed for the sake of rough comparability. Due to the vastly different questions, the row percentages are not directly comparable (see Table 3.4; please also note the explanatory text). However, the ranking of the genres gives us some indication as to what is popular in the given country, and what is not. There are some obvious country specifics—for example, strategy games are wildly popular in Germany (something that is already known from sales figures; see, for example, the figures published on a regular basis in the trade journal *GamesMarkt*).

Furthermore, some genres receive surprisingly low support, for example, shooter games, and, to some extent, also role-playing games (RPGs). One would expect these titles to be of higher relevance, based on the public discussion, the media resonance, and the number of AAA titles in the respective genre. However, it seems plausible that this expectation is based on a stereotypical view of "the gamer"; that is, a strong identification of gaming with the core gamer group (where these genres are of higher importance). In contrast to this, the figures for puzzle and card games are high, which might surprise as well. This could be linked to the large number of casual gamers, as many puzzle and card games are titles that are typically played *once in a while*, and not for extended periods of time. Again, this is somewhat speculative. As a point of comparison, the Finnish survey asked about the most recent game the respondents had played, and the classic puzzle game *Solitaire*, available on every PC with the Windows operating system, received 152 mentions in the 2011 survey, whereas the

Table 3.4 Genres (Percentage of Gamers)

	Flanders*	Germany*	Singapore**
Role-playing games	10.0	43.3	8.8
Strategy games	18.5	72.9	8.0
Sports games	22.7	46.6	6.8
Racing games	27.7	40.9	2.4
First-person shooters	24.3	28.7	6.3
Action games	19.0	37.4	5.1
Simulation games	16.5	40.3	3.4
Adventure games	19.8	48.2	7.5
Music and party games	13.0	38.2	2.0
Puzzle/card games	47.7	59.6	33.0

Notes
* Percentage of players indicating that they are playing the respective genre (in the case of Germany, at least a medium preference is shown for the genre on a five-point scale).
** Respondents reported genres of the games they played most often in the past six months; categories were recoded: role-playing games include MMOGs and single-player, role-playing games, puzzle games also include Flash-based games (such as *Solitaire* and *Tetris*); action games include all action genres with the exception of the other categories, i.e., fighting and survival horror games; not all genres reported here (so this does not add up to 100%).

most popular sports game (the *NHL* series by Electronic Arts, 1991–2012) got 25 mentions, and the most popular action game (*Call of Duty* series by Infinity Ward, Treyarch et al., 2003–2012) 23 mentions. The popularity of *Solitaire* has been at an equally high level in all three Player Barometer surveys carried out in Finland so far (Karvinen and Mäyrä, 2009, 2011; Kuronen and Koskimaa, 2010).

It should be noted that many puzzle and card games are solo games, whereas many shooter games (such as *Counter-Strike* by Valve Corporation, 1999) and some RPGs (such as *World of Warcraft* by Blizzard Entertainment, 2004) are multiplayer titles, which fuels the assumption that multiplayer gaming might be more popular among the core gamers. The free and easy availability of a game can also be a significant factor, as in the case of Windows *Solitaire*, as contrasted to games that require money and specific effort to acquire and install.

Gender and Age

In the last section, we discussed some findings for the overall group of gamers. However, from the diffusion rates, one could already deduce that gaming is very much dependent on socio-demographic and other personal factors. In this overview article, we will restrict the discussion to the most basic differentiating factors: gender and age.

36 *Quandt, Chen, Mäyrä, and Van Looy*

When examining the game duration (see Table 3.5), it becomes obvious that some gender-based differences have persisted in gaming. While the diffusion rates indicated a closure of the *gaming gap* between men and women, these figures underline that men still play much more than women in all countries under analysis.

Consistent with these findings, the frequency data from Finland and Germany (see Table 3.6) reveal that male gamers are not only playing more, but also more frequently than their female counterparts. About half of the female gamers can be regarded as being *casual gamers* in both countries.

Genre use also varies with gender, and there are patterns that can be compared across regions; in this case, for Flanders, Germany, and Singapore (see Table 3.7). There is one genre in particular that shows a stark contrast between male and female gamers—first-person shooters (and to some extent, the related genre of action games). This genre is very unpopular among the female players. The opposite is true for puzzle and card games: Women have a clear preference for this genre in all three countries, at a much higher level than men. For another genre—music and party games—women's interest surpasses that of men in all countries. These findings can be related to gender-specific preferences, but are also connected to the higher percentage of casual gamers among women (as puzzle/card games are more of a *casual* genre).

The influence of gender on game use follows similar patterns across countries, and the same is true—to an even more obvious extent—for age (see Table 3.8). The game duration is the highest for the young players, and

Table 3.5 Gaming Duration and Gender (Minutes per Day)

	Finland*	Flanders	Germany	Singapore
Men	46.0	122.0	58.0	74.9
Women	22.3	87.0	38.6	54.2

Note
* Recalculated to daily use; item was minutes/week.

Table 3.6 Gaming Frequency and Gender (Percentage of Gamers)

	Finland			Germany	
	Male	Female		Male	Female
Daily	26.7	16.8	Daily	23.7	20.5
Weekly	38.7	32.1	Several times a week	35.6	29.3
About once a month	16.1	20.7	Several times a month	19.1	20.8
Seldom	18.5	30.4	Seldom	21.7	29.5

Table 3.7 Gaming Genre and Gender (Percentage of Gamers)

	Flanders		Germany		Singapore	
	Male	Female	Male	Female	Male	Female
Role-playing games	15.9	3.7	50.0	34.5	11.8	5.3
Strategy games	27.4	8.7	76.5	68.2	11.0	4.6
Sports games	30.8	28.9	52.9	38.4	10.1	3.0
Racing games	38.5	15.8	51.2	27.4	3.6	1.0
First-person shooters	39.6	7.4	43.9	7.9	9.4	2.8
Action games	28.4	8.8	51.1	19.5	6.9	3.1
Simulation games	16.5	16.4	48.1	30.0	3.4	3.5
Adventure games	25.0	14.1	51.7	43.6	7.4	7.6
Music and party games	12.5	13.4	32.3	46.0	1.6	2.6
Puzzle/card games	37.8	58.6	44.0	79.9	24.2	42.9

then decreases with age (with the exception of Germany, where the two top groups have a slightly higher use time than the younger groups).

The gaming-frequency data primarily follow this pattern, with frequent use among the young gamers, and then decreasing use frequency for the older groups. However, for the two countries where age-dependent frequency information is available, we find an interesting deviation from the expected pattern: Daily use goes up again for the two oldest groups, whereas occasional use goes down (see Table 3.9).

This effect might be related to more stable spare-time contingents for the older and retired gamers—something that is also known in television viewing and other forms of media use. Depending on societal developments, it is likely that this effect might become more pronounced in the future, with aging generations of digital natives who regard digital gaming as an integral part of their existence, and who gain more time for it again

Table 3.8 Gaming Duration and Age (Minutes per Day)

	Finland*	Flanders	Germany	Singapore
15–20	67.8	201	67.7	–
21–30	32.2	115	64.0	77.6
31–49	24.5	113	40.0	53.4
50–64	23.8	108	42.6	52.8
65+	21.1	68	45.5	50.0

Note
* Recalculated to daily use; item was minutes/week; the group of 10–14 years old was left out of this comparison, as it was not available in any other country survey.

Table 3.9 Gaming Frequency and Age (Percent)

Finland [Germany]	15–20	21–30	31–49	50–64	65+
Day*	34.5 [28.9]	21.5 [19.9]	13.1 [18.8]	17.4 [22.2]	28.1 [33.2]
Week	39.0 [36.1]	35.0 [34.1]	33.1 [28.5]	33.0 [34.7]	32.6 [40.4]
Month	18.4 [15.4]	22.7 [22.5]	21.1 [23.6]	17.4 [16.2]	13.1 [12.3]
Seldom	8.1 [19.7]	20.9 [23.5]	32.7 [29.1]	32.3 [26.9]	26.2 [14.1]

Note
* Reference point for frequency; please note the difference between the scales in Finland and Germany; see Table 3.3.

in the later phases of their life. For example, the Finnish Player Barometer studies already show a statistically significant increase in game playing among the oldest 70- to 75-year-old demographic. In 2009, the segment of active game players was 75% of the respondents, whereas in 2011 this figure was already 91% (p = 0.02), when analog and digital game play were considered together (the results are not statistically significant when digital play is considered separately, even when digital play had also increased among elderly people during the period, as in the surveyed Finnish population in general; Karvinen and Mäyrä, 2011).

Finally, age effects are also visible when examining preferences and genres. The interest in RPGs, sports games, and shooter games decreases with age. In contrast to this, it goes up for puzzle and card games (with a slight decline for the oldest group in Finland and Germany).[7]

This pattern could be the outcome of the interplay between several factors—a more general reduction in playing time with age, the above-mentioned gain of more regular spare-time patterns with age (leading to a gain in frequency), and an age-related preference for less action-oriented, more casual genres. However, the reasons cannot be identified with the current data sets. It should be noted that the increasing interest in casual games in many different demographics has been noted in the game culture as a more general trend (Juul, 2010).

That said, a genre-mediated effect on multiplayer gaming is plausible: Puzzle games are typically single-player games, whereas shooter games, massively multiplayer online role-playing games (MMORPGs), and many console sports games offer multiplayer modes. An age-related decline in multiplayer gaming is also plausible on the basis of the more generally low diffusion rate of gaming in the older groups: Older gamers have much fewer options for finding co-players in their own peer group, as gaming is a rare hobby in the respective age segment. And finally, some multiplayer titles (for example, first-person shooters and sports games) depend on reaction time and "skills," which may adversely affect older gamers (in contrast to many puzzle games where reaction time is irrelevant).

Table 3.10 Selected Genres and Age (Percentage)

	15–20	*21–30*	*31–49*	*50–64*	*65+*
Role-playing games					
Flanders	17.5	23.8	6.2	2.6	5.8
Germany	64.3	61.8	42.0	22.8	12.6
Singapore	–	11.6	7.0	3.2	0.0
Sports games					
Flanders	45.9	34.1	23.3	11.2	3.5
Germany	60.6	49.0	48.6	34.7	29.3
Singapore	–	8.9	5.5	1.1	12.5
First-person shooters					
Flanders	55.7	39.0	25.0	9.4	0.0
Germany	53.6	46.9	23.8	8.1	3.7
Singapore	–	7.7	5.5	3.2	0.0
Puzzle and card games					
Flanders	36.1	39.0	47.5	62.1	49.4
Germany	35.1	52.0	65.1	73.2	65.5
Singapore	–	24.1	38.9	49.0	62.5

Multiplayer and Social Gaming

In the previous section, we have discussed some findings from four national surveys on digital gaming. There were some indications of socio-demographic effects on the multiplayer and/or social aspects of gaming, but the conclusions were indirect and speculative. Unfortunately, specific questions regarding socially relevant gaming modes are missing from most surveys. Basically, dependable representative data on the phenomenon are missing (which is true for many other aspects of digital gaming as well).

In the case of the German survey, the bus study questionnaire included some more detailed questions regarding gaming modes: solo gaming, online gaming, or co-located gaming with others (i.e., playing in front of a console or PC with co-present other players). Naturally, individuals are not limited to playing in just one way—while some might prefer only to play solo, others might play together with others both in front of their console, and via the Internet with their PCs. The different options and the percentage of players belonging to the respective groups can be arranged in a Venn diagram (see Figure 3.1).

The diagram reveals an uneven distribution between the various options, with three major groups: solo only players (32%); solo/co-located players (27%); and a group we labeled omnivores (17%)—gamers who actually play via all available modes. All other combinations are negligible: Only a very small number of gamers solely play online or co-located games, or

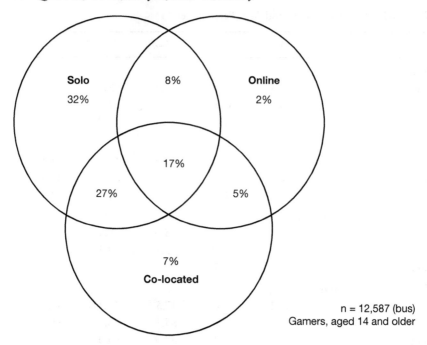

Figure 3.1   Gaming Modes (Germany, All Players, Bus Study).

both in combination, but not in single-player mode. In that sense, solo gaming can be seen as a base mode of digital gaming, as nearly every gamer does it once in a while.

However, the relatively low number of pure solo gamers shows that the stereotypical, socially inept, "lonely" gamer does not make up the majority of gamers: Most of the players take part in some sort of social gaming in addition to solo gaming. The solo/co-located gamers are most likely the more casual gamers who play with their console or sometimes alone at their PC, whereas the omnivores seem to be primarily core gamers who play anything. However, these plausible considerations would need to be tested in future analyses and studies. There is already some evidence available that the solo preference of casual gamers exists, yet also that the practice of playing alone may also have a significant social component (Kallio, Mäyrä, and Kaipainen, 2011; Stenros, Paavilainen, and Mäyrä, 2011).

Reconstructing the Global Gamersphere: Toward a Comparative Research Program

In the previous sections, we discussed some of the findings from the surveys in the four countries. On the positive side, such comparisons help us to learn about "the others" and widen the perspective of the research, even in one's own country context (see Berger, 1997).

However, as we saw, not only do the findings from the various country contexts differ vastly, but so do the theoretical and methodological backgrounds of the studies. While all of them offered some base data that seem to be roughly comparable as a reference on a very general level, analyses that are more detailed are difficult due to these differences. The problems begin with the very definition of who a gamer is and with what constitutes "use" in the context of digital games (see also Blake and Klimmt, 2012), continue with the choice of samples, with data collection, and do not end with the in-/exclusion of specific gaming modes, and specialized, unstandardized scales. Naturally, the problems become more severe when examining specific phenomena, such as in this volume—questions on multiplayer or social gaming are mostly not included in the surveys, at least not directly. Some information could be indirectly retrieved from other questions, but some of the conclusions are just plausible speculations (for example, based on genre information). Only in one case—the German survey—were several questions directed toward multiplayer and social gaming (which is not surprising, as this was one of the aims of this specific national study).

This leads to pressing methodological and theoretical questions: Can we really identify cultural/national differences when the aims, methods, and theories of the respective studies differ at the same time? Can findings be transferred between countries and regions when we realize that gaming as a social activity has a vastly different presence and status in the countries under analysis?

When examining the problem more systematically, one can differentiate between various types of comparative research, as described in relation to other fields in previous literature. For example, the level of similarity between the units under analysis plays an important role, as this is relevant for comparisons to be made. Przeworski and Teune (1970) identify two different strategies here: The most similar and the most different systems approach, based on the similarities among, and the contrast between the units under analysis. Hanitzsch (2008), building on previous systematizations of comparative research (such as Przeworksi and Teune, 1970; Kohn, 1989), names three general approaches: safari research, application, and assembly. As the name implies, safari research involves carrying out research in a cultural context that is at least partially different from the researcher's own home context. Application is quite the opposite: Here, the researcher applies studies from another cultural context to her/his own home context. Assembly is, in its best form, a collaborative research effort, where researchers from different cultural contexts join forces in designing the research, including the development of the instruments, analysis strategies, and the publication of the findings. Hanitzsch (2008) notes that all of these approaches have their strengths and weaknesses. Naturally, if the logistics and practical aspects allow for it, then undertaking assembly research is the most desirable route, as the research is not ripped out of its context and not applied to phenomena that it was not meant for.

The overview of surveys presented here does not really fall into that category: Although the researchers joined forces for some (limited) analysis and a publication, the actual planning and implementation of the studies was undertaken by individual teams, using different instruments (therefore, we only used overview tables without applying more advanced statistical analysis, which would simply be inappropriate in the given context). Furthermore, the selection of countries does not follow theoretical considerations, but practical ones, and in the end, the availability of data. Naturally, the result is not a "global" study in the sense of a comprehensive overview of gaming populations all over the planet; rather, it spotlights some aspects in some countries.

This is obviously not an ideal solution: Many aspects, even early on in the research process, are not comparable. In many ways, we are still groping in the dark, even when it comes to such basic things as diffusion rates across countries. Therefore, more unified approaches on an international level are needed, with a theory-driven selection of countries, and some standardization regarding:

- definitional criteria as to what and who gamers are, including all kinds of gaming (i.e., PC/computer gaming, consoles, mobile games, etc.);
- sampling procedures and methods;
- questions on game use and frequency;
- personality variables;
- gaming modes (online vs. offline, solo vs. multiplayer, etc.);
- internationally applicable game genre lists;
- questions on gaming behavior, preferences, experience;
- questions on attitudes toward one's own or others' gaming, or toward talking about one's gaming to others.

There are certainly some difficulties involved with such a standardization process, but the benefits would be manifold. Most obviously, one would get comparable base data for gaming across nations, cultures, and societies. Naturally, this would widen the perspective of the research, which is often confined by the national viewpoint; however, at the same time, we would learn about our own gamer culture through contrasting it with that of other regions and cultures. Identifying reasons for the observed differences would lead to the discovery of more general underlying factors governing the role of digital games in the lives of different peoples. Additionally, we could identify not only changes in the level of gaming per se, but also for specific modes such as multiplayer gaming. From the exploratory data presented here, one can deduce that there is a growing importance for social gaming modes—obviously, digital gaming as a whole appears highly different from the stereotypes associated with lonely solo gamers. However, more international, comparative research would be needed to further support these ideas, and to give the current work on multiplayer gaming and other social uses of games more context.

Acknowledgments

Frans Mäyrä expresses thanks to his co-author and research assistant Juho Karvinen, who provided invaluable help while conducting some further analyses of Player Barometer data that were needed for the purposes of this article. The Player Barometer study was carried out with a grant from the Academy of Finland. Thorsten Quandt expresses special thanks to Ruth Festl and Michael Scharkow for their help in preparing the German data. The German study is part of the larger ERC (European Research Council) project "The Social Foundations of Online Gaming." It received funding from the European Union's Seventh Framework Programme (FP/2007–2013) under grant agreement no. 240864 (SOFOGA).

Notes

1   The games industry claims to have surpassed the film industry for several years now, after having compared computer and console games with box office returns in the USA. However, according to several comparisons (such as the estimated worldwide revenue), overall, the film industry is still economically more important than the games industry. For a more in-depth discussion on this issue see Kerr (2006, p. 50) or Dovey and Kennedy (2006, p. 45).

2   Even single-player games are adapted to national markets: Written text or spoken words are translated, sometimes the content is adapted to local customs and experiences, sometimes parts of the game (especially brutal and gory content, but also sexually explicit scenes) are cut to reflect the respective legal and societal situation, and so on. However, these changes usually do not radically alter the games' content and feel, including the in-game interactions.

3   There is a discussion in psychology about the applicability of findings from lab research and its typical samples to other groups of society (Henrich, Heine, and Norenzayan, 2009), so this is not merely specific to games research.

4   An *omnibus* or *bus* study is a large-scale survey where multiple clients can "book" their questions to be asked during the interviews. The socio-demographic data and some base data are shared by the clients (as it just needs to be asked once during the interview). Usually, such surveys are done on a regular or ongoing basis by media and market research institutes. These studies have the benefit of a large sample size, the high speed of data gathering (as the survey institutes usually have dozens or even hundreds of interviewers working on the omnibus), and of saving costs through sharing the bus. However, they are primarily used to gather information regarding a few aspects, but on a large scale.

5   A panel study is a longitudinal study where the same respondents are interviewed several times at specified intervals (for example, annually). The individual incarnations of the study are called *waves* (so if the respondents are interviewed three times, the panel has three waves).

6   One could argue that the mental concept triggered by these questions equals to *day, week, month,* and *more rarely.*

7   Singapore deviates from this pattern in the case of sports games. However, due to the small sample size in the respective age group, this may be the result of individual outliers.

References

Anderson, C. A. and Bushman, B. J. (2001). Effects of violent games on aggressive behavior, aggressive cognition, aggressive affect, psychological arousal, and prosocial behavior. A meta-analytic review of scientific literature. *Psychological Science*, 12, 353–359.

Berger, P. (1997). Epistemological modesty: An interview with Peter Berger. *The Christian Century*, *114*(30), 972–978.

BIU, Bundesverband interaktiver Unterhaltungssoftware (2013). Marktzahlen. Retrieved from http://www.biu-online.de/de/fakten/marktzahlen.html

Blake, C. and Klimmt, C. (2012). The challenge of measuring the use of computer games. In J. Fromme and A. Unger (Eds.), *Computer games and new media cultures. A handbook of digital games studies* (pp. 357–369). Berlin: Springer.

Cassell, J., and Jenkins, H. (Eds.). (1998). *From Barbie to Mortal Kombat. Gender and computer games*. Cambridge: MIT Press.

Chee, F. (2005). *Understanding Korean experiences of online game hype, identity, and the menace of the "Wang-tta"*. Retrieved from http://www.digra.org/dl.

De Pauw, E., Pleysier, S., Van Looy, J., and Soetaert, R. (2008). *Jongeren en gaming: Over de effecten van games, nieuwe sociale netwerken en educatieve kansen*. Leuven: ACCO.

Dovey, J. and Kennedy, H. W. (2006). *Games cultures: Computer games as new media*. Maidenhead: Open University Press.

ESA, Entertainment Software Association (2013). *Essential facts about the computer and video game industry. 2012 sales, demographic and usage data*. Retrieved from http://www.theesa.com/facts/pdfs/esa_ef_2012.pdf.

Ferguson, C. J. (2007). The good, the bad and the ugly: A meta-analytic review of positive and negative effects of violent video games. *Psychiatric Quarterly*, 78, 309–316.

Festl, R., Scharkow, M., and Quandt, T. (2013). Problematic computer game use among adolescents, younger and older adults. *Addiction*, *108*(3), 592–599.

Fritz, J., Lampert, C., Schmidt, J., and Witting, T. (Eds.). (2011). *Kompetenzen und exzessive Nutzung bei Computerspielern: Gefordert, gefördert, gefährdet*. Berlin: Vistas.

Fromme, J. and Unger, A. (Eds.) (2012). *Computer games and new media cultures: A handbook of digital games studies*. Heidelberg, London, New York: Springer.

Griffiths, M. D., Davies, M. N. O., and Chappell, D. (2003). Breaking the stereotype: The case of online gaming. *CyberPsychology and Behavior*, *6*(1), 81–91.

Hanitzsch, T. (2008). Comparing journalism across cultural boundaries: State of the art, strategies, problems and solutions. In M. Löffelholz and D. Weaver (Eds.), *Global journalism research: Theories, methods, findings, future* (pp. 93–105). Oxford: Blackwell.

Hartmann, T. (2006). Gewaltspiele und Aggression – aktuelle Forschung und Implikationen. In W. Kaminski (Ed.), *Clash of Realities. Computerspiele und soziale Wirklichkeit*. (pp. 81–99). München: KoPäd.

Henrich, J., Heine, S. J., and Norenzayan, A. (2010). The weirdest people in the world? *Behavior and Brain Sciences*, *33*(2/3), 1–23.

Hjorth, L. and Chan, D. (2009). *Gaming cultures and place in Asia-Pacific*. London: Routledge.

iMinds-iLab.o. (2010). *Digimeter report 3*. Gent: iMinds-iLab.o.

Juul, J. (2010). *A casual revolution: Reinventing video games and their players*. Cambridge, MA: MIT Press.

Kallio, K. P., Mäyrä, F., and Kaipainen, K. (2011). At least nine ways to play: Approaching gamer mentalities. *Games and Culture*, 6(4), 327–353.

Karvinen, J., and Mäyrä, F. (2009). *Pelaajabarometri 2009: Pelaaminen Suomessa*. Tampere: University of Tampere. Retrieved from http://urn.fi/urn:isbn:978-951-44-7868-0.

Karvinen, J., and Mäyrä, F. (2011). *Pelaajabarometri 2011: Pelaamisen muutos*. Tampere: University of Tampere. Retrieved from http://urn.fi/urn:isbn:978-951-44-8567-1.

Kerr, A. (2006). The business of making digital games. In J. Rutter and J. Bryce (Eds.), *Understanding digital games* (pp. 36–57). London: Sage.

Kohn, M. L. (1989). Introduction. In M. L. Kohn (Ed.), *Cross-national research in sociology* (pp. 17–31). Newbury Park, CA: Sage.

Kuronen, E. and Koskimaa, R. (2011). *Pelaajabarometri 2010*. Jyväskylä: University of Jyväskylä. Retrieved from https://www.jyu.fi/erillis/agoracenter/julkaisut/verkkosivut/pelaajabarometri2010.pdf.

Lee, T. and Willnat, L. (2009). *Media research and political communication in Singapore*. Retrieved from http://dspace.cigilibrary.org/jspui/.

Lenhart, A. (2008, September 16). *Teens, video games and civics*. PEW Internet and American Life Project. Retrieved from http://www.pewinternet.org/Reports/2008/Teens-Video-Games-and-Civics.aspx.

Lenhart, A., Jones, S., and Macgill, A. (2008, December 7). *Adults and video games*. PEW Internet and American Life Project. Retrieved from http://www.pewinternet.org/Reports/2008/Adults-and-Video-Games.aspx.

Przeworski, A. and Teune, H. (1970). *The logic of comparative inquiry*. New York: Wiley.

Quandt, T. (2010). Computer- und Konsolenspiele. Ein Forschungsüberblick zur Nutzung und Wirkung von Bildschirmspielen. In Kommission Jugendmedienschutz der Landesmedienanstalten (KJM) (Ed.), *Umstritten und umworben: Computerspiele – ein Herausforderung für die Gesellschaft (KJM-Schriftenreihe, Band 2)* (pp. 113–114). Berlin: Vistas.

Quandt, T., Festl, R., and Scharkow, M. (2011). Digitales Spielen – Medienunterhaltung im Mainstream. GameStat 2011: Repräsentativbefragung zum Computer- und Konsolenspielen in Deutschland. *Media Perspektiven*, 9/2011, 414–422.

Quandt, T., Scharkow, M., and Festl, R. (2010). Digitales Spielen als mediale Unterhaltung: Eine Repräsentativstudie zur Nutzung von Computer- und Videospielen in Deutschland. *Media Perspektiven*, 11/2010, 515–522.

Quandt, T., Wimmer, J., and Wolling, J. (Eds.). (2009). *Die Computerspieler. Studien zur Nutzung von Computergames* (2nd ed.). Wiesbaden: Verlag für Sozialwissenschaften.

Ritterfeld, U., Cody, M., and Vorderer, P. (Eds.). (2009). *Serious games: Mechanisms and effects*. New York/London: Routledge.

Sherry, J. L. (2001). The effects of violent video games on aggression. A meta-analysis. *Human Communication Research*, 27(3), 409–431.

Stenros, J., Paavilainen, J., and Mäyrä, F. (2011). Social interaction in games. *International Journal of Arts and Technology*, 4(3), 342–358.

Toyad, J. (2011). *Game development in Singapore: A primer.* Retrieved from http://www.gamespot.com/features/game-development-in-singapore-a-primer-6323728/.

Vorderer, P. and Bryant, J. (Eds.). (2006). *Playing video games. Motives, responses, and consequences.* Mahwah, NJ: Lawrence Erlbaum Associates.

Games Cited

Armor Projects (1986-2012). Dragon Quest (series), Square Enix.

Blizzard Entertainment (2004). *World of Warcraft,* Vivendi Activision Blizzard.

Electronic Arts (1991–2012). *NHL* (series), Electronic Arts.

Infinity Ward, Treyarch et al. (2003–2012). *Call of Duty* (series). Activision/Aspyr Media.

Remedy Entertainment (2001). *Max Payne,* Gathering of Developers.

Remedy Entertainment (2010). *Alan Wake,* Remedy Entertainment.

Rockstar (2006). *Canis Canem Edit*, Rockstar/Take-Two Interactive.

Rovio Entertainment (2009). *Angry Birds,* Rovio Entertainment.

Square Enix (1987-2013). Final Fantasy (series), Square Enix.

Valve Corporation (1999). *Counter-Strike,* Valve Corporation.

Part II

Social Interaction in Virtual Worlds

4 Methodology of Measuring Social Immersion in Online Role-Playing Games

Exemplary Experimental Research on Social Interactions in Virtual Worlds

Georg Valtin, Daniel Pietschmann, Benny Liebold, and Peter Ohler

Social Science Research in Virtual Worlds

Computer games studies is a broad field with a great number of contributing disciplines. As a result, a great variety of research approaches and methods are being used. While questionnaires clearly dominate the field (e.g. Axelsson and Regan, 2006; Quandt, Wimmer, and Wolling, 2008), other methods applied include laboratory experiments (e.g. Yee, 2007), ethnography (e.g. Taylor, 2006), and qualitative approaches (see Vermeulen and Van Looy, Part II; Kowert and Oldmeadow, Part III). The choice of a suitable method naturally depends on the discipline as well as the research question, and every method is impaired by drawbacks and caveats.

From the perspective of media psychology, the experiment is the preferable method, since it allows us to explain the experience and behavior of users based on the relations of cause and effect. So far, most of the experiments have been conducted in a controlled laboratory setting and, therefore, they lack external validity. This is a major problem for the research on virtual worlds, such as massively multiplayer online role-playing games (MMORPGs), since it is almost impossible to induce natural playing behavior in the participants. Therefore, it can be concluded that laboratory experiments are not an optimal solution for the research of users' behavior in online role-playing games, especially regarding social interaction between the players.

The Methodology of *in situ* Experiments

However, the problem of low external validity in laboratory experiments is not new and can be solved by conducting field experiments. It is often argued that the results of field experiments are less accurate because of their vulnerability to confounding variables (e.g. Bortz and Döring, 2006, pp. 49 ff.). In contrast to the "real world," this problem is rather manageable in virtual environments, because game worlds are less complex, and, most of all, less dynamic. For example, many environmental factors remain constant; that is, the spatial–temporal configuration of game elements. This allows researchers to use exactly the same setup for every participant (e.g. performing an interaction in the same location under the same conditions). To emphasize the fact that we measure the behavior of users in natural situations without the typical drawbacks relating to internal validity, we call this kind of field experiment in virtual environments an *in situ* experiment.[1]

Most of the MMORPGs offer tools (e.g. scripts and macros) allowing an unchanging course of action and standardized responses during interaction and communication between the researchers and the participants. Furthermore, these tools and computer technology in general offer effective and reliable means of data collection: Log-files, screenshots, and even video captures can automatically gather all the relevant information and thus enable the researchers to focus on the interaction itself. Another advantage of this method is the possibility for comparative cultural research: Most MMORPGs offer servers with localized versions of the game. For *World of Warcraft (WoW)* (Blizzard Entertainment, 2004), there are, for instance, servers for North America, Russia, and China. If the research team has adequate language abilities, the experiments can be conducted with samples from different cultures, which may lead to broader scientific findings.

Having rather easy access to many potential participants is another positive aspect of *in situ* experiments. Generally, this method is highly economical regarding financial, logistic, and time investments: The required equipment is already available and the research takes place in a virtual environment where you can easily recruit participants.

Prerequisites for the Use of *in situ* Experiments

As mentioned above, every scientific method has its own characteristics, assets, and drawbacks. Those will be discussed after some considerations regarding the prerequisites for using this method. First of all, *in situ* experiments require a deep knowledge of the given virtual world. The researchers must not only be able to control their avatar smoothly in every situation, but they must also be familiar with the game world, and the rules of interaction between players. That includes the "slang" as well as the behavior in groups and the implicit rules that are established in every shared virtual environment. Otherwise, the behavior of the researchers would appear as inappropriate, or even wrong, and could easily cause participants to change their behavior or cease communication altogether. Our recommendation is to play the game thoroughly for an extended period of time to prepare for the *in situ* experiments.

Social Immersion

To illustrate the application of the *in situ* method, we report on a study that was conducted at the Department of Media Psychology at Chemnitz

University of Technology examining social behavior as a major aspect of the user experience in online role-playing games. The user experience during gameplay is a key question in the field of computer game studies. Researchers suggested several concepts and determinants to explain this phenomenon, for example, control, interactivity, effectance, presence, involvement, and immersion (e.g. Murray, 1997; Ryan, 2001; McMahan, 2003; Zimmerman, 2004; Klimmt, 2006; Tamborini and Skalski, 2006; Pietschmann, 2009). In the field of game studies, immersion is one of the most discussed terms regarding the gameplay experience with many different approaches, for example, from literature studies (e.g. Murray, 1997), or presence research (e.g. Slater and Wilbur, 1997). As a result of the heterogeneous approaches, there is a lack of a generally accepted definition of the term "immersion" (Pietschmann, 2009, p. 76). To our understanding, immersion has to be considered as a psychological state of the user, similar to concepts such as flow (Csikszentmihalyi, 1973/2005), presence (Tamborini and Skalski, 2006), and cognitive absorption (Agarwal and Karahanna, 2000).[2] Several definitions of immersion relate to perceiving oneself as "[being] enveloped by, included in, and interacting with an environment that provides a continuous stream of stimuli and experiences" (Witmer and Singer, 1998, p. 227), with the consequence that users are captured by a story and its world, and shut out the "real" world around them (Gander, 1999, p. 1).

Presence is a similar concept originating from virtual reality research to describe "a feeling of being there" (Biocca, 1997). As opposed to immersion, presence is about the extent "to which the unification of simulated sensory data and perceptual processing produces a coherent 'place' that you are 'in'" (Slater, 2003). It is not about the quality of involvement or engagement of the user toward the media.[3] According to Slater (2003), one can be present but not involved, for example, in many everyday life situations. However, one can also be involved but not present, for example, when watching a movie in the living room. Thus, when we talk about immersion, we mean both the perceptual processing that generates presence, and the remainder of psychological processing (e.g. imagination processes) that occurs during gameplay.

Independent of the approaches to conceptualize immersion, researchers agree on the existence of different forms of immersion that contribute to the feeling of immersion as a whole. Examples include audio-visual immersion (e.g. Held and Durlach, 1992), temporal immersion, emotional immersion, sensomotoric immersion (e.g. Ermi and Mäyrä, 2005), and social immersion (Thon, 2008). For the research on social aspects of the user experience during gameplay, the concept of social immersion is obviously the most relevant form of immersion.

Thon (2008, p. 39) defines social immersion as "a shift of attention to the other players as social actors and the relationships between them." Within presence research, there is also a subtype concerning social aspects of perception processes: Social presence is widely understood as the "degree of salience of the other person in [an] interaction and the consequent salience of the interpersonal relationships" (Short, Williams, and Christie, 1976, p. 65). Biocca, Harms, and Burgoon (2003) argue that social presence is constituted by the perception of another copresent being, psychological involvement, or behavioral engagement. These aspects go beyond solely perceptual processing, so they refer more to our definition of immersion than to presence. The authentic reproduction of human social behavior through different communication channels and nonverbal expressions of avatars or agents are key factors to induce social immersion during game-play. Additionally, there is a sense of responsibility and community with the other players.

Social immersion should induce authentic social interactions within the virtual world, as other avatars or agents should be recognized as intelligent beings instead of merely game characters. Online role-playing games are highly social places,[4] where many diegetic and nondiegetic elements of the game support social immersion. The highest degree of social immersion should occur in real-world interactions. A high level of social immersion within a virtual world should mean that a player's social behavior should be very similar to their real-world social behavior. Therefore, social psychology findings should be transferable to the game world. As an example of highly socially immersive situations, we studied altruistic behavior within several games.

We employed *in situ* experiments as a methodology to study these social interactions within the game worlds, because they provide both a high internal and external validity.

Exemplary Study: The Role of Avatar Attractiveness in Prosocial Behavior

The goal of the study was to find out more about similarities and differences of real-life and virtual-life social behavior, particularly the social interaction revolving around a digital self-representation of the users via avatars, which can be altered in dramatic ways. Several theories concerning social interaction have been successfully applied to virtual environments (e.g. Behavioral Confirmation; Snyder, Tanke, and Berscheid, 1977; or Self-Perception Theory; Bem, 1972) and new forms of interaction unique to virtual worlds have been found (e.g. the Proteus Effect; Yee and Bailenson, 2007). In our study, we focused on prosocial and altruistic behavior in online role-playing games and tried to reproduce findings from evolutionary and social psychology (e.g. West and Brown, 1975; Wilson, 1978). Therefore, we employed the method of *in situ* experiments in online environments, such as *Second Life* (Linden Lab, 2003), *WoW*, *The Lord of the Rings Online: Shadows of Angmar* (Turbine Inc., 2007), and *Age of Conan* (Funcom, 2008). Physical attractiveness is an influential mediator for prosocial behavior. We used a variation of avatar attractiveness as the independent variable and asked other players to help us in performing in-game tasks to decide whether prosocial behavior was displayed or not.

Our main hypothesis assumed that players of online games help attractive avatars more often than unattractive avatars.

In preparation for the *in situ* experiments, suitable avatars were created in the respective game worlds and their attractiveness was evaluated during a pretest to create a ranking of attractiveness, ranging from low (1) to high attractiveness (6). Next, we decided on the prosocial behavior-inducing situation, which involved asking for help with certain quests/missions in the game world. The recruitment method and criteria for the participants were defined as well as a standardized address. Furthermore, we specified the interaction and communication with the participants and the methods of data logging. Lastly, the avatars were prepared for the in-game situation by getting them to the required minimum level and location for the chosen quests and equipping them with appropriate items to realize the intended visual appearance according to their desired attractiveness.

As measurements, we defined basic interaction protocols (whether the player helped when doing the quest or not), recorded chat logs, and took screenshots of the situation. Server-side data included relevant avatar information (e.g. level, race, class, etc.).

We conducted several *in situ* experiments in *WoW* (N = 60) and *Age of Conan* (N = 120) to test our hypotheses concerning avatar attractiveness (see Figure 4.1). In all experiments, attractive female avatars did receive significantly more help than attractive male or unattractive female avatars. One could argue that players infer characteristics of other players from their representation in the virtual environment. This also supports the fact that online role-playing games are highly socially immersive, as players project the image of other players' presentations on the actual user. The social behavior we found was often unconscious and automatic, which leads us to believe that from a cognitive viewpoint, players do not interact with other avatars, but rather, they interact directly with the other users. This can only occur in highly socially immersive environments.

 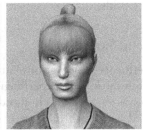 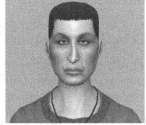

Figure 4.1 Avatars Used in the *Age of Conan In situ* Experiment from Left to Right: High Attractiveness (Rating 5.7), Medium Attractiveness (Rating 3.3), and Low Attractiveness (1.0).

Drawbacks and Caveats of *in situ* Experiments

It is not possible to conduct the experiment with randomized sampling. Instead, in most cases a convenient sample (accidental sampling) is used. Thus, the results cannot be generalized automatically because of issues concerning representativity. However, convenient samples are regarded as suitable for pilot studies, as in the exemplary study described above, since they offer a rather easy way to obtain a sample (Gravetter and Forzano, 2011). Through the variation of the time of the day, server, server type, and so on during the course of the experiment, the researchers can greatly increase the representativity of the convenience sample.

Another disadvantage is the fact that this specific *in situ* experiment only allows us to connect the data to the avatars of the participants and not to the actual participants. Obviously, the gender of the avatar is not necessarily the same as the gender of the player, and based on the nature of a MMORPG, we should expect a certain degree of role-playing behavior that does not reflect the typical response of the player. Yet, we are interested in the behavior during the gaming sessions in the virtual worlds, and thus a separation between player and avatar can even be considered as a useful feature. For research questions that focus on the players or the relationship between players and their avatars, *in situ* experiments can only be one of several ways to collect relevant data.

Finally, *in situ* experiments are constrained by the limits of the given virtual environment. This is an important factor when it comes to the question of how the variations of the independent variable can be realized. In laboratory experiments, it is often possible to create a specific environment and to design the experimental conditions accurately in the way the researchers want them to be. This is impossible in shared virtual environments that are hosted by commercial companies, allowing only a variation within the given parameters. This problem occurred when we tried to vary the attractiveness of avatars in *World of Warcraft*. The game did not allow for the alteration of the physique of the avatar and only provided very few preset faces and hairstyles. Researchers thus have to be sure that the degree of variation is sufficient for the given research question and independent variable, respectively, which is a shared characteristic of all kinds of experimental research in virtual worlds.

Ethical Considerations and Summary

Finally, some thoughts on ethical considerations: Since the participants were not aware of their contribution in our experiment, some might consider this method a violation of ethical research standards. Additionally, the participants were not asked for their "informed consent" before or after the experiment. Regarding research in real-world environments, there is no doubt that research must not take this path to avoid potential damage to a participant's psyche or reputation, which is the ultimate goal of ethical research standards. However, conducting experiments in virtual environments might not have negative effects on the participants' equivalent, real-world scenarios. Thus, to answer the question as to whether this procedure can be considered ethically justified or not, we have to look at the potential resulting damage to the players' psyche or reputation. In our opinion, this is not the case for the methodology of *in situ* experiments.

This conclusion results from two major arguments: First, players are not present in person in virtual environments but are mediated by their agent or avatar. Consequently, players benefit from a certain degree of anonymity that is constituted by the nature of most virtual environments. Considering this fact, we can rule out damage to a participant's reputation due to the missing link between a player's behavior in a virtual world and the person behind the respective avatar or agent. Second, players did not—at least in our specific research—have to show any other types of behavior that were not expected in the specific virtual environment due to its very nature. In fact, it is a quite common phenomenon in typical gaming sessions to be asked by low-level players to aid them in a quest. Hence, there were no extraordinary psychological strains on the questioned participants. Overall, employing *in situ* experiments (e.g. counting frequencies of behavior) without subsequent debriefing of the participants should be ethically justified in most cases, as long as the term *in situ* is understood literally; that is, that there are no additional data linking the avatar or agent to the player, and that there are no changes to the player's behavior that might result in types of behavior that are not expected within the specific virtual world.

By and large, *in situ* experiments can be considered as a favorable research method for virtual worlds and they should be applied more often. In doing so, scientists could rebut the argument of collecting rather useless data in laboratory settings. Instead, we would gain insight into actual behavior, free of the well-known biases that occur in artificial situations. This is, of course, generally interesting for social sciences and other disciplines, even though *in situ* experiments are more difficult to execute in real social situations. However, our method can obviously be combined or adapted respectively for many other settings involving computer-mediated communication. Even though it requires more work than other methods, the results are worth the effort.

Notes

1 This Latin phrase (meaning "in position") is frequently used in many scientific disciplines, such as archeology, biology, and literature.
2 For a more detailed discussion of both concepts, see McMahan (2003), Slater (2003), or Pietschmann (2009).
3 The terms engagement, involvement, and immersion are often mixed together, but resemble different scientific concepts in presence research, game studies, or marketing. McMahan (2003) and Pietschmann (2009) differentiate these terms on a more detailed level.
4 For an overview, see Ducheneaut et al. (2006).

References

Agarwal, R., and Karahanna, E. (2000). Time flies when you're having fun: Cognitive absorption and beliefs about information technology usage. *MIS Quarterly, 24*(4), 665–694.

Axelsson, A., and Regan, T. (2006). Playing online. In P. Vorderer and J. Bryant (Eds.), *Playing video games: Motives, responses, and consequences* (pp. 291–307). Mahwah, NJ: Lawrence Erlbaum.

Bem, D. J. (1972). Self perception theory. In L. Berkowitz (Ed.), *Advances in experimental social psychology (Vol. 6)*. New York City, NY: Academic Press.

Biocca, F. (1997): The cyborg's dilemma: Progressive embodiment in virtual environments. *Journal of Computer-Mediated Communication, 3*(2), 12–26.

Biocca, F., Harms, C., and Burgoon, J. K. (2003). Toward a more robust theory and measure of social presence: Review and suggested criteria. *Presence: Teleoperators and Virtual Environments, 12*(5), 456–480.

Bortz, J., and Döring, N. (2006). *Forschungsmethoden und Evaluation für Human- und Sozialwissenschaftler* (4th ed.). Berlin, Heidelberg, New York: Springer Verlag.

Csikszentmihalyi, M. (2005). *Das Flow Erlebnis: Jenseits von Angst und Langeweile: Im Tun aufgehen* (9th ed.). Stuttgart, Germany: Klett-Cotta.

Ducheneaut, N., Yee, N., Nickell, E., and Moore, R. J. (2006). Conference proceedings of the Conference on Human Factors in Computing Systems (CHI): *Alone together? Exploring the social dynamics of massively multiplayer games*. Montreal, PQ.

Ermi, L., and Mäyrä, F. (2005). Conference proceedings of the DiGRA Conference 2005: *Fundamental components of the gameplay experience: Analysing immersion*. Vancouver, University of Vancouver. Retrieved from http://www.digra.org/dl/db/06276.41516.pdf.

Gander, P. (1999). Two myths about immersion in new storytelling media. *Lund University Cognitive Studies, 80*, 1–16.

Gravetter, F. J., and Forzano, L. B. (2011). *Research Methods for the Behavioral Sciences* (4th ed.). Belmont, CA: Wadsworth.

Held, R., and Durlach, N. I. (1992). Telepresence. *Presence: Teleoperators and Virtual Environment, 1*(1), 109–112.

Klimmt, C. (2006). *Computerspielen als Handlung: Dimensionen und Determinanten des Erlebens interaktiver Unterhaltungsangebote*. Köln, Germany: Halem.

McMahan, A. (2003). Immersion, engagement, and presence: A method for analyzing 3-D video games. In M. J. P. Wolf and B. Perron (Eds.), *The video game theory reader* (pp. 67–87). New York City, NY: Routledge.

Murray, J. (1997). *Hamlet on the holodeck: The future of narrative in cyberspace*. Cambridge, MA: MIT Press.

Pietschmann, D. (2009). *Erleben in virtuellen Welten*. Boizenburg, Germany: Verlag Werner Hülsbusch.

Quandt, T., Wimmer, J., and Wolling, J. (2008). *Die Computerspieler. Studien zur Nutzung von Computergames*. Wiesbaden, Germany: VS Verlag.

Ryan, M.-L. (2001). *Narrative as virtual reality: Immersion and interactivity in literature and electronic media*. Baltimore, London: Johns Hopkins University.

Short, J. A., Williams, E., and Christie, B. (1976). *The social psychology of telecommunications*. New York City, NY: John Wiley & Sons.

Slater, M. (2003). A note on presence terminology. *Presence Connect, 3,* 3.

Slater, M., and Wilbur, S. (1997). A framework for immersive virtual environments (FIVE): Speculations on the role of presence in virtual environments. *Presence: Teleoperators and Virtual Environments, 6*(6), 603–616.

Snyder, M., Tanke, E. D., and Berscheid, E. (1977). Social perception and interpersonal behavior: On the self-fulfilling nature of social stereotypes. *Journal of Personality and Social Psychology, 35*(9), 656–666.

Tamborini, R., and Skalski, P. (2006). The role of presence in the experience of electronic games. In P. Vorderer and J. Bryant (Eds.), *Playing video games: Motives, responses, and consequences* (pp. 225–241). Mahwah, NJ: Lawrence Erlbaum Associates.

Taylor, T. L. (2006). *Play between worlds: Exploring online game culture.* Cambridge, MA: MIT Press.

Thon, J.-N. (2008). Immersion revisited: On the value of a contested concept. In A. Fernandez, O. Leino, and H. Wirman (Eds.), *Extending experiences: Structure, analysis and design of computer game player experience* (pp. 29–43). Rovaniemi, Lapland: Lapland University Press.

West, S. G., and Brown, T. J. (1975). Physical attractiveness, the severity of emergency and helping: A field experiment and interpersonal simulation. *Journal of Experimental Social Psychology, 11,* 531–538.

Wilson, D. W. (1978). Helping behavior and physical attractiveness. *The Journal of Social Psychology, 104,* 313–314.

Witmer, B. J., and Singer, M. J. (1998). Measuring presence in virtual environments: A presence questionnaire. *Presence: Teleoperators and Virtual Environments, 7*(3), 225–240.

Yee, N. (2007). *The Proteus Effect: Behavioral modification via transformations of digital self-representation.* Retrieved from http://www.nickyee.com/pubs/Dissertation_Nick_Yee.pdf.

Yee, N., and Bailenson, J. N. (2007). The Proteus Effect: The effect of transformed self-representation on behavior. *Human Communication Research, 33,* 271–290.

Zimmerman, E. (2004). Narrative, interactivity, play, and games: Four naughty concepts in need of discipline. In N. Wardrip-Fruin and P. Harrigan (Eds.), *First person: New media as story, performance, and game* (pp. 154–164). Cambridge, MA: MIT Press.

Games Cited

Blizzard Entertainment (2004), *World of Warcraft,* Vivendi Activision Blizzard.

Funcom (2008), *Age of Conan,* Eidos Interactive.

Linden Lab (2003), *Second Life,* Linden Lab.

Turbine Inc. (2007), *The Lord of the Rings Online: Shadows of Angmar,* Turbine Inc.

5 Happy Together?

A Gender-Comparative Study into Social Practices in Digital Gaming

Lotte Vermeulen and Jan Van Looy

Massively multiplayer online games (MMOs) attract a wide variety of players. This is due to the fact that these games afford a wide range of playing styles and encourage players to explore various modes of social interaction. For instance, Bartle (1996) distinguished between four types of multi-user dungeon (MUD) players; namely, achievers (goal oriented), explorers (discovery oriented), socializers (social contact oriented), and killers (annoyance oriented). In general, online games offer players opportunities to connect with like-minded others, build significant relationships, and form strong networks. However, although these social aspects may open new venues for women to participate in gaming culture, their participation is still lagging behind that of their male counterparts (Behnke, 2012). Accordingly, several studies have observed a lower participation rate of females in digital gaming (e.g., Williams, Yee, and Caplan, 2008; Willoughby, 2008).

An explanation for this is that digital games have traditionally been seen as boys' toys. Since the introduction of digital games, male teenagers have been perceived as their main target audience, and have largely continued to be so until recently (Laurel, 2008). Over the years, several attempts have been made at creating games specifically for girls, yet most of these efforts have not succeeded (Graner Ray, 2004). Researchers therefore continue looking for the ideal girl game by trying to identify gendered patterns of playing styles in order to rethink game design (e.g. Kafai, Heeter, Denner, and Sun, 2008). A central element, thereby, is the emphasis on game features that afford social interaction (AAUW, 2000). However, a detailed picture of the differences in preference of social features across gender is still lacking. The aim of this paper is to present an empirically grounded exploration of the differences in social gaming experience between men and women. This brings us to our research question:

RQ: Are there differences in social gaming preferences between male and female players, and how are they distributed?

We will tackle this subject on four levels; namely, the preference for in-game social interaction, the inclination to interact in real life during gaming, the urge to socially compete against others, and the importance of social contact as a motivation for playing in relation to other gaming motivations. Finally, we will narrow our focus to the MMO genre to see whether gender differences in social interaction are still present among players of this inherently social game genre.

Social Interaction

Social interaction in digital games is crucial to many players (De Vocht, Van Looy, Courtois, and De Marez, 2011). Social contact is seen as one of the most important motivations for playing games (e.g. De Pauw et al., 2008; Kolo and Baur, 2004). This social experience surrounding digital games is a multilayered concept that includes a variety of possibilities for social interaction. First, there is the possibility of communicating with others in online gaming environments. The most basic understanding of this online communication is in terms of "chat," which can be casual, but can also lead to long-term meaningful relationships, such as marriages between characters (in-role or not), or having regular friends and hunting/fighting/trading partners (Taylor, 2003). These interpersonal connections can also stimulate players to form groups with others in clans or guilds, for example, for attacking a group of monsters together (Ducheneaut, Yee, Nickell, and Moore, 2007). A second type of interaction in social game play concerns the possibility of out-of-game socializing. This implies communicating and spending time with offline relations who are involved in the game in a particular way (Taylor, 2003). There is the possibility of playing with people in the same physical location either by playing the same game together or by watching the other play. Moreover, people play with others they know well, such as family members, friends, or partners, as well as with strangers (e.g., at local-area network (LAN) parties). The third and last type of interaction in game play involves online, out-of-game socializing. Even when gamers are not playing, they often stay connected through comments about the game on discussion boards and websites, or by writing reviews and "walk-throughs" for the game (Pew, 2008).

Research has shown that women prefer other game genres than men and that they have different playing styles. Fewer women than men are attracted to action-based games that require high-level gaming skills and a strong commitment (Kerr, 2003). They tend to prefer abstract, short, and easier-to-master games, such as casual and social network games (IGDA, 2009; Nielsen, 2009). A study by Jenson and de Castell (2005) found that women tend to play games mostly on their own.

Furthermore, several studies have indicated that MMOs, which are typically social games, have a large majority of male players (Yee, 2008). These findings suggest a lesser tendency toward social game play for women than for men. The study by the BBC (2005), however, showed that party games are particularly popular among women. These games primarily aim to bring people together and encourage a social experience. This indicates that women do appreciate social interaction during game play, but not necessarily in the same context as men (De Pauw et al., 2008).

Some researchers have contended that social interaction in games is of considerable importance to women. According to Taylor (2003), the growing population of women in MMOs can partly be attributed to the sense of community and social structure these games offer. In the study by Hartmann and Klimmt (2006), three content-related factors were given to explain females' dislike of popular contemporary games: (1) stereotypical images of female avatars, (2) an abundance of in-game violence, and (3) few opportunities for social interaction. The results showed that the third reason was the most dominant feature in women's evaluation of games. Likewise, the AAUW (2000) emphasized the importance of numerous opportunities to interact with others in order to attract a female audience. The girls who participated in the study indicated that they liked having the chance to build new relationships through gaming.

Other studies, however, have contradicted the claim that female players have a stronger interest in social interaction than men do. Jansz, Avis, and Vosmeer (2010) conducted research into gender differences in motivations for playing *The Sims 2* (Maxis, 2004) and found that male players scored higher on the social interaction motivation than female players. Whereas Jansz et al. (2010) focused on one game title, Lucas and Sherry (2004) looked at multiple game genres for explaining gender differences in game play. Like Jansz et al., they found that women were less motivated by social interaction than men were. Lucas and Sherry explained this difference by contending that playing games is generally seen as appropriate for men, but not for women. Gender-stereotyped playing patterns have emerged due to the persistent view of digital games as boys' toys. Consequently, girls who deviate from this norm risk being rejected by their peers.

Social Spaces

Bertozzi (2008) has used a similar line of reasoning, claiming that access to online spaces is also confined by traditional societal gender roles that women and men are supposed to fulfill. Whereas virtual spaces provide an opportunity for women to anonymously compete against males (Bryce and Rutter, 2001), Bertozzi argues that virtual certainty of cross-gender competition deters women from digital games due to the difficulty in transgressing cultural norms. For instance, female players who are overtly aggressive and competitive against others in virtual spaces, often experience harassment as a result of their mismatch with feminine roles. Furthermore, Bryce and Rutter (2001) identified several other thresholds of access in public and domestic spaces that prevent girls from engaging in social gaming activities. LAN parties are an example of gendered public spaces where males dominate the space and girls are treated as an anomaly (Beavis and Charles, 2007; Bryce and Rutter, 2001). Although domestic spaces provide a less gendered gaming environment for female gamers, men are also likely to dominate this space. Bryce and Rutter (2001) refer to the work by Schott and Horrell (2000), who found that men consider themselves as "experts" in gaming situations. Even if the console is owned by the girl, men take access by justifying their play as collaborative or supportive, while they are, in fact, undermining the girl's skills. Finally, the study of Schott and Horrell also indicated that female players generally do not extend their playing habits outside the home, nor do they participate in the wider game culture.

The goal of this study is to elaborate on the above findings and explore in what way social experiences differ across gender. This brings us to our first hypothesis:

H1: Female players are less motivated by social contact in digital games than male players

   H1.1: Female players are less attracted to online communication during game play than male players

   H1.2: Female players are less attracted to gaming with others in the same physical space than male players

Competition

Another aspect of social gaming that needs to be taken into account is the possibility of competing against other players. As Sweetser and Wyeth (2005) have indicated, social competition as a motivation, which implies gaining satisfaction from competing against other people, is also an important aspect of social game play. Literature about gender differences in game preferences has indicated that male players are more strongly motivated by competition than female players (e.g. Hartmann and Klimmt, 2006). Taking into account the stronger interest of men in social interaction and competition in games, we predict that:

H2: Male players are fonder of social competition in digital games than female players

Genre

Like Lucas and Sherry (2004), we will focus on multiple gaming genres to gain insight into gender differences in social interaction. However, we will also look more closely at MMOs, in which social interaction is a crucial aspect (Chen, Duh, Priscilla, and Lam, 2006) and which is therefore a well-suited game genre to inquire into gender differences in social experience. We expect that the "social contact" motivation of female and male MMO players will be in line with hypothesis 1, stating:

H3: Female MMO players are less motivated by social contact in digital games than male MMO players

However, we expect that this gender difference will be smaller among MMO players compared to the overall sample because of similar interests and experience.

The Survey Study

Two exploratory focus groups with girls were undertaken to guide the design of the survey questionnaire. Afterwards, we recruited 983 respondents who indicated that they regularly play/have played digital games. The survey was distributed on online forums, on a gaming website, on (women-specific) forums, on social network sites, via e-mailing, and by handing out flyers. After data cleaning, we retained 962 valid and usable cases. Respondents were asked to rate each item on a five-point Likert scale, ranging from *strongly disagree* to *strongly agree*. In addition, an ordinal five-point scale was used for measuring playing frequency of specific game genres, ranging from *never* to *every day*. To test the general "social contact" motivation, we used the *Video Game Intrinsic Motivation Questionnaire* designed by Van Looy (2010). This five-point Likert motivation scale is based on the previous work of Van Looy, Schuurman, De Moor, De Marez, and Courtois (2010), who, in turn, revised the original gameflow heuristics by Sweetser and Wyeth (2005).

Results

Demographics

The mean age of our respondents was 24 years (SD = 6.49), ranging from 11 to 65. Moreover, the sample comprised more male (64.20%) than female gamers (35.80%). Interestingly, men were more deeply involved in their hobby, playing more than two times the number of game hours than women did per week (M = 16.70 hours for men versus M = 7.93 hours for women, t = 12.536, df = 805.220, p < .001). Furthermore, by means of Mann–Whitney tests, we found that men play fighting, shooting, adventure, action-adventure, survival horror, role-playing, MMO, strategy, racing, and sports games significantly more often than women. Women, on the other hand, more often play platform, simulation, party, casual, and social network games. The strongest effect size was found for shooting games (r = –.58) and the smallest significant effect size for platform games (r = –.09).

Motivation

By means of the *Video Game Intrinsic Motivation Questionnaire* of Van Looy (2010), we looked into motivations for playing games. More concretely, we were interested in the respondents' scores for the "social contact" motivation to test hypothesis 1, which stated that female players are less motivated by social contact in games than male players.

By means of a principal component analysis (PCA, varimax rotation) on 31 Likert items, we found five intrinsic game motivation components: (1) social contact, (2) challenge, (3) immersion, (4) freedom/control, and (5) competition. All components had eigenvalues greater than 1.0 and the total variance explained was 57.74%. Three items were removed because of factor loadings smaller than 0.5. All Cronbach's alphas were above .70, showing high levels of internal consistency.

Figure 5.1 illustrates the means of both male and female respondents on all five motivations. These results show that female gamers (M = 3.01) are least motivated by social contact, while male gamers (M = 3.84) are most driven by this compared to other intrinsic motivations. When performing an independent t-test, the mean difference between women and men for the social contact motivation seemed to be statistically significant ($t(620.610) = 14.027, p < .001$). However, men scored significantly higher on all intrinsic motivations, and the effect size of social contact was the largest ($d = .94$) compared to the other motivations ($d_{challenge} = .83; d_{immersion} = .63; d_{freedom} = .5; d_{competition} = .43$). This finding supports hypothesis 1.

However, as in the study of Lucas and Sherry (2004), we suspect that the social contact motivation was confounded with the amount of game play, because male gamers' means for all motivations were significantly higher. Therefore, in line with Lucas and Sherry, we performed an ANCOVA test with total minutes play per week as the covariate. However, the results showed that the amount of time spent on gaming is significantly related to the social contact motivation ($F(1,959) = 152.187, p < .001$), and gender continued to have a significant effect ($F(1,959) = 105.444, p < .001$). The mean difference, however, decreased (adjusted male M = 3.75 versus adjusted female M = 3.17).

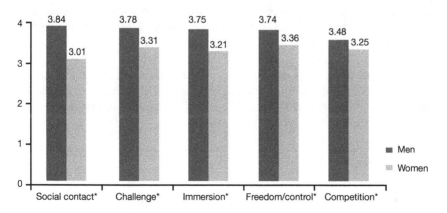

Figure 5.1 Means for Men and Women for Gaming Motivation Factors.
Note: Independent t-tests were performed. *$p < .05$

Online Communication

Hypothesis 1.1 stated that female players were less attracted to online communication than male players. We tested this statement on the basis of three items (see Table 5.1). We found that male gamers have a stronger inclination toward in-game interaction compared to female gamers. Table 5.1 reports medium to large effect sizes for all items, which supports hypothesis 1.1. This is particularly the case for respondents' preference for playing games online with others ($d = 1.03$).

Social Interaction in Real Life

Furthermore, we looked into gender differences in preferences for social interaction surrounding the game (i.e. physically being with others when playing a game). Hypothesis 1.2, that female players prefer to game with others in the same physical space less than male players do, was tested by the means of two items (see Table 5.2). Again, both statements significantly differed between male and female players, indicating that women are less inclined to get together with others to play games than are men. Whereas the first item suggests a strong effect size for gender ($d = .81$), the second one reveals a medium-sized effect ($d = .52$). However, both variables support hypothesis 1.2, as the scores of women are positive (> 3.00), suggesting that interaction with others is also important to them.

Social Competition

Hypothesis 2 stated that male players were fonder of social competition in games than female players were. To test this, we drew a comparison between male and female players based on items that focus on competition with other players (see Table 5.3). The scores on the first two items highlight that male gamers are more interested in social competition than female gamers. The largest effect size was found for the importance of competition against other players ($d = .52$). However, women's high mean on the item "I like to win against other players" suggests that they too are (socially) competitive. The last item ("I like to compete against friends by means of movement games") is even more strongly preferred by female gamers compared to their male counterparts. This is probably because women are fonder of party games than men (cf. part demographics). Hypothesis 2 is thus partly supported.

MMO Players

As with hypothesis 1, we used the *Video Game Intrinsic Motivation Questionnaire* of Van Looy (2010) to test hypothesis 3, which posited that female MMO players were less motivated by social contact than male MMO players were. Figure 5.2 illustrates the mean scores on motivation

Table 5.1 Independent *t*-tests for Gender Concerning Online Communication Preferences

Likert statements	Means		Cohen's d
	Male	Female	
I like to play with others online $t(584.583) = 14.688*$	4.00	2.78	1.03
I think it is fun communicating with others while gaming $t(650.444) = 8.844*$	3.72	3.09	0.60
In-game contact with other players is important to me $t(960) = 9.511*$	3.60	2.94	0.63

* $p < .001$

Table 5.2 Independent *t*-tests for Gender Concerning Social Interaction in Real Life

Likert statements	Means		Cohen's d
	Male	Female	
I like to come together with friends for gaming $t(574.716) = 11.542*$	4.03	3.22	0.81
I like to play a video game together with others $t(960) = 7.862*$	3.65	3.13	0.52

* $p < .001$

Table 5.3 Independent *t*-tests for Gender Concerning Social Competition

Likert statements	Means		Cohen's d
	Male	Female	
I like to win against other players $t(960) = 6.842*$	4.28	3.92	0.45
Competition against other players is essential to me $t(767.558) = 7.852*$	3.25	2.70	0.52
I like to compete against friends by means of movement games $t(960) = 6.325*$	3.16	3.61	0.43

* $p < .001$

for both men and women who play MMOs at least once a month. As with the general sample, "social contact" is the strongest motivation for men to play MMO games. When performing an independent *t*-test, we found that the mean difference between men (M = 4.14) and women (M = 3.82) on the "social contact" motivation was statistically significant ($t(107.234) = 3.091$, p = .003), confirming hypothesis 3. Apart from the challenge motivation ($t(318) = 2.058, p = .04$), no other significant differences were found between men and women. The effect size (d = .43) of social contact, however, was larger than the effect size of challenge (d = .33). Nevertheless, the gender effect of social contact for MMO players was smaller than the effect size for the general sample (d = .83). In the case of MMO players, the results also indicate that "social contact" (besides "immersion") is the most important motivation for female MMO players. This is also different from the overall sample, in which women were least motivated by social contact.

Discussion

In the past few decades, digital gaming has become a mainstream pastime. As a result, gaming has generated new relationships and networks between players existing alongside and intermingling with current social networks in real life. This study explored social experiences of players and focused on identifying gender patterns in social game play.

Our analyses revealed a consistent pattern of women being less interested in social game play than their male counterparts. On a general level, female players were the least attracted to social contact as an intrinsic gaming motivation. Furthermore, we narrowed our focus to MMO players to investigate whether gender differences in social interaction are still present among players with similar interests. However, even though female MMO players

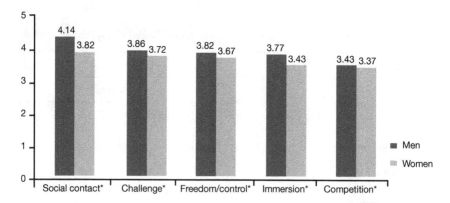

Figure 5.2 Means for Male and Female MMO Players for Gaming Motivation Factors.

Independent *t*-tests were performed.* $p < .05$

stated that social contact was the most important motivation for playing MMOs, male MMO players were still more interested in social interaction. One possible explanation for the gender differences found is that game play is negotiated by the social context. Accordingly, Lin (2008) argues that women often experience harassment and flirtation from male players, combined with attempts to find out their real gender. Furthermore, women have learned that it is dangerous to reveal their real gender because of the risk of being branded as incompetent. These practices constantly remind women that they are trespassing in a male-dominated environment (Yee, 2008). As a result, it may be that women keep out of gaming activities to fulfill their social needs, and rather use other means such as e-mail, the telephone, etc. In other words, we suspect that women are less involved in social gaming activities due to the difficulty in transgressing culturally gendered playing lines; that is, gaming as a traditionally male pastime. Further research should therefore focus on social interaction during game play between male and female gamers as a way to explore the gap in social drivers between men and women thoroughly.

Finally, we need to mention some limitations of the current study. Methodologically, the sample does not represent the whole population of gamers because answers to the survey items may have been affected by respondents' self-selection. Moreover, this study took an exploratory step toward quantitatively examining gender differences in social interaction in games, which led us to use non-validated items. Furthermore, we acknowledge that social contact in games is a multidimensional concept and therefore difficult to make operational in a survey. Further research should find other ways to look at various social game discourses and the way they are experienced by both men and women. Accordingly, it is important for future studies to investigate other forces that shape gendered social behavior in games instead of solely concentrating on intrinsic differences between men and women in gaming preferences.

References

AAUW (Ed.) (2000). *Tech-savvy: Educating girls in the new computer age.* Washington, DC: American Association of University Women Educational Foundation.

Bartle, R. (1996). *Hearts, clubs, diamonds, spades: Players who suit MUDs. MUSE.* Retrieved from http://www.mud.co.uk/richard/hcds.htm.

BBC (Ed.). (2005). *Gamers in the UK. Digital play, digital lifestyles.* Retrieved from http://open.bbc.co.uk/newmediaresearch/files/BBC_UK_Games_Research_2005.pdf.

Beavis, C., and Charles, C. (2007). Would the 'real' girl gamer please stand up? Gender, LAN cafes and the reformulation of the 'girl' gamer. *Gender and Education, 19*(6), 691–705.

Behnke, K. A. (2012). *Ladies of warcraft: Changing perceptions of women and technology through productive play.* Proceedings of the International Conference on the Foundations of Digital Games, Raleigh, NC.

Bertozzi, E. (2008). 'You play like a girl!': Cross-gender competition and the uneven playing field. *Convergence: The International Journal of Research into New Media Technologies, 14*(4), 473–487.

Bryce, J. O., and Rutter, J. (2001). Gender dynamics and the social and spatial organization of computer gaming. *Leisure Studies, 22*(1), 1–15.

Chen, V., Duh, H., Priscilla, P., and Lam, D. (2006). Enjoyment or engagement? Role of social interaction in playing massively multiplayer online role-playing games (MMORPGs). *Lecture Notes in Computer Science, 4161*, 262–267.

De Pauw, E., Pleysier, S., Van Looy, J., Bourgonjon, J., Rutten, K., Vanhooven, S., and Soetaert, R. (February 2008). *Ze krijgen er niet genoeg van! Jongeren en gaming, een overzichtstudie.* Study by viWTA order, Brussels, Belgium.

De Vocht, M., Van Looy, J., Courtois, C., and De Marez, L. (2011). Sociaal contact in een MMORPG: Een exploratief onderzoek naar de motivaties voor het spelen van *World of Warcraft* vanuit de uses and gratifications-benadering. *Tijdschrift voor Communicatiewetenschap, 39*(1), 44–63.

Ducheneaut, N., Yee, N., Nickell, E., and Moore, R. J. (2007). Proceedings from the SIGCHI conference on human factors in computing systems: *The life and death of online gaming communities: A look at guilds in World of Warcraft.* New York City, NY.

Graner Ray, S. G. (2004). *Gender inclusive game design: Expanding the market.* Hingham, MA: Charles River Media.

Hartmann, T., and Klimmt, C. (2006). Gender and computer games: Exploring females' dislikes. *Journal of Computer-Mediated Communication, 11*(4), 910–931.

IGDA (2009). *2008–2009: Casual games white paper.* Retrieved from 2008–2009: Casual games white paper. igda.

Jansz, J., Avis, C., and Vosmeer, M. (2010). Playing *The Sims* 2: An exploration of gender differences in players' motivations and patterns of play. *New Media & Society, 12*(2), 235.

Jenson, J., and de Castell, S. (2005). Proceedings from the Proceedings of DiGRA 2005 Conference: Changing Views – Worlds in Play: *Her own boss: Gender and the pursuit of incompetent play.* Vancouver, Canada.

Kafai, Y. B., Heeter, C., Denner, J., and Sun, J. Y. (2008). Preface: Pink, purple, casual, or mainstream games: Moving beyond the gender divide. In Y. B. Kafai, C. Heeter, J. Denner, and J. Y. Sun (Eds.), *Beyond Barbie and Mortal Kombat. New perspectives on gender and gaming* (pp. xi–xxv). Cambridge, MA: MIT Press.

Kerr, A. (2003, November). Proceedings from the Level Up: Digital Games Research Conference: *Women just want to have fun: A study of adult female players of digital games.* Utrecht, The Netherlands.

Kolo, C., and Baur, T. (2004). Living a virtual life: Social dynamics of online gaming. *Game Studies, 4*(1), 1–31.

Laurel, B. (2008). Notes from the utopian entrepreneur. In Y. B. Kafai, C. Heeter, J. Denner, and J. Y. Sun (Eds.), *Beyond Barbie and Mortal Kombat. New perspectives on gender and gaming* (pp. 21–31). Cambridge, MA: MIT Press.

Lin, H. (2008). Body, space, and gendered gaming experiences: A cultural geography of homes, cybercafes, and dormitories. In Y. B. Kafai, C. Heeter, J. Denner, and J. Y. Sun (Eds.), *Beyond Barbie and Mortal Kombat. New perspectives on gender and gaming* (pp. 67–81). Cambridge, MA: MIT Press.

Lucas, K., and Sherry, J. L. (2004). Sex differences in video game play. *Communication Research, 31*(5), 499–523.

Nielsen (2009). *Insights on casual games: Analysis of casual games for the PC.* Unpublished research report.

Pew (2008, 16 September). *Teens' gaming experiences are diverse and include significant social interaction and civic engagement.* Retrieved from http://pewinternet.org/Reports/2008/Teens-Video-Games-and-Civics.aspx.

Schott, G. R., and Horrell, K. R. (2000). Girl gamers and their relationship with the gaming culture. *Convergence, 6*(36), 36–53.

Sweetser, P., and Wyeth, P. (2005). GameFlow: A model for evaluating player enjoyment in games. *ACM Computers in Entertainment, 3*(3), 1–24.

Taylor, T. L. (2003). Multiple pleasures: Women and online gaming. *Convergence, 9*(1), 21–46.

Van Looy, J. (2010). *Video game intrinsic motivation questionnaire.* Internal report, Ghent; Faculty of Communication Studies, University of Ghent, Belgium.

Van Looy, J., Schuurman, D., De Moor, K., De Marez, L., and Courtois, C. (2010). Proceedings from the Etmaal van de Communicatiewetenschap: *Freewheelers, solo- en social competers. Een driewegsclassificatie van heavy gamers op basis van een vijfdimensionele gameflow-schaal.* Ghent, Belgium.

Williams, D., Yee, N., and Caplan, S. (2008). Who plays, how much, and why? A behavioral player census of virtual world. *Journal of Computer-Mediated Communication, 13*(4), 993–1018.

Willoughby, T. (2008). A short-term longitudinal study of Internet and computer game use by adolescent boys and girls: Prevalence, frequency of use, and psychosocial predictors. *Developmental Psychology, 44*(1), 195.

Yee, N. (2008). Maps of digital desires: Exploring the topography of gender and play in online games. In Y. B. Kafai, C. Heeter, J. Denner, and J. Y. Sun (Eds.), *Beyond Barbie and Mortal Kombat: New perspectives on gender and gaming* (pp. 83–96). Cambridge, MA: MIT Press.

Games Cited

Maxis (2004). *The Sims 2*, Redwood City, USA: EA Games.

6 Player-Centered Game Design

Expectations and Perceptions of Social Interaction in RPGs and FPSs as Predictors of Rich Game Experience

Christina Schumann

Introduction

Social interaction in video games has mainly been studied under the perspective of human-to-human interaction in massively multiplayer online role-playing games (MMORPGs), online first-person shooters (FPSs), or browser-based games (Fritz, 2009; Pena and Hancock, 2006; Wright, Boria, and Breidenbach, 2002). It is often forgotten that a special form of social interaction also occurs in single-player games as human-to-system interaction (McMillan, 2006): Players interact, on the one hand, with opponents, for example, in a battle, or also in "verbal combat," and, on the other hand, with so-called NPCs (non-player characters), for example, by trading, talking, trying to convince the NPC to do something, or even engaging in a romantic relationship. Krotz calls this communication type "interactive communication" and describes it as a "simulation of a conversation" (Krotz, 2009, p. 33), in which both the human and the computer system participate in a communication process. Concerning Laird and van Lent, the design of challenging artificial intelligence (AI) characters, which show human-like behaviors and allow rich social interaction, has become one of the main points of competition for successful game design (Laird and van Lent, 2005). They argue that the "challenge of competing and cooperating with another intellect" (Laird and van Lent, 2005, p. 205) is one of the main factors that captivates the player and enhances the game experience.

When taking a closer look at the theoretical game design approaches (for a good overview see Salen and Zimmerman, 2004; Salen and Zimmerman, 2006), it becomes obvious that there is little known about *how* the AI characters should be designed and *if* simulated rich social interaction with them is really a main factor in captivating the player and enhancing the game experience. Or as Sykes (2006, p. 83) puts it: "A predictive theory of game design is still some way off." Due to the lack of research in this area, the uncertainty of "what works" (Costikyan, 2006, p. 193) and which design implementations might be successful remains high.

The paper focuses on this lack of knowledge and will concentrate on the general research interest of how social interaction with non-human players (NPCs and opponents) should be designed to enhance the game experience.

To answer this question, the study will focus exclusively on role-playing games (RPGs) and FPSs, as the interaction with AI characters has been found to be particularly important for a good game experience in these game types (Laird and van Lent, 2005).

Game Experience

Game experience is understood as a complex and multidimensional construct (LeBlanc, 2006, p. 213; Salen and Zimmerman, 2004, p. 90; Sherry, 2004, p. 330). Therefore, studies in media entertainment, but also video game research, have placed great focus on describing the experience during game play: Enjoyment, for example, is seen as the pleasure that derives from media reception (Raney, 2004, p. 348; Vorderer, Klimmt, and Ritterfeld, 2004, p. 388); and transportation is defined as a mental process that leads to a melding of attention, imagery, and feelings (Green and Brock, 2000, p. 701). However, from an empirical point of view, these concepts are difficult to operationalize because of their broad definitions. Thus, the present study will focus on two concepts that are first defined more precisely, and second, are seen as very suitable in defining game experience: flow and presence.

Based on the work of Csikszentmihalyi (1987), flow is defined as an autotelic experience of intense pleasure, characterized by the merging of action and awareness, intense and focused concentration, and the loss of reflective self-consciousness (Nakamura and Csikszentmihalyi, 2002, p. 90). It is seen as a fruitful concept with which to define the game experience (Sherry, 2004, p. 339; Weber, Tamborini, Westcott-Baker, and Kantor, 2009), as video game use—compared to the use of other media—is somehow difficult, and therefore challenging, but it also provides clear feedback about the player's progress. Both feedback and difficulty of the task are seen as prerequisites for a flow state.

Presence is defined as the "perceptual illusion of non mediation" (Lombard and Ditton, 1997, p. 9) or just as "being there" (Reeves, 1991). Recipients experiencing presence report a "compelling sense of being in a mediated space other than where their physical body is located" (Biocca, 1997, p. 9). With the differentiation in spatial- (Wirth et al., 2007) or physical (IJsselsteijn, de Ridder, Freeman, and Avons, 2000, p. 3), social (Lee, 2004; Tamborini and Skalski, 2006, p. 230), and self-presence (Lee, 2004; Lee, Park, Jin, and Kang, 2005), the concept has become clearly characterized: The three differentiations describe special forms of presence, where virtual objects, virtual social actors, and the virtual self are experienced as actual and real (Lee, 2004, p. 44).

It is obvious that there are clear parallels between the two approaches: Both regard the complete melding of the recipient's awareness with his task. The differentiation in spatial, social, and self-presence, however, can be regarded as a more precise description of what is happening while the recipient is completely focused on the task. For this study, it is assumed that the game experience is good when the player experiences flow and presence.

The Theory of Subjective Quality Assessments

For this study, the focus will be on the *players* of video games, as it is the user—and not the designer—for whom video games are made, and it is the players who judge the implemented AI characters. From this, the Theory of Subjective Quality Assessments (TSQA) (Emmer, Vowe, and Wolling, 2011, p. 269; Wolling, 2009; Wolling, 2004; Vowe and Wolling, 2004) is presented: The TSQA uses "quality" as a synonym for a media attribute or characteristic that can be perceived and judged by the recipients. In contrast to a normative understanding of quality (Ruß-Mohl, 1992; Schatz and Schulz, 1992), quality is seen as a neutral term. According to this theory, the interaction with the AI characters in video games would be called a quality. With the *quality expectation* (QE) and the *quality perception* (QP), two of the theory's three main concepts will be used to answer the research interest: The QE deals with the question of what idea the recipients have of an ideal medium and its attributes. Here, it will be used to scrutinize how the interaction with the AI characters should be designed according to the players. The QP asks how the recipients perceive the qualities of a certain medium and, inter alia, what media experience derives out of this perception. For this study, we will analyze if the game experience—namely, flow and presence—can be explained by the perception of a certain interaction with AI characters. Based on this, the general research interest is divided into three main research questions (RQ):

RQ 1:   What expectations do players of RPGs and FPSs have concerning an ideal interaction with the AI characters (NPCs and opponents)?
RQ 2:   How important are these expectations for the players and how do they perceive actual games on the market? Where are the differences between the expectations and perceptions?
RQ 3:   To what extent can the game experience (flow and presence) be explicated by the QPs of the implemented AI characters in the games?[1]

RQ 1: Qualitative Pre-study

To the best of the author's knowledge, the TSQA has not yet been applied to the study of video games, and RQ1 was answered by a qualitative pre-study: Eight focus groups (four per genre) were formed with up to seven experienced core-gamers of RPGs and FPSs. They took place at Ilmenau University of Technology or were realized online via Skype; the duration was one to two hours. Participants had to imagine that they were a group of game designers and that they could create an ideal RPG or FPS. To avoid the participants mentioning game characteristics indiscriminately without any reflection, the task was linked to the condition that they should agree about the game's most important attributes and how these should be designed.

Results show that the interaction with the AI entities is intensively discussed: For the opponents, the participants concentrated on two dimensions: the *level of hazardousness* and *strategic and realistic behavior.*

Concerning the level of hazardousness, the players require that the opponents should always be a challenge. Thus, they favor adaptive game balancing, meaning that the difficulty in defeating an opponent adapts individually in accordance with the skill of each player. Furthermore, especially the RPG players feel insulted when they are attacked by an opponent they deem to be below their station. For instance, Susanne (RPG) says, "I take it as an insult when a boar attacks my 'level 40 character.' I always think: Hey man—look at me!" Concerning the opponent's behavior, the participants wish for a more strategic component. First, that means that the player has to act more strategically with different enemies, or as Markus (FPS) puts it: "I miss that I do not have to use different tactics to fight different enemies." And second, that enemies should behave defensively when they "realize" that they have no chance of winning a fight. Daniel (RPG) argues: "I also expect defensive behavior from time to time." Therefore, opponents who show unrealistic behavior are explicitly criticized: "I hate it when an opponent runs full-speed toward the hail of bullets! No one would do that" (Marco, FPS).

The interaction with the NPCs is of special importance too: Players discuss *authenticity, human-like behavior,* and *profound reactions.* An NPC is perceived as authentic when it shows a pronounced personality: "NPCs should be designed with loving care and have their own minds" (Daniel, RPG). Concerning the human-like behavior, Frank (RPG) praised the NPCs in the game *Baldur's Gate* (Bioware, 1998): "They had real personalities, commented on everything that was going on around them, and even quarreled among themselves." In this context, players criticize the so-called looping behavior (Laird and van Lent, 2005, p. 209), which means that an NPC always does the same thing. Manuela (RPG) says, "It is strange when an NPC stands around every day at the same place. And when I talk to it, it says: 'I have lots of things to do. Make it short!' And I think: What do you have to do? Hang around all day long?"

However, under a theoretical perspective, the claimed, profound reactions of the NPCs are the most interesting category. Here, the players mention the clearest gap between their expectations and their perception of the status quo in the market. For example, NPCs are criticized for being too apathetic when something dangerous happens next to them. Susanne (RPG) says, "I think that games do not react sufficiently to the actions of the players. For example, when I'm attacked and there are guards around, they should help me. But they just stand around and do nothing." Another example is mentioned by Nina (RPG): "In a game I played, there was a scientist in the swamps. And when I was killed he just walked 'through'[2] my corpse. If he does not want to help me, at least he should run away." Furthermore, the participants criticized the NPCs for being too unthankful if the player has helped them in a difficult or dangerous situation. Frank

(RPG) complains: "Why don't they react like this: Oh my dear, this is our hero who has helped us with this and that."

Quantitative Survey: Method

Measures

To scrutinize these results in a quantitative study, a first draft of items for the QEs and QPs was designed based on the qualitative results. These items were tested in four think-aloud interviews with players of FPSs and RPGs. While they filled in the first draft of the questionnaire, interviewees were asked to express everything that came into their mind. By this means, problematic items were revised, and a second draft of the questionnaire was pretested in a quantitative survey with N = 198 players of RPGs and FPSs. For completion, the scales were tested with factor analysis and Cronbach's alphas were calculated. In the main study, a nine-item, six-point Likert-scale was used.

For the operationalization of flow and presence, existing scales were used: Flow items were taken out of the game experience questionnaire.[3] To evaluate presence, items were partially based on the single-item scale of Schneider et al. (Schneider, Lang, Shin, and Bradley, 2004, p. 368).

In the main study, participants first filled in the items for the QEs. Afterward, a list of FPSs and RPGs, which came onto the market in 2009 and 2010, was presented. Participants stated which games they had played and were asked to fill in the questions for the dependent variables as well as for the QPs for at least one of these titles. As the data presented in this paper were part of a larger study, the survey used the complete quality scales just for the QPs. To measure the QEs, a shortened scale was used: For this, the two items with the highest factor loadings from the quantitative pretest were integrated into the survey. Otherwise, the survey would have taken too long to fill in. More information about this will be given when the results are presented.

Frequency of genre use (FPS and RPG) was used as the control variable, as it is seen as an indicator for genre preference: The more the players are fascinated by the games of a special type, the more likely they are to experience flow and presence. Age was also considered, as younger players might be more enthusiastic about video games and may find it easier to immerse themselves in the game world. Finally, the perception of a high technical standard of a game—that is, high-end graphics, a sophisticated physics engine, and real-world sound—was controlled. In recent years, particularly high-end graphics have been considered as the main factor for competition in the video game market—especially for the FPSs (Laird and van Lent, 2005, p. 206). So it is plausible that a perceived high technical standard might influence the game experience.

As one can argue that a game might also be perceived as ideal when undesired qualities are missing, the questionnaire ended with an open question.

There, participants were to mention everything that they did *not* want to have in an ideal RPG or FPS.

Procedure and Participants

For data collection, an online survey was distributed in late winter and early fall 2011 in Germany. The invitation to participate was posted in the news section of several topic-oriented websites, such as gamestar.de and spieletipps.de, with a link pointing to the survey. Participation was anonymous and not promoted by a raffle. After data cleansing, N = 2086 surveys for the FPS players and N = 3085 surveys for the RPG players were found to be suitable for analysis. The majority of the participants were male (FPS: 98%, N = 2029; RPG: 95%, N = 2916) and proportionally young (FPS: mean = 22 years, *SD* = 6.5; RPG: mean = 25 years, *SD* = 11.4). Participants showed a high amount of video game use, as 92% of the FPS players (N = 1919) and 91% of the RPG players (N = 2807) reported that they played daily or several times a week, with the average time spent playing each "session" being three hours (FPS: mean = 2.8 h, *SD* = 1.7, N = 2024; RPG: mean = 2.9, *SD* = 1.5, N = 3040).

Analytical Strategy

For both the independent and the dependent variables, factor analysis was carried out. As the factors remain stable when calculated separately for each subsample (one for the RPG players and one for the FPS players), or for the whole sample, results will be presented for the latter. For RQ2, the frequency distributions of the QEs and QPs are compared and linear regression analysis is used to answer RQ3.

Results will be presented for the following games: *Bioshock 2* (2K Games, 2004) (N = 128) and *Call of Duty: Black Ops* (Treyarch, 2010) (N = 308) for the FPSs, and *Two Worlds II* (Reality Pump, 2010) (N = 614) and *Arcania: Gothic 4* (Spellbound Entertainment, 2010) (N = 149) for the RPGs, as for these games there are enough cases to run the analyses. While *Bioshock 2*, a science-fiction FPS, takes place in the fictional underwater dystopia of "Rapture," *Call of Duty: Black Ops* chooses a real-world scenario where the player slips into the role of a US soldier during the Cold War. *Two Worlds II* and *Arcania: Gothic 4* are both so-called high-fantasy RPGs (Kücklich, 2009, p. 36) that show strong parallels to J.R.R. Tolkien's Middle Earth.

Results

Factor Analysis

For the QPs, two factors were found (see Table 6.1): one for the NPCs and one for the opponents. Thus, the dimensions that were presumed from the qualitative results (level of hazardousness, and strategic and realistic behavior for the opponents; authenticity, human-like behavior, and profound reactions for the NPCs) all belong to one concept, respectively. The first factor—*lifelike NPCs*—is about the authentic design of the NPCs, which have a personality, show realistic reactions, and generally behave in a lifelike manner. The major focus of the second factor is on the intelligence and cleverness of the opponents: They show different tactics, but also defensive behavior in combat, and challenge the player by their level of hazardousness.

Table 6.2 presents the factor analysis for the game experience scales.

The results confirm the two concepts: flow and presence. The first factor is composed of the items that were operationalized for the flow, the second of those for presence. It should be stressed that the second factor is composed of the three facets of presence, due to the operationalization with single items. The item "I felt completely absorbed" (flow scale) loaded on both factors and was dropped.

RQ2: Comparison of QEs and QPs

Figure 6.1 shows the QEs for the lifelike NPCs and the intelligent and on-par opponents, and how their design is perceived in the four games.

Table 6.1 QPs of the AI Characters: Factor Analysis

In game X ...	Lifelike NPCs	Intelligent and on-par opponents
(NPCs) behave in a lifelike way[a]	0.88	
(NPCs) behave as if they were real people/creatures	0.87	
(NPCs) have their own personality and are not just empty shells	0.80	
(NPCs) react to me as if they were real people/creatures[a]	0.76	
(NPCs) have an authentic appearance	0.73	
(opponents) show different strategies in combat		0.76
(opponents) sometimes show defensive behavior and withdraw[a]		0.73
(opponents) are not below the level of my avatar[a]		0.61
(opponents) show a level of hazardousness that is suitable to the role they play		0.58
Cronbach's alpha	0.91	0.65

Principal component analysis, varimax rotation, listwise, eigenvalue > 1, 64% variance explained, KMO: .9

[a] Items that are written in italics were used in the expectations scale.

Table 6.2 Game Experience: Factor Analysis

In game X ...	Flow	Presence
I forgot everything around me	0.80	
I lost track of time	0.80	
I lost connection with the outside world	0.67	
I was fully occupied with the game	0.54	
I felt like my avatar was a real person		0.82
I felt like the game world was real		0.80
I felt like the other characters in the game were real people		0.80
I felt like I was in a real place		0.73
Cronbach's alpha	0.70	0.82

Principal component analysis, varimax rotation, listwise, eigenvalue > 1, 59% variance explained, KMO: .83

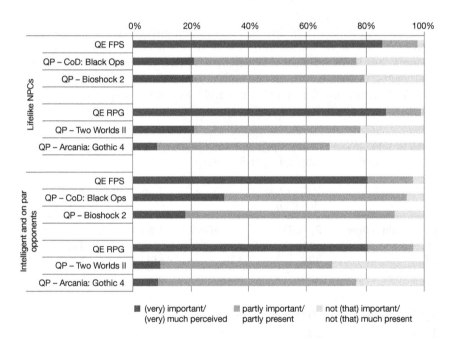

Figure 6.1 QEs and QPs: Comparison.

With regard to the QEs, it becomes obvious that both qualities are judged as important or very important by a majority of the players. The lifelike NPCs score a little higher in both genres. However, the QPs fail to come up to the expectations in both categories and for all games. Although a large proportion of the participants at least perceived that lifelike NPCs and intelligent and on-par opponents are partly present in the four games, the gap between the expectations and perceptions is wide. This is all the more remarkable as *Call of Duty: Black Ops* and *Bioshock 2*, as well as *Two Worlds II* and *Arcania: Gothic 4* are all ranked as Triple A titles.

In general, *Arcania: Gothic 4* has major differences between the QE and QP. Furthermore, concerning the intelligent and on-par opponents, differences are larger in the RPGs. *Call of Duty: Black Ops* achieved the best results for both qualities.

RQ3: Explication of Game Experience

In the following, the paper will scrutinize if flow and presence can be explained by the perception of the lifelike NPCs, and the intelligent and on-par opponents. Table 6.3 shows the results for the flow experience.

With regard to the "amount" of flow that was experienced when playing the different games, the highest scores were reported for *Bioshock 2*, while *Arcania: Gothic 4* had the lowest scores.

In general, a high perception of lifelike NPCs is a significant positive predictor of the flow experience in all four games. Betas are highest for *Arcania: Gothic 4*. Additionally, for *Bioshock 2* and *Arcania: Gothic 4*, a significant association between the perception of intelligent and on-par opponents, as well as of high-end technical standards and flow was found. Concerning age, no clear pattern is visible, as both younger (*Call of Duty:*

Table 6.3 Impact of Lifelike NPCs and Intelligent and On-Par Opponents (QP) on Flow: Multiple, Linear Regression

	Call of Duty: Black Ops	Bioshock 2	Two Worlds II	Arcania: Gothic 4
Mean values flow	2,7 (SD=0,8)[a]	3,0 (SD=0,9)[a]	2,6 (SD=0,9)[a]	2,4 (SD=0,8)[a]
R^2	12%	25%	20%	30%
N	308	128	614	149
	beta	beta	beta	beta
Quality perceptions				
Lifelike NPCs	0.18**	0.30**	0.32***	0.45***
Intelligent and on-par opponents	n.s.	0.25*	n.s.	0.21**
Control variables				
Perception of high-end technics	0.13*	n.s.	0.12**	n.s.
Age	−0.15*	n.s.	n.s.	0.21**
Genre preference (FPS or RPG)	0.19*	0.16*	0.18***	n.s.

Method: enter, $*p < .05$, $**p < .01$; $***p < .001$
[a] scales from '1=very low' to '5=very high'

Black Ops) and older players (*Arcania: Gothic 4*) might experience more flow. Genre preference, however, had a significant impact in both FPS models and for *Two Worlds II*.

Table 6.4 shows the results for presence.

For *Bioshock 2*, the players reported the highest amount of presence, while *Arcania: Gothic 4* again had the lowest scores.

A higher presence was significantly associated with the perception of lifelike NPCs. The betas are remarkably high in all models. Apart from *Call of Duty: Black Ops*, age was also a significant predictor, as younger players experience a higher feeling of presence. However, the perception of intelligent and on-par opponents did not show a significant impact in any of the models. Additionally, genre preference is not a suitable predictor, as only one model (*Two Worlds II*) showed a significant effect on presence.

Discussion

For the explication of both flow and presence, the perception of lifelike NPCs was the main predictor: In the theory, it is argued that the feeling of flow is probable whenever the challenge of a task and the skill that is essential to master the challenge are well balanced (Nakamura and Csikszentmihalyi, 2002, p. 94; Csikszentmihalyi, 1987, p. 77). Based on this, it might be

Table 6.4 Impact of Lifelike NPCs and Intelligent and On-Par Opponents (QP) on Presence: Multiple, Linear Regression

	Call of Duty: Black Ops	*Bioshock 2*	*Two Worlds II*	*Arcania: Gothic 4*
Mean values flow	2,5 (SD=1,0)[a]	2,7 (SD=1,0)[a]	2,5 (SD=1,0)[a]	2,4 (SD=0,8)[a]
R^2	23%	29%	29%	38%
N	310	130	614	154
	beta	beta	beta	beta
Quality perceptions				
Lifelike NPCs	0.42***	0.44***	0.49***	0.39***
Intelligent and on-par opponents	n.s.	n.s.	n.s.	n.s.
Control variables				
Perception of high-end technics	0.12*	n.s.	n.s.	0.28***
Age	n.s.	−0.23**	−0.15***	−0.17**
Genre preference (FPS or RPG)	n.s.	n.s.	0.12***	n.s.

Method: enter, *$p < .05$, **$p < .01$; ***$p < .001$
[a] scales from '1=very low' to '5=very high'

argued that the perception of lifelike NPCs may lead to a feeling of challenge. *Bioshock 2* is used as an example to clarify this argumentation: The NPCs of this FPS were lauded because they actively pursue the story and are not just decorative accessories. The player is often left in the dark about their aims, the role they play, and if they are friends or foes. Furthermore, the story may have different endings depending on how the player interacts with some of the NPCs (Schmitz, 2010). Therefore, the interaction with them might be perceived as a challenge to bring the game to a good conclusion.

The interpretation of the effect on presence might follow a similar argumentation: If the NPCs are perceived as lifelike, they might be experienced as if they were real interactive partners. This makes it easier for the players to forget about the artificiality of the gaming world and to feel totally present in the game.

Compared to this "overall effect," the influence of the perception of intelligent and on-par opponents is quite low. This is surprising, because in game design literature it is argued that the opponents play a key role in video games and therefore have to be designed very carefully (Birdwell, 2006, p. 215). Furthermore—in theoretical terms—it would have been plausible that they are especially suitable to explain the flow experience, as they might be seen as the main component of challenge for the players. Although the design of the opponents should not be neglected, the results indicate that the game industry should focus more on the design of lifelike NPCs.

Furthermore, the influence of the high-end technical perception also fell considerably short of the perception of lifelike NPCs. This is remarkable, as the game industry has put some effort into making video games more "high-end" in the last few years (Laird and van Lent, 2005, p. 206). It would be premature to say that the game industry has backed the wrong horse, because the perception of high-end technical standards was also a significant predictor in some models. Furthermore, it is highly probable that a poor technical standard in a game would be explicitly criticized by the players. However, it must be underlined that compared to the technical aspects, the focus should be stronger on the design of lifelike NPCs.

As was seen in the comparison of QEs and QPs, there still is a major gap between the ideal and the reality. This leads to the question as to what the game industry can do to design more lifelike NPCs. With the results of the focus groups, some ideas have already been presented. Besides, the answers in the open question at the end of the questionnaire give some further hints and ideas. Participants were asked how AI entities should *not* be designed. For the NPCs, constant babbling (sample RPG) was as much criticized as NPCs always repeating the same expressions such as "Kill them!" or "I was wounded" (sample FPS). Furthermore, players dislike it if NPCs give the impression that they are "too stupid to harvest a sugar beet" (sample RPG). Especially for the female NPCs, players complained about the exaggeration of sexual traits and nudity. Even if these are qualitative results, which should be verified in a quantitative study, the game industry should consider the presented aspects.

Limitations and Future Research Directions

While the study shows some promising relationships between the perception of the AI entities (especially the lifelike NPCs) and the game experience, this work can be improved and extended.

First, the study focuses exclusively on the FPS and RPG genres, but there is little reason for the results to be limited to these game types. Therefore, further research should also concentrate on the role of the AI characters in other genres and determine if the results remain stable.

Second, the results presented here give some initial ideas about the perceived interaction with the AI entities and the influence on the game experience. With regard to the results, the importance of lifelike NPCs has to be underlined. Therefore, further research should examine the interplay of the perception of lifelike NPCs and the game experience more precisely. Questions that should be focused on are what—besides the already mentioned aspects—leads to the perception of lifelike NPCs? *How* lifelike should NPCs be? Should the industry concentrate on making them more and more lifelike or are there any limitations? With regard to the so-called uncanny valley effect (Mori, 1970), it is plausible that making the NPCs too lifelike might also have negative effects on the game experience. To concentrate on these questions, again, a qualitative approach is recommended. Furthermore, as different types of NPCs exist (e.g. companion NPCs that fight together with the players, NPCs that serve as purchasers for quests, NPCs that just populate the game world), it must be determined if players have different expectations and perceptions for different types of NPCs and how these are interwoven with the game experience.

Conclusion

Based on the TSQA, the data serve to contribute to a better understanding of the player's expectations and perceptions of the interaction with AI characters. It was demonstrated that especially the perception of lifelike NPCs is highly associated with self-reported flow and presence during game play. So, results show that social interaction plays an important role not just in multiplayer games, but also in "classical," offline single-player games: Here, a highly lifelike simulation of social interaction with AI characters is of special importance for the players and leads to a good game experience. But, with regard to actual games on the market, it has been shown that perceptions still fail to come up to expectations. Therefore, in the future, the games industry should concentrate more on the human-to-system interaction in order to simulate a lifelike social interaction with the AI entities and, through this, to strengthen the social side of "classical" single-player games.

Scholars and practitioners continue to focus on understanding game experiences and the factors representing what mostly constitutes a good game. As the approach of this study seems to be a fruitful contributor to answering these questions, future research should concentrate on deepening the presented results and understandings.

Notes

1 The third main concept, the quality judgment, will not be considered in this study: Its calculation follows complex rules (Wolling, 2009) and it would be beyond the scope of this article to explain the procedure in detail. Furthermore, it was found before (Emmer et al., 2011; Wolling, 2004) that media experience/media selection can be explained as well or even better just by regarding the QPs and not the quality judgments. The multivariate models that are presented later have been tested with both the QPs and the quality judgments as predictors. The results showed that the quality-perception models explain flow and presence during game play as well, or even better than the quality judgments.
2 Here, Nina refers to a so-called glitch. Glitches are little bugs that can, inter alia, be mistakes in the graphics that make it possible to walk through static objects.
3 For more information please consider http://www.gamexplab.nl/index. php?page=home.

References

Biocca, F. (1997). The cyborg's dilemma: Progressive embodiment virtual environments. *Journal of Computer-Mediated Communication, 3*(2). Retrieved from http://jcmc.indiana.edu/vol3/issue2/biocca2.html.

Birdwell, K. (2006). The cabal: Valve's design process for creating half-life. In K. Salen and E. Zimmerman (Eds.), *The game design reader: A rules of play anthology* (pp. 212–225). Cambridge, MA: MIT Press.

Costikyan, G. (2006). I have no words and I must design. In K. Salen and E. Zimmerman (Eds.), *The game design reader: A rules of play anthology* (pp. 192–211). Cambridge, MA: MIT Press.

Csikszentmihalyi, M. (1987). *Das Flow-Erlebnis: Jenseits von Angst und Langeweile: Im Tun aufgehen* (2nd ed.). Stuttgart, Germany: Klett-Cotta.

Emmer, M., Vowe, G., and Wolling, J. (2011). *Bürger Online: Die Entwicklung der politischen Online-Kommunikation in Deutschland*. Konstanz, Germany: UVK Verl.-Ges.

Fritz, J. (2009). Spielen in virtuellen Gemeinschaften. In T. Quandt, J. Wimmer, and J. Wolling (Eds.), *Die Computerspieler: Studien zur Nutzung von Computergames* (2nd ed., pp. 135–147). Wiesbaden, Germany: VS Verlag.

Green, M. C., and Brock, T. C. (2000). The role of transportation in the persuasiveness of public narratives. *Journal of Personality and Social Psychology, 79*(5), 701–721.

IJsselsteijn, W. A., de Ridder, H., Freeman, J., and Avons, S. E. (2000). *Presence: Concept, determinants and measurement*. Retrieved from http://www.ijsselsteijn.nl/papers/SPIE_HVEI_2000.pdf.

Krotz, F. (2009). Computerspiele als neuer Kommunikationstypus.: Interaktive Kommunikation als Zugang zu komplexen Welten. In T. Quandt, J. Wimmer, and J. Wolling (Eds.), *Die Computerspieler: Studien zur Nutzung von Computergames* (2nd ed., pp. 25–40). Wiesbaden, Germany: VS Verlag.

Kücklich, J. (2009). Narratologische Ansätze – Computerspiele als Erzählungen. In T. Bevc and H. Zapf (Eds.), *Wie wir spielen, was wir werden: Computerspiele in unserer Gesellschaft* (pp. 27–48). Konstanz, Germany: UVK Verlag.

Laird, J. E., and van Lent, M. (2005). The role of artificial intelligence in computer game genres. In J. Raessens and J. H. Goldstein (Eds.), *Handbook of computer game studies* (pp. 205–215). Cambridge, MA: MIT Press.

LeBlanc, M. (2006). Tools for creating dramatic game dynamics. In K. Salen and E. Zimmerman (Eds.), *The game design reader: A rules of play anthology* (pp. 438–459). Cambridge, MA: MIT Press.

Lee, K. M. (2004). Presence, explicated. *Communication Theory, 14*(1), 27–50.

Lee, K. M., Park, N., Jin, S.-A., and Kang, S. (2005). Proceedings from the International Communication Association Annual Meeting: *Effects of narrative on feelings of presence in computer-game playing* (1–42).

Lombard, M., and Ditton, T. (1997). At the heart of it all: The concept of presence. *Journal of Computer-Mediated Communication, 3*(2).

McMillan, S. J. (2006). Exploring models of interactivity from multiple research traditions: User, documents, systems. In L. A. Lievrouw and S. M. Livingstone (Eds.), *Handbook of new media: Social shaping and consequences of ICTs* (Updated Student Edition, pp. 205–229). London, United Kingdom: SAGE.

Mori, M. (1970). The Uncanny Valley. *Energy, 7*(4), 33–35.

Nakamura, J., and Csikszentmihalyi, M. (2002). The concept of flow. In C. R. Snyder and S. J. Lopez (Eds.), *Handbook of positive psychology* (pp. 89–105). New York City, NY: Oxford University Press.

Pena, J., and Hancock, J. T. (2006). An analysis of socioemotional and task communication in online multiplayer video games. *Communication Research, 33*(1), 92–109.

Raney, A. A. (2004). Expanding disposition theory: Reconsidering character liking, moral evaluations, and enjoyment. *Communication Theory, 14*(4), 348–369.

Reeves, B. R. (1991). "Being there": Television as symbolic versus natural experience. Unpublished manuscript; Institute for Communication Research, Stanford University, CA.

Ruß-Mohl, S. (1992). "Am eigenen Schopfe ... ": Qualitätssicherung im Journalismus – Grundfragen, Ansätze, Näherungsversuche. *Publizistik, 37*(1), 83–96.

Salen, K., and Zimmerman, E. (2004). *Rules of play: Game design fundamentals.* Cambridge, MA: MIT Press.

Salen, K., and Zimmerman, E. (2006). *The game design reader: A rules of play anthology.* Cambridge, MA: MIT Press.

Schatz, H., and Schulz, W. (1992). Qualität von Fernsehprogrammen: Kriterien und Methoden zur Beurteilung von Qualität im dualen Fernsehen. *Media Perspektiven, 11*, 690–712.

Schmitz, P. (2010). *Bioshock 2 im Test: Gute Shooter Fortsetzung ohne große Neuerungen.* Retrieved from http://www.gamestar.de/spiele/bioshock–2/test/ bioshock_2,44349,2312484.html.

Schneider, E. F., Lang, A., Shin, M., and Bradley, S. D. (2004). Death with a story: How story impacts emotional, motivational, and physiological responses to first-person shooter video games. *Human Communication Research, 30*(3), 361–375.

Sherry, J. L. (2004). Flow and media enjoyment. *Communication Theory, 14*(4), 328–347.

Sykes, J. (2006). A player-centered approach to digital game design. In J. Rutter and J. Bryce (Eds.), *Understanding digital games* (pp. 74–91). London, United Kingdom: SAGE.

Tamborini, R., and Skalski, P. (2006). The role of presence in the experience of electronic games. In P. Vorderer and J. Bryant (Eds.), *Playing video games. Motives, responses, and consequences* (pp. 225–240). Mahwah, NJ: Lawrence Erlbaum.

Vorderer, P., Klimmt, C., and Ritterfeld, U. (2004). Enjoyment: At the heart of media entertainment. *Communication Theory, 14*(4), 388–408.

Vowe, G., and Wolling, J. (2004). *Radioqualität – was die Hörer wollen und was die Sender bieten: Vergleichende Untersuchung zu Qualitätsmerkmalen und Qualitätsbewertungen von Radioprogrammen in Thüringen, Sachsen-Anhalt und Hessen*. München, Germany: Kopaed.

Weber, R., Tamborini, R., Westcott-Baker, A., and Kantor, B. (2009). Theorizing flow and media enjoyment as cognitive synchronization of attentional and reward networks. *Communication Theory, 19*(4), 397–422.

Wirth, W., Hartmann, T., Böcking, S., Vorderer, P., Klimmt, C., Schramm, H., Saari, T., Laarni, J., Ravaja, N., Ribeiro Gouveia, F., Biocca, F., Sacau, A., Jäncke, L., Baumgartner, T., and Jäncke, P. (2007). A process model of the formation of spatial presence experiences. *Media Psychology, 9*(3), 493–525.

Wolling, J. (2004). Qualitätserwartungen, Qualitätswahrnehmungen und die Nutzung von Fernsehserien: Ein Beitrag zur Theorie und Empirie der subjektiven Qualitätsauswahl von Medienangeboten. *Publizistik, 49*(2), 171–192.

Wolling, J. (2009). The effect of subjective quality assessments on media selection. In T. Hartmann (Ed.), *Media choice. A theoretical and empirical overview* (pp. 84–101). New York City, NY: Routledge Taylor & Francis.

Wright, T., Boria, E., and Breidenbach, P. (2002). Creative player actions in FPS online video games: Playing *Counter-Strike*. *Game Studies, 2*(2). Retrieved from http://www.gamestudies.org/0202/wright/.

Games Cited

Bioware (1998). Baldur's Gate, CA: Interplay Entertainment.

2K Games (2004). *Bioshock 2*, Novato, California, US: 2K Games.

Treyarch (2010). *Call of Duty: Black Ops*, Santa Monica, California, US: Activision, Inc.

Reality Pump (2010). *Two Worlds II*, Paradise, Nevada, US: TopWare Interactive.

Spellbound Entertainment (2010). *Arcania: Gothic 4*, Rottenmann, Austria: JoWooD.

7 Analyzing AI in NPCs

An Analysis of Twelve Games

Magnus Johansson, Björn Strååt,
Henrik Warpefelt, and Harko Verhagen

Introduction

When *Baldur's Gate: Dark Alliance* (Vivendi, 2001) was released in 2001 for the PlayStation 2 console, it was received with enthusiastic approval. When starting the first mission in the game, a mission that consisted of clearing out a cellar of giant rats and vermin in the Elfsong Tavern, it was obvious how extraordinary the graphical detail was compared to contemporary games. After finishing the first mission, it was time to head back to the Elfsong Tavern to sell some loot and get another mission. The vendor in the tavern greets you with a long monologue about his products; a sales pitch to make players spend their gold on his merchandise. Even the vendor, a nonplayer character (NPC) in the game, was, when compared to contemporary standards, both detailed and believable, the first ten times. However, after going to the same vendor for the fiftieth time, his monologue was starting to become annoying ...

In Bartle (2003), the history of virtual worlds is documented, ranging from the multi-user dungeons (MUDs) of the seventies, to the game worlds of 2003. Shortly after this, *World of Warcraft (WoW)* (Blizzard Entertainment, 2005) was released, but the question is whether *WoW* really changed everything. Bartle (2003) claims that the major difference between MUDs and modern virtual worlds is the graphics—under the surface, they still function pretty much the same, and the same social phenomena can be observed in both. Among the unchanged aspects is the unfulfilled potential of artificial intelligence (AI) in games: "From the point of view of world design, AI promises great things. If virtual worlds could be populated by intelligent NPCs, all manner of doors would open" (Bartle, 2003, p. 616). Castronova (2006) also suggests further improvement in game AI.

The believability of NPCs is one area that has an impact on the interaction between players and between players and NPCs. In this chapter, we investigate how game AI has developed over the last 15 years, with a focus on the social believability of NPC behavior. The chapter will discuss the game AI in 12 games, focusing on the complexity of the behavior of NPCs. We also discuss different roles for and types of NPCs.

NPCs

In Johansson and Verhagen (2011), we discussed the limitations in game AI by observing NPCs in *WoW* in general. For NPCs, acting as a means to communicate something in the game world or to fulfill the specific task they have been designed for, complexity of behavior (i.e. unpredictable yet understandable behavior) is not needed. Some of the most usual tasks NPCs fill in game worlds are described in Bartle (2003, p. 287):

- Buy, sell, and make stuff
- Provide services
- Guard places
- Get killed for loot
- Dispense quests (or clues for other NPCs' quests)
- Supply background information (history, lore, cultural attitudes)
- Do stuff for players
- Make the place look busy.

These are perhaps the most common tasks for NPCs in the massively multiplayer online game (MMOG) genre. In first-person shooter (FPS), third-person shooter games, role-playing games (RPGs), and real-time strategy (RTS), NPCs are usually allies or enemies, where enemies are part of the intrigue of the game. Sometimes the allied NPCs are so-called persistent NPCs that are also part of cut-scenes to reveal information or parts of the plot in the game (Pinchbeck, 2009).

If NPCs in the future should be able to perform other tasks than the automated actions above, we need to start to think about what traits the NPCs of today lack. To answer this, we investigate 12 games released between 1996 and 2011.

Data Collection

To explore certain aspects of video games, different kinds of observation methods can be used. Based on ethnographic methods, observations made in study 1 were made in pairs, where one person is playing the game and the other is taking "field notes." Three pairs performed the studies. Gameplay lasted up to five hours per session. In study 2, games were played individually and video recorded. Game sessions lasted one to three hours. The video recordings were analyzed in pairs; one research pair was used for the whole study. Complementary data collecting consists of recordings of the game sessions for in-depth analysis after the observations.

We studied AI from a "black-box" perspective, since the code was not accessible. It also underlines an important aspect of game AI; namely, that the actual implementation is not important as long as the result is believable game AI that does not disturb the game play. In some cases, we used cheat codes to trigger some typical behaviors of NPCs for some game scenarios.

These scenarios were influenced by the categorization derived from the social fractionation matrix developed by Carley and Newell (1994) (referred to as C&N from here on) to see what parts of the model social agent could be found in NPC behavior and what parts were missing. The matrix consists of several categories of knowledge and processing capabilities that together span all types of agents from omnipotent agents to model social agents. In Johansson and Verhagen (2011), we analyzed a regular NPC from *WoW* as a mix between a bounded rational agent and a cognitive agent. This chapter uses the same method to study how capable NPCs in different games are at interacting with the player and each other. The first study takes a more holistic perspective focused on biological attributes such as hearing and sight, whereas the second study focuses on the social actions taken by the NPCs.

Study 1

Using C&N's social fractionation matrix, we identified different situations for NPCs. The tasks can be either non-social, multiple agents, or real-time interaction. For the processing internals of the NPCs, we selected the omnipotent agent, rational agent, bounded rational agent, and cognitive agent as the potential categories to consider. Finally, we added game-typical aspects, such as path finding, and biological aspects, such as line of sight and hearing, where applicable.

The games that have been studied in this chapter can be arranged into the following categories:

FPSs

- *Quake* (Id Software, 1996)
- *Duke Nuke'em 3D* (3D Realms, 1996)
- *Deus Ex* (Ion Storm Inc., 2000).

Third-Person Shooters

These games are usually divided into subgenres. In our study, the first three games are "stealth" games ("stealth" in the sense that a large part of the challenge in the game is to remain hidden from the NPC enemies in the game, while solving tasks), while the last two games are "sandbox" games (sandbox games are games with an open virtual world, where the player can travel freely around, and often also freely choose how to approach game tasks, etc.).

- *Metal Gear Solid* (Microsoft Game Studios, 1998)
- *Splinter Cell* (Ubisoft Montreal, 2002)
- *Assassins Creed: Brotherhood* (Ubisoft Montreal, 2011)
- *Mafia: The City of Lost Heaven* (Illusion Softworks, 2002)
- *Grand Theft Auto 4* (Rockstar North, 2008).

Multiplayer Online Battle Arena

The multiplayer online battle arena (MOBA) is a fairly new game genre that, from certain perspectives, has much in common with the RTS genre. The NPCs that have been part of the MOBA observation are monsters and minions, where there are four different types of minions for each team, and ten different types of neutral monsters that can be killed in order to get experience points and gold. Throughout this chapter, we focus on the AI of the minions, the towers of each team. Only one game was part of the study.

- *League of Legends* (Riot Games, 2009).

Results for Study 1

FPSs

Quake. The NPCs (named ogres) are opponents to fight. They have a limited set of strategies and always react in the same way in fighting situations. For example, when being attacked, they always flinch back and get stunned for a while, and they always attack the player that attacked them last, even if this is not a strategically sound choice. The NPCs have a defined set of weapons that is static during the game, and the way that they use weapons is unvaried as well. The path-finding algorithm is very limited; NPCs walk into walls and have problems with utilizing the different levels of the map. The path-finding algorithm seems to ignore the routes available to the player. Their line of sight is fairly realistic, since they do not see players attacking from behind and cannot see through walls or obstacles. The social aspects of NPCs are limited to not attacking each other. They do not have any cooperative strategies whatsoever, apart from sharing vision in some sense. If all NPCs in a group have the line of sight of the player, and one NPC sees the player, all NPCs discover the player. However, if an NPC in a group does not have line-of-sight vision, it will not discover the player, even if the other group members see the player.

Duke Nuke'em. Here, NPCs (assault troopers) are opponents as well. They have similar traits to the NPCs in *Quake*. The NPCs can see through windows, but do not discover the player from reflections in mirrors in the game. However, once the NPC discovers the player, the line of sight seems to become infinite and the NPC can see through walls. Before the player is spotted, the path-finding algorithm acts in a limited way. Once the player is spotted, NPC mobility in the game increases, even though they can run into walls and obstacles without resolving the situation. The NPCs have no restrictions when it comes to friendly fire and attack their allies without hesitating. If an NPC gets in the line of fire between another NPC and the player, it will keep on shooting. They have no means of communication, and if one NPC in the proximity of other NPCs is attacked, there is no reaction to the attack.

Deus Ex. Here, the NPCs (terrorists) are less limited than the NPCs in the previous games. They are equipped with many types of weapons and adapt the choice of weapon to the situation. The NPCs have no precautions with respect to other NPCs and may fire rounds that hit their allies. They can notify other NPCs if they have spotted the player, but do not have any strategies to cooperate with the player. The path-finding algorithm seems to be less restricted than in the previous cases.

Third-Person Shooters

The stealth games

In all three stealth games in this study, the NPCs have three basic modes that direct their behavior. The first mode is "patrolling" and could be interpreted as a neutral mode. The NPCs have not yet discovered anything suspicious, but they will if the players get in the NPCs' line of sight, or if the NPCs hear the player. Once a player has been discovered, the NPCs change mode and become suspicious. The last mode for the NPCs of this genre is offensive, and this is the active mode, where the NPCs will chase and try to kill the player.

Metal Gear Solid. The NPCs depend on their line of sight to see and give pursuit to a spotted player. Apart from the above-mentioned general stealth modes, the NPC will be in "suspicious" mode during a cool-down period until it gets back to the initial "neutral" mode if it cannot perceive the player anymore. However, while playing, the cool-down period feels like the NPC is suffering from amnesia. The path-finding algorithm does not resolve problems with obstacles encountered during the chase. The NPCs do not seem to cooperate.

Splinter Cell. Here, NPCs also activate the "suspicious" mode after hearing, for example, footsteps, gunshots, etc. The line of sight of the NPCs is cone-shaped and feels realistic, and is complemented with 360-degree hearing. An NPC that has spotted a player, and is in "offensive" mode, will not "forget" the player to return to being suspicious or neutral. The path-finding algorithm is efficient as long as the path for the NPC is not blocked with high obstacles. If one NPC spots the player, all nearby NPCs will start to chase the player as well, which is the only element of cooperation.

Assassin's Creed: Brotherhood. This game offers different types of NPCs, such as civilians (creating an atmosphere of crowded city streets) and guards (patrolling the streets). It takes some player effort to trigger the suspicious and offensive mode of the NPCs, and if the player does not attack the NPC, it will remain in the "patrol" mode. However, if the player attacks the NPC, kills a civilian, or climbs the roofs, the NPCs will quickly become offensive and chase the player. A player that has once been spotted by an NPC in offensive mode will be recognized and activate the offensive mode of that NPC. The path-finding algorithm of the NPCs is highly efficient, in terms of both the routes the NPCs patrol and how NPCs solve the path-finding task when chasing players. The player can only be attacked by one NPC at a time, a strategy to regulate the difficulty of an attack by multiple NPCs.

The sandbox games

In the sandbox games, the NPCs are either neutral or offensive toward the player character, and different actions trigger the offensive mode of the NPCs in the game.

Mafia: The City of Lost Heaven. The NPCs (law-enforcement personnel) are in neutral mode by default. If a player kills a civilian in the game without any NPCs being in the vicinity, nothing happens. If NPCs observe a killing, they will change into "offensive" mode and the player will be "wanted." If the player manages to kill the NPC during the chase, the "wanted" alert disappears. Thus, NPCs do not cooperate or communicate their mode or the status of the player. The path-finding algorithm of the NPCs cannot deal with blocked paths.

Grand Theft Auto 4. The NPCs (police officers) are in neutral mode by default. The "wanted" mode is invoked after an observed killing and remains active when the player is within the limits of a circular area. All NPCs will chase the player when spotted in this mode. If the player manages to escape the area, there is a cool-down period until the NPCs return to their neutral mode. When in neutral mode, the NPCs do not recognize the player, even if the player just attacked an NPC and escaped. NPCs in a gunfight try to duck for cover if possible. Different NPCs have different responses to player actions, for instance, if the player attacks a civil NPC, the police NPCs will try to arrest him; on the other hand, if the player aims a gun at a police NPC, the police NPCs will open fire. The path-finding algorithm is similar to the one in *Mafia*.

Multiplayer Online Battle Arena

In the MOBA genre, there is a priority system for some of the NPCs. When the special NPCs (heroes and minions) get attacked, a call for help is sent to allied NPCs. The priority system is static, with preset values for when to intervene and send help. However, the status check does not take place continuously. If hero B from the opposing team attacks hero A, the allied minions will continue to attack hero B even if he withdraws. An assumption is that computer-controlled heroes share this priority system and the AI of minions.

The difficulty level of the game session can be changed and this alters some of the NPCs behaviors slightly. The aggressiveness of their behavior differs; the NPCs' strategic decision-making varies, etc.

The cooperation between the NPCs is not that of team play, nor do they try to get tactical benefits from tactical formations in the game, or prioritize and change their target once it is locked on an opponent.

Study 2

The first study showed that there were some limitations in what could be observed; namely, how NPCs interacted with each other and with the player on a level beyond that of pure action. Thus, this second study (presented in more detail in Warpefelt and Strååt, 2012) is aimed at finding the finer details of NPC social behavior; that is, where they display convincing behavior. We also encountered situations where the behavior of the NPCs was so unrealistic that it could be considered as game breaking. It is important to note that we did not attempt to trick the NPCs into performing aberrant behaviors, but rather played the game as it was intended by the developer (i.e. following the story with some extra exploration of the game world where it was allowed).

The identified social situations were also recorded here using a screen-capture utility. The recorded videos were then analyzed in pairs, where the attributes listed in C&N were compared to the behavior of the NPCs. However, here we utilized all the 74 attributes found in the matrix, rather than the subset of overarching categories used in study 1. The attributes in the model were assumed to be exhaustive.

The games were selected using three criteria:

- Recently released (i.e. between November 2010 and November 2011).
- Used AI behavior and/or technology as a selling point, and/or had positive reviews of the same.
- Must be a Triple-A title (i.e. a big budget, high-quality studio title).

The games chosen using this method were:

- *Skyrim* (Bethesda, 2011)
- *RAGE* (Id Software, 2011)
- *L.A. Noire* (Team Bondi/Rockstar Leeds, 2011).

Results of Study 2

In essence, we found that these games were similar in their capabilities. *Skyrim* and *RAGE* had ten positive attributes in common, *RAGE* and *L.A. Noire* had seven, and *Skyrim* and *L.A. Noire* had eight in common. As for the total number of positive attributes, *Skyrim* had 15 in total, and *RAGE* and *L.A Noire* had 12 and 9, respectively. It should be noted that these results do not transfer between pairs, so *Skyrim* and *L.A Noire* having a similarity value of eight bears no relation to *RAGE* and *L.A. Noire* having a similarity value of seven.

In Table 7.1, we present some of our findings in more detail. In addition to the results described above, we will also describe the previously mentioned game-breaking behavior. We have categorized the findings as *combat, non-combat situations,* and *irrational behavior.*

Table 7.1 Values from Study 2

Game	Combat	Non-combat situations	Irrational behavior
Skyrim	Crisis response Group making Rapid emotional response Use of tools Use of language Group think Mob action Goal-directed behavior Adaptation Automatic response to status cues	Use of tools Production of goods Use of language Advertising Face-to-face	The player witnesses a hunter chasing a refugee, both being oblivious of the player. The hunter ignores the player, even when she is blocking his view. When talking to the king in one town, other NPCs talked at the same time, addressing the player.
RAGE	Use of tools Use of language Models of others Adaptation Interruptability Crisis response Mob action Goal-directed Cooperation Automatic response to status cues Group think	Face-to-face	We were unable to find any irrational behavior in *RAGE*.
L.A. Noire	Use of tools Mob action Group think	Turn taking Use of language Face-to-face Rapid emotional response Automatic response to status cues Crisis response	*L.A. Noire* is not as complex as *Skyrim* but there are still some situations in which the NPCs act irrationally, such as in traffic situations. For example, if the player collides with a car driven by an NPC, the NPC may get out and start signaling displeasure by making gestures. However, the player cannot interact with the NPC in any manner. The NPC will run its animation, enter its car and drive off, ignoring the player. This signals a distinct lack of models of others.

Skyrim. The game is a typical sandbox type of RPG. NPCs that exist are story-essential NPCs, companions that will follow the player and fight for her, storekeepers, special storekeepers, such as blacksmiths, ambient NPCs, such as strolling city people, working farmers, guards, wild animals (friendly or hostile), monsters, and several kinds of human antagonists, such as bandits.

It appears that the NPCs do not have the following attributes:

- Acquires information (omniscient guards always know about a crime).
- Models of others (hunter ignoring player when shooting a refugee).
- Turn taking (NPCs talking at the same time—quest-related cues do not overtake context/proximity triggered cues).

RAGE. The game is a mission-driven FPS with some racing and role-playing elements. The player is more or less forced to follow the story in order to progress and is given step-by-step goals to achieve in order to finish each step of the quest line. It is possible to roam the game world, but this is mostly used to travel between locations and provide bonus quests, rather than as a key component to the story. NPCs are either friendly and passive or hostile and active. The friendly NPCs provide the player with quests and services (such as access to racing tracks and repairs), and act as storekeepers who sell supplies to the player. The hostile NPCs are exclusively out to kill the player and never provide any other interaction possibilities.

L.A. Noire. The game is a missions-based, third-person shooter game. The game has an action element (combat criminals) and a racing element (chase criminals). The action elements can be skipped. The only NPCs that can be interacted with are the criminals in a combat or an interrogation situation. To successfully interrogate a criminal NPC, players must observe the NPC's face and decide if it is lying, withholding the truth, or actually telling the truth when asked a question. The quality of the arguments that the player can present to the NPC is based on the amount of evidence collected from crime scenes and through interrogation. Other NPCs (traffic and pedestrians) populate the game world, but the interaction between the player and these NPCs is limited to the use of car sounds or vocal utterances.

Analysis

The analysis of the data in study 1 shows that path-finding algorithms have developed. The NPCs in the oldest games in this study had problems with a changing environment, while newer games seem to have solved this problem. Only *Assassin's Creed* seems to have solved the problem with NPCs navigating a truly three-dimensional space.

An open problem is the total amnesia NPCs display when it comes to actions performed by the player character, also noted by Pinchbeck in his study on persistent NPCs (Pinchbeck, 2009). A memory function would be motivated for persistent NPCs and the NPCs' players interact with and expect to act in certain ways. However, in the action genre where NPCs are always hostile toward the player, there is no need for a memory function for believability reasons.

Regarding the knowledge situation (the x-axis in C&N), NPCs do not cooperate or communicate with other NPCs. NPCs are slightly harder to locate on the information-processing axis. Of course, the environment limits the possible actions of an agent. Some of the traits of NPCs are similar to the bounded rational agent, such as being rational in their attempts to achieve their goals, and having a limited attention span, making it hard for the agent to process all the information in its task environment. However, NPCs lack some of the components of the "bounded rational agent," the "cognitive agent," and the "emotional cognitive agent." NPCs typically lack a memory function; thus, NPCs form a separate class in the matrix. Most typical NPC-interacting scenarios show patterns similar to the behavior of state machines, where NPCs typically behave in a stimulus–response manner. Most NPCs, however, could be described with some of the traits common to both the "cognitive agent" and the "bounded rational agent," in line with the conclusions drawn in Johansson and Verhagen (2011).

Even though study 2 analyzed NPCs from various genres, the NPCs have similar social abilities. This is an interesting result, since the games studied differ in many aspects, especially in the gameplay experience. However, the NPCs in study 2 had more believable cooperation, while in other respects the NPCs displayed irrational behavior that threatened the gameplay experience from a player perspective.

Discussion and Conclusions

The believability of NPC behavior is crucial for immersion in games and enables seamless interaction between players and between players and NPCs. In this chapter, we have analyzed 12 games in two studies. The scope of the initial nine games in study 1 with the additional three games in study 2 is too narrow to be used as proof of the complexity of NPCs and game AI in general, but served its purpose in evaluating the categories, and in helping to pinpoint some obvious shortcomings of the games studied, and of the analytical values of C&N for game studies. In study 2, the shortcomings of study 1 were adjusted to contain all the attributes of C&N, which resulted in the possibility of comparing NPCs from a social-complexity perspective across games and genres.

Inspired by C&N on social behavior, we tested it to analyze NPCs. However, the matrix is designed with a close approximation of a human agent in mind. Thus, NPCs that are not designed to be social have a hard time fitting in or living up to that expectation. Perhaps NPCs are more a product of the vision of what particular gameplay NPCs are designed to cater for, than trying to create truly believable NPCs. Game AI is mostly designed to be smart enough to keep the illusion of intelligent behavior alive, as mentioned in Lidén (2003). NPCs in general are not as dynamic and believable as needed if we start having expectations other than those from current games. If we were to aim at designing games where the interaction with NPCs is deeper, or where NPCs need to be socially apt and believable, then we need to start developing strategies to cater for these new needs. One way is by adapting the strategies behind games such as *Façade* (Procedural Arts, 2005), with a focus on how to enrich the dialogue, or with design patterns as presented in Lankoski, Johansson, Karlsson, Björk, and Dell'Acqua (2011), or in Campbell, Grimshaw, and Green (2009) and their review of relational agents. Yet another solution to this problem would be to start implementing an internal mode that can be mapped to theories on human decision-making and behaviors, as in Johansson, Verhagen, and Eladhari (2011).

As for the limitations to the use of C&N to categorize NPC behaviors, the adaptation in study 2 to include all attributes in the matrix proved useful both for the analysis and to compare NPCs, and even to compare game AI across genres. However, the method may need to be refined to better differentiate NPCs' social abilities when comparing games. Applying a graded measurement of the attributes in C&N instead of the binary values is one way forward. This may enable us to evaluate how well an attribute is represented.

The irrational behavior observed in study 2 could possibly be related to a poorly constructed social model, or perhaps even the lack of one. It would also be useful to create an extended model that can describe *how and why* the AI fails, rather than just when.

Future work will be directed at implementing a model social game agent that closely maps to the theories of Carley and Newell, as described in Johansson et al. (2011). The expanded method used in study 2 will be further investigated and used to collect data from more games and more genres to fill the gap, as this chapter only introduces an inconclusive and sketchy picture of the current status of NPCs.

Acknowledgments

This study would not have been possible without the help of five bachelor students collecting empirical data for this article. Thanks to Jimmie Westerberg, Fredrik Jansson, Hampus Ekelin, Oscar Falk, and Mattias Lundman for your expertise and efforts.

References

Bartle, R. (2003). *Designing virtual worlds*. Indianapolis, IN: New Riders.
Campbell, R. H., Grimshaw, M. N., and Green, G. M. (2009). Relational agents: A critical review. *The Open Virtual Reality Journal, 1*(1), 1–7.
Carley, K. M., and Newell, A. (1994). The nature of the social agent. *Journal of Mathematical Sociology, 19*(4), 221–262.

Castronova, E. (2006). *Synthetic worlds: The business and culture of online games.* Chicago, IL: University of Chicago Press.

Johansson, M., and Verhagen, H. (2011). "Where is my mind?"—The evolution of NPCs in online worlds. In J. Filipe and A. L. N. Fred (Eds.), *Proceedings of ICAAI 2011*, (2), 359–364.

Johansson, M., Verhagen, H., and Eladhari, M. (2011). Model of social believable NPCs for teacher training. *CGames 2011*, 270–274.

Lankoski, P., Johansson, A., Karlsson, B., Björk, S., and Dell'Acqua, P. (2011). AI design for believable characters via gameplay design patterns. In M. Cruz-Cunha, V. H. Carvalho, and P. Tavares (Eds.), *Business, technological, and social dimensions of computer games* (15–31). Hershey, PA: IGI Global.

Lidén, L. (2003). Artificial stupidity: The art of intentional mistakes. In S. Rabin (Ed.), *AI game programming wisdom II* (41–48). Hingham, MA: Charles River Media.

Pinchbeck, D. (2009). An analysis of persistent non-player characters in the first-person gaming genre 1998–2007: A case for the fusion of mechanics and diegetics. *Eludamos. Journal for Game Culture, 3*(2), 261–279.

Warpefelt, H., and Strååt, B. (2012). A method for comparing NPC social ability. In E. Prakash (Ed.), *Proceedings of Computer Games and Allied Technologies 2012* (58–63).

Games Cited

Bethesda Game Studios (2011), *Skyrim*, Bethesda Softworks.

Blizzard Entertainment (2005), *World of Warcraft.* Blizzard Entertainment (EU-release).

Id Software (1996), *Quake*, Activision/Valve Corporation (Steam).

Id Software (2011), *RAGE*, Bethesda Softworks.

Illusion Softworks (2002), *Mafia: City of Lost Heaven*, Gathering of Developers (EU-release).

Ion Storm Inc. (2000), *Deus Ex*, Eidos Interactive (EU-release).

KCEJ (2008), *Metal Gear Solid*, Microsoft Game Studios.

Procedural Arts (2005), *Façade*, Procedural Arts. Retrieved from http://interactivestory.net/download/.

Riot Games (2009), *League of Legends*, Riot Games.

Rockstar North (2008), *Grand Theft Auto 4*, Rockstar Games (EU-release).

Snowblind Studios (2001), *Baldur's Gate: Dark Alliance*, Vivendi Universal.

Team Bondi, Rockstar Leeds (2011), *L.A. Noire,* Rockstar Games.

Ubisoft Montreal (2002), *Splinter Cell*, Ubisoft.

Ubisoft Montreal (2011), *Assassin's Creed*, Ubisoft (EU-release).

3D Realms (1996), *Duke Nuke'em 3D*, GT Interactive (EU-release).

Part III
Online Gaming

8 Party Animal or Dinner for One
Are Online Gamers Socially Inept?

Rachel Kowert and Julian A. Oldmeadow

Introduction

Interpersonal communication is the number one use of the Internet at home (Kraut et al., 1998). Video games have adapted to this trend with great success, as the popularity of online video games is on the rise (Wu, 2010). However, along with the success of online gaming has come a growing concern about the possible consequences of prolonged interaction within these new social spaces. Aspects of social competence, or rather incompetence, have become one of the primary concerns in relation to this new social media. Despite the fact that online games are highly social spaces, the players of such games have become anecdotally and empirically characterized as socially reclusive, inept individuals (Kowert, Griffiths, and Oldmeadow, in press; Kowert and Oldmeadow, 2012; Williams, 2005; Williams, Yee, and Caplan, 2008). Although numerous demographic studies have refuted these negative characterizations of online gamers, the prominence of these stereotypes has not diminished (see Axelsson and Regan, 2002; Cole and Griffiths, 2007; Griffiths, Davies, and Chappell, 2003; Kowert and Oldmeadow, 2012; Williams, Ducheneaut, Xiong, Yee, and Nickell, 2006; Williams et al., 2008; Yee, 2006).

The earliest suggestion that video games may negatively impact an individual's sociability comes from Senlow (1984) who coined the term "electronic friendship" to suggest that electronic games (e.g., arcade machines) have the ability to replace one's real-world friends. Senlow's (1984) suggestion has recently been expanded to propose that one's electronic friends (i.e. friends met over the Internet) may replace one's real-world friends, fuelling concerns that these social spaces are displacing civic and social institutions (Putnam, 2000). In society and media alike, there are even signs of moral panic surrounding the impact of social interaction online. Jim Hightower, an ABC radio commentator, expressed this concern when he stated, "While all this razzle-dazzle connects us electronically, it disconnects us from each other, having us interfacing more with computers and TV screens than looking in the face of our fellow human beings" (Fox, 1995, p. 12).

This chapter will outline the current state of research examining the relationship between social competence and online gaming. After providing a general overview of social competence, the emerging theories that explain the mechanisms by which sociability can be affected by online gaming will be discussed, along with the methodologies, findings, conclusions, and limitations of selected empirical work within this area.

What Is Social Competence?

Social competence is difficult to characterize. Numerous definitions have been presented for this concept, which range from the very broad "social success" (Atteli, 1990, p. 241) to the more narrow "attainment of relevant social goals in specified social contexts" (Ford, 1982, p. 323). Despite the varied definitions of this concept, it is generally agreed upon that social competence requires some element of being effective in social interaction (Dodge, 1985; Rose-Kransor, 1997). To assess this "social effectiveness," social competence can be broken down into more specific levels of classification (Anderson and Messick, 1974). Most commonly, this has been done through operationalizing social competence as a measure of sociometric status (popularity), relationship quality and quantity, functional outcomes, and/or social skills.

This chapter will primarily focus on the social skills approach, as this approach has been predominantly employed throughout the broader social competence literature (for a review of the different methodologies see Rose-Kransor, 1997) and social skills form the foundation for social competence in most social competence models (e.g., Cavell, 1990; DuBois and Felnder, 1996; Rose-Kransor, 1997).

Social Skills Approach

The social skills approach operationalizes social competence as either having or not having certain skills (Rose-Kransor, 1997). Not surprisingly, researchers regularly disagree on which skills should be included under the umbrella of social skills (Hops and Finch, 1985). As Liberman, DeRisi and Mueser (1989) state, "Trying to define social skills in one sentence is like trying to define a complex motor skill, such as being a good baseball player, in one sentence" (p. 136). To account for this, researchers often employ broad, overarching, measures of social skills, such as the Social Performance Survey Schedule (Lowe and Cautela, 1978) or the Social Skills Inventory (SSI) (Riggio, 1989). Measures such as these allow one to administer a single inventory to obtain a comprehensive picture of the range of skills an individual may possess as well as pinpoint possible social strengths and weaknesses.

Even though the social skills approach has been criticized for excluding a direct measurement of the transitional nature of social communication (that is, the real-time interaction between individuals), validity evidence has demonstrated significant relationships between self-report measures of social skill and performance-based assessments (Baron and Markman,

2003; Riggio, 2005; Riggio and Riggio, 2001). This suggests that the self-report methodology often used in the social skills approach is a valid measurement of both social skills and social performance.

Social Competence and Online Gaming

In general, greater social use of the Internet has been associated with a variety of social declines, such as declines in the size of one's social circle (Cole and Griffiths, 2007; Shen and Williams, 2010) and the extent of social involvement (Cole and Griffiths, 2007; Kraut et al., 1998; Shen and Williams, 2010). These findings, in combination with the rise in popularity of video games, have sprouted new concerns for the possible social consequences of participating in online gaming environments (Affonso, 1999). This seems paradoxical, as online games are social spaces, in which players consistently rate social motivations as one of the primary reasons for continued play (Axelsson and Regan, 2002; Ducheneaut, Yee, Nickell, and Moore, 2006; Griffiths et al., 2003; Hussain and Griffiths, 2009a; Kolo and Baur, 2004; Ng and Wiemer-Hastings, 2005). How is it that these highly social environments could be associated with social declines?

One suggestion is that the increase in time spent in online gaming environments replaces real-world contacts with online contacts (Cole and Griffiths, 2007; Hussain and Griffiths, 2009b; Lo, Wang, and Fang, 2005; Morahan-Martin and Schumacher, 2003; Shen and Williams, 2010). If so, this could hinder the development and maintenance of various aspects of social competence, including the ability to maintain real-world interpersonal relationships (Cole and Griffiths, 2007; Hussain and Griffiths, 2009b; Lo et al., 2005; Morahan-Martin and Schumacher, 2003; Shen and Williams, 2010) and the development of social and emotional skills (Andrew, 2009; Chiu, Lee, and Huang, 2004; Griffiths, 2010; Kim, Namkoong, Ku, and Kim, 2008; Morahan-Martin and Schumacher, 2003; Smyth, 2007). This theory, referred to as the Displacement Hypothesis, is based on the supposition that Internet communities thrive at the expense of face-to-face interactions (Chiu et al., 2004; Kraut et al., 1998; Morahan-Martin and Schumacher, 2003; Nie, 2001; Nie and Erbring, 2002; Williams, 2006).

Empirical support has led credence to this theory. For example, Smyth (2007) found that individuals who played online games (massively multiplayer online games in particular) steadily reduced the time spent socializing with real-world friends in order to spend more time online, a pattern that was not found for players of offline games. Moreover, the online players reported more interference with real-world socializing in conjunction with a greater development of online friendships. Though these individuals may be thriving in the elaborate social world of their online game, it appears to come at the expense of pre-existing, real-world relationships (Morahan-Martin and Schumacher, 2003; Williams, 2006). As having and maintaining relationships is integral to developing effective social skills and learning socially appropriate behavior (Bartholomew and Horowitz, 1991;

Cassidy et al., 1996; Engles et al., 2001), becoming socially disengaged or isolated due to play could substantially hinder the development, or stimulate the deterioration, of effective "offline" social skills, over time.

A second theoretical model, referred to as Social Compensation Hypothesis, has also gained support within the literature. Unlike the Displacement Hypothesis, Compensation theorists attempt to delineate the sequence of events that motivate individuals to initiate and continue prolonged interaction within online gaming environments. It is the sequence itself that explains why online gamers may be less socially competent than their non-gaming counterparts.

The Social Compensation Hypothesis asserts that players begin to engage with these virtual, social environments due to particular predispositions (such as depression, loneliness, social anxiety, or a lack of social skill), which may have contributed to poor real-world interpersonal relationships. Individuals are drawn to this alternative social environment as the anonymity that is granted within it alleviates fears of social repercussions while decreasing self-consciousness and social anxiety (Morahan-Martin and Schumacher, 2003). While this may initially seem beneficial, over time individuals may begin to place more value on their in-game social networks (Williams, 2006), simultaneously increasing their sense of online community and depriving themselves of their connections with real-world contacts (Morahan-Martin and Schumacher, 2003). This process can exacerbate and intensify psychosocial predispositions (Lemmens, Valkenburg, and Peter, 2011; Lo et al., 2005; Morahan-Martin and Schumacher, 2003) and further discourage individuals from forming stable face-to-face relationships (Caplan, Williams, and Yee, 2010; Griffiths, 2010).

Empirical evidence has also lent support to this theory. In regards to promoting online video game play, social anxiety, loneliness, shyness, depression, and low self-esteem have all been found to initiate online gaming activity (Barnett et al., 1997; Caplan et al., 2010; Chak and Leung, 2004; Griffiths, 2010; Kim et al., 2008; Morahan-Martin and Schumacher, 2003; Peters and Malesky, 2008; Williams et al., 2008; Yee, 2002). This in and of itself may negatively impact social skills, as depression has been linked to social skills deficits (Segrin, 2000; Tse and Bond, 2004; Wierzbicki, 1984) and social anxiety has been linked to (often inaccurate) self-perceptions of social deficits (Caplan, 2003; Cartwright-Hatton, Tschernitz, and Gomersall, 2005; Lucock and Salkovskis, 1988). Therefore, the social deficits that online gamers may appear to have, or report to have, could be attributable to pre-existing dispositions, rather than displacement effects. However, it remains unclear whether any further deterioration of social skills occurs over time due to an exacerbation of these psychosocial predispositions, or if something specific to online gaming directly impairs social skills.

The Social Displacement and Compensation Hypotheses both provide explanations as to why we may see social deficits in online gaming populations, but how would one explain the findings that suggest social improvements due to gaming (Chak and Leung, 2004; Griffiths et al., 2003; Hussain and Griffiths, 2009a; Kolo and Baur, 2004; Morahan-Martin and Schumacher, 2003; Peters and Malesky, 2008)? Online gaming environments are inherently social spaces, which are conducive to various forms of social learning as they promote socialization with fellow players in order to progress through the games' content (Ducheneaut and Moore, 2005; Jakobsson and Taylor, 2003; Moore, Ducheneaut, and Nickell, 2007). For instance, in multiplayer first-person shooting games (such as *America's Army, Left 4 Dead,* and *Team Fortress 2*), players can compete in teams to more easily complete objectives. In the multiplayer mode of the *Battlefield* series, individuals are assigned to teams and must work together to achieve their goals that range from winning a game of capture the flag to matches to the death. In the massively multiplayer online role-playing game, *World of Warcraft* (Blizzard Entertainment, 2004), individuals must work together to complete group activities, which are necessary to progress through the environment and obtain the most exclusive rewards (Ducheneaut and Moore, 2005; Moore et al., 2007).

This need for social participation in online games (Jakobsson and Taylor, 2003) may provide individuals with opportunities to learn (and perfect) social skill (Ducheneaut and Moore, 2005), both directly and indirectly. Direct learning, through socialization with other players, can promote the learning of effective socialization strategies (Spence, 2003), regardless of whether the communication occurs face-to-face or virtually. In the absence of direct socialization, indirect social learning can arise through the observation of social interactions occurring between other individuals. The opportunity for observation of social interactions between other players occurs frequently within these gaming environments. Similar to observing real-world models, players have the opportunity to observe social behaviors modelled by others in a wide variety of situations. From this, individuals can learn socially appropriate (and inappropriate) behaviors from which to draw upon in their future social experiences (Bandura, 1977; Rogoff, Paradise, Arauz, Correa-Chávey, and Angelillo, 2003).

Overview of Empirical Work: Social Skills Approach

Research examining links between online gaming and social interaction has produced varied and mixed results, ranging from findings that online interactions contribute to increases in interpersonal difficulties (Kim et al., 2008) and social awkwardness (Andrew, 2009), while reducing the importance of real-world friends (Kraut et al., 1998) to determining that online gaming may contribute to increased real-world leadership skills (Yee, 2006).

One of the most comprehensive evaluations of the relationship between social competence and online game play comes from Loton (2007). Focusing on uncovering the possible foundations of problematic game play, Loton presented online gamers with the SSI and the Problematic Video Game Playing Scale (PVP), hypothesizing that deficient social skills may underpin the development of problematic playing behaviors. Loton found a small inverse relationship (r = −.084, *p* = .037) between the overall SSI scores and outcome scores on the PVP. However, he later discredited these findings due to the small effect size.

In one of our own studies (Kowert and Oldmeadow, under review), we examined the relationship between video game involvement and social skills, as measured by the SSI. However, we conceptualized video game involvement more broadly than Loton (2007), choosing to enlist a composite score of involvement derived from participants' reported weekly play frequency, game-play variety, and social identity, rather than categorizing them based upon problematic play behaviors. The integration of objective (i.e., play frequency and variety) and subjective (i.e., social identity) measures of involvement was thought to provide a more systematic assessment of game involvement than has been previously employed within the literature and more appropriately assess the degree to which participants are involved in gaming as a form of activity. After controlling for age and gender, regression analyses showed that all three emotional subscales of the SSI (Emotional Expressivity, Sensitivity, and Control) significantly predicted higher game involvement amongst the broad population of active video game players. However, none of the SSI subscales significantly predicted Involvement amongst the subgroup of online exclusive players. The lack of consistent, negative relationships between social outcomes and increased Involvement amongst online exclusive players disputes the all-encompassing, maladaptive social skills that are anecdotally attributed to online video game players (e.g., Griffiths et al., 2003; Kowert et al., in press; Kowert and Oldmeadow, 2012; Williams, Yee, and Caplan, 2008) and indicates the unlikelihood that players are suffering severe social consequences due to engagement within these spaces. However, further research is needed to confirm these findings.

Other investigations have enlisted more narrow assessments of social skills. For instance, Barnett, Coulson, and Foreman (2009) compared how non-gamers and MMO gamers would react to a series of hypothetical real-life potential anger-causing provocations such as "You are talking to someone and they are not listening to you" (taken from the Novaco Provocation Inventory; Novaco, 2003). The results showed that the majority of both gamers and non-gamers chose constructive (assertive) rather than destructive (aggressive) responses, leading to the conclusion that gamers are not socially deficient as compared to non-gamers. Utilizing a slightly broader measure, Griffiths (2010) administered the Social Situations Questionnaire (Bryant and Trower, 1974) among high and low frequency online players. This measure assesses the extent to which individuals feel anxious or uncomfortable (i.e., socially anxious) in a variety of hypothetical situations. The results indicated that more frequent game players reported a greater difficulty with the presented social situations, signifying a higher degree of social inadequacy than low frequency players.

While only a few studies have been highlighted here, in general the negative social repercussions of online gaming remain widely publicized despite a lack of considerable evidence to support the validity of this claim. While preliminary evidence suggests that there are some inverse relationships between online video game play and social competence, in general, the empirical results do not support the magnitude of these claims. Furthermore, there is a small, but noteworthy, amount of literature contradicting the contention that online video game players are somehow socially deficient. For instance, researchers have uncovered some positive social effects of online gaming, including declines in loneliness (Williams, 2006) and increases in real-world leadership skills (Yee, 2006).

Summary

The Internet gaming industry continues to flourish, as people choose to spend a substantial amount of their time playing games together (Heydon, 2010; Wu, 2010). However, along with the success of online gaming has come growing concern about the possible effects of prolonged interaction within these spaces, particularly in relation to social competence. Although a considerable amount of research has investigated the relationship between social competence and online gamers, consistent relationships have yet to be established.

For some, these social spaces are "safe havens" that provide an alternative social outlet for individuals who may have social difficulties in their offline lives (Griffiths et al., 2003; Hussain and Griffiths, 2009a; Kolo and Baur, 2004; Morahan-Martin and Schumacher, 2003), while others have branded the success of online gaming as a sign of a broken society (Putnam, 2000). Online games seem to have created a "communication paradox" (Shen and Williams, 2010). That is, the core qualities of online games themselves (i.e., communication with other players, player networks), which strongly suggest that online gaming environments promote interaction and sociability, have been found to be associated with worse psychosocial outcomes (Ng and Wiemer-Hastings, 2005; Shen and Williams, 2010).

The possible loss of (or failure to develop) social skills remains one of the most actively debated social effects of online video game interaction. Based on single measures of social competence, Barnett et al. (2009) concluded that no differences in social competence exist between gamers and non-gamers, whereas Griffiths (2010) would contest that conclusion. However, as social competence is a multi-faceted concept that is difficult to evaluate (Rose-Kransor, 1997), it is tenuous to draw conclusions from singular measures, as negative outcomes on one measure of sociability do not necessarily show that online gamers are socially incompetent as compared to non-gamers. Both Loton (2007) and Kowert and Oldmeadow (under review) attempted to overcome these limitations by employing broad measures, but still reached conflicting conclusions. While Loton found a negative relationship between social competence and online gaming, he discredited his findings due to a weak, albeit significant, relationship. Kowert and Oldmeadow, however, uncovered positive, moderately strong effects, but only amongst the broad video game-playing population.

Despite these inconsistencies, and the promising findings that online gaming may be socially beneficial, the picture of a socially inept, reclusive, online gamer remains firmly within popular culture. It remains unclear whether negative social consequences are an inevitable by-product of participation within these environments or if it is simply an assumption motivated by the stereotype of this population. For those who believe negative social consequences abide, it is still uncertain whether individuals who suffer from social difficulties turn to online gaming for a social outlet (as is suggested by the Social Compensation Hypothesis), or if the activity of online gaming directly affects one's social competence (as suggested by the Displacement Hypothesis).

In general, studies show that online gamers are somehow socially different as compared to non-gamers, although further research is needed to help uncover the exact nature of the relationship between social competence and online gaming. Until that happens, the prevailing belief that online gaming somehow negatively impacts one's social competence will remain. One thing for certain, however, is that the idea of a globally socially inept individual, as portrayed by the stereotype of the population, is unfounded.

References

Affonso, B. (1999). *Is the Internet affecting the social skills of our children?* Sierra Source.

Anderson, S., and Messick, S. (1974). Social competency in young children. *Developmental Psychology, 10,* 282–293.

Andrew, C. (2009). The real-world effects of online gaming: Socially inept. Retrieved from http://www.associatedcontent.com/article/1712963/the_real-world_effects_of_online_gaming_pg3.html?cat=41.

Atteli, G. (1990). Successful and disconfirmed children in the peer group: Indices of social competence within an evolutionary perspective. *Human Development, 33,* 238–249.

Axelsson, A., and Regan, T. (2002). *How belonging to an online group affects social behaviour – a case study of Asheron's Call.* Redmond, WA: Microsoft Research.

Bartholomew, K. and Horowitz, L. M. (1991). Attachment styles among young adults. *Journal of Personality and Social Psychology, 61*(2), 226–244.

Bandura, A. (1977). *Social learning theory.* New York City, NY: General Learning Press.

Barnett, J., Coulson, M., and Foreman, N. (2009). *Testing the efficacy of the General Aggression Model: Exploring responses to provocations in non-gamers, and gamers after violent online play.* Unpublished doctoral dissertation, Middlesex University, United Kingdom.

Barnett, M., Vitaglione, G., Harper, K., Quackenbush, S., Steadman, L., and Valdez, B. (1997). Late adolescents' experiences with and attitudes towards videogames. *Journal of Applied Social Psychology, 27*(15), 1316–1334.

Baron, R., and Markman, G. (2003). Beyond social capital: The role of entrepreneurs' social competence in their financial success. *Journal of Business Venturing, 18*(1), 41–60.

Bryant, B., and Trower, P. (1974). Social difficulty in a student sample. *British Journal of Educational Psychology, 44,* 13–21.

Caplan, S. (2003). Preference for online social interaction: A theory of problematic Internet use and psychosocial well-being. *Communication Research, 30,* 625–648.

Caplan, S., Williams, D., and Yee, N. (2010). Problematic internet use and psychosocial well-being among MMO players. *Computers in Human Behavior, 25*(6), 1312–1319.

Cartwright-Hatton, S., Tschernitz, N., and Gomersall, H. (2005). Social anxiety in children: Social skills deficit or cognitive distortion? *Behaviour Research and Therapy, 43*(1), 131–141.

Cassidy, J., Kirsh, S., Scolton, K., and Parke, R. (1996). Attachment and representations of peer relationships. *Developmental Psychology, 32*(5), 892–904.

Cavell, T. (1990). Social adjustment, social performance, and social skills: A tricomponent model of social competence. *Journal of Child Psychology, 19*(2), 111–122.

Chak, K., and Leung, L. (2004). Shyness and locus of control as predictors of Internet addiction and Internet use. *CyberPsychology and Behavior, 7*(5), 559–570.

Chiu, S., Lee, J., and Huang, D. (2004). Video game addiction in children and teenagers in Taiwan. *CyberPsychology and Behavior, 7*(5), 571–581.

Cole, H., and Griffiths, M. (2007). Social interactions in massively multiplayer online role-playing games. *CyberPsychology and Behavior, 10*(4), 575–583.

Dodge, K. A. (1985). Facets of social interaction and the assessment of social competence in children. In B. H. Schneider, K. H. Rubin, and J. Ledingham (Eds.), *Children's peer relations: Issues in assessment and intervention* (pp. 3–22). New York: Springer-Verlag.

DuBois, D., and Felnder, R. (1996). The quadripartite model of social competence: Theory and applications to clinical intervention. In M. Reinecke, F. Dattilio, and A. Freeman (Eds.), *Cognitive therapy with children and adolescents: A casebook for clinical practice* (pp. 12–152). New York City, NY: Guilford Press.

Ducheneaut, N., and Moore, R. (2005). More than just 'XP': Learning social skills in massively multiplayer online games. *Interactive Technology and Smart Education, 2*(2), 89–100.

Ducheneaut, N., Yee, N., Nickell, E., and Moore, R. (2006). *"Alone together?": Exploring the social dynamics of massively multiplayer online games.* Paper presented at the SIGCHI conference on Human Factors in computing systems, New York City, NY.

Engles, R., Finkenauer, C., Meeus, W., and Dekovic, M. (2001). Parental attachment and adolescents' emotional adjustment: The associations with social skills and relational competence. *Journal of Counseling Psychology, 48*(4), 428–439.

Ford, M. (1982). Cognition and social competence in adolescence. *Developmental Psychology, 18*(3), 323–340.

Fox, R. (1995). Newstrack. *Communications of the ACM, 38*(8), 11–12.

Griffiths, M. (2010). Computer game playing and social skills: A pilot study. *Aloma, 27,* 301–310.

Griffiths, M., Davies, M., and Chappell, D. (2003). Breaking the stereotype: The case of online gaming. *CyberPsychology and Behavior, 6*(1), 81–91.

Heydon, P. (2010). Disruption = value creation in games. Paper presented at the Edinburgh Interactive Festival: Avista Partners.

Hops, H., and Finch, M. (1985). Social competence and skill: A reassessment. In B. Schneider, K. Rubin, and J. Ledingham (Eds.), *Children's peer relations: Issues in assessment and intervention* (pp. 23–39). New York City, NY: Springer-Verlag.

Hussain, Z., and Griffiths, M. (2009a). Excessive use of massively multi-player online role-playing games: A pilot study. *International Journal of Mental Health and Addiction, 7*(4), 563–571.

Hussain, Z., and Griffiths, M. (2009b). The attitudes, feelings, and experiences of online gamers: A qualitative analysis. *CyberPsychology and Behavior, 12*(6), 747–753.

Jakobsson, M., and Taylor, T. L. (2003). *The Sopranos meets EverQuest: Social networking in massively multiplayer online games.* Paper presented at the 2003 Digital Arts and Culture (DAC) conference, Melbourne, Australia.

Kim, E., Namkoong, K., Ku, T., and Kim, S. (2008). The relationship between online game addiction and aggression, self-control, and narcissistic personality traits. *European Psychiatry, 23*(3), 212–218.

Kolo, C., and Baur, T. (2004). Living a virtual life: Social dynamics of online gaming. *International Journal of Computer Game Research, 4*(1).

Kowert, R. and Oldmeadow, J. (2012). *The stereotype of online gamers: New characterization or recycled prototype?* Conference proceedings of the Nordic DiGRA: Games in Culture and Society, Tampere, Finland.

Kowert, R., Griffiths, M.D., and Oldmeadow, J. (2012). Geek or Chic? Emerging Stereotypes of Online Gamers. *Bulletin of Science, Technology, and Society, 32*(6), 471 – 479.

Kowert, R. and Oldmeadow, J. (2013). (A)Social Reputation: Exploring the Relationship between Online Video Game Involvement and Social Competence. *Computers in Human Behavior, 29*(4), 1872–1878.

Kraut, R., Patterson, M., Lundmark, V., Kiesler, S., Mukopadhyay, T., and Scherlis, W. (1998). Internet paradox: A social technology that reduces social involvement and psychological well-being?. *American Psychologist, 53*(9), 1017–1031.

Lemmens, J., Valkenburg, P., and Peter, J. (2011). Psychological causes and consequences of pathological gaming. *Computers in Human Behavior, 27*(1), 144–152.

Liberman, R., DeRisi, W., and Mueser, K. (1989). *Social skills training for psychiatric patients.* Needham Heights, MA: Allyn & Bacon.

Lo, S., Wang, C., and Fang, W. (2005). Physical interpersonal relationships and social anxiety among online game players. *CyberPsychology and Behavior, 8*(1), 15–20.

Loton, D. (2007). *Problem video game playing, self esteem, and social skills: An online study.* Unpublished Honours thesis; Victoria University, Melbourne, Australia.

Lowe, M., and Cautela, R. (1978). A self report measure of social skill. *Behavior Therapy, 9*, 535–544.

Lucock, M., and Salkovskis, P. (1988). Cognitive factors in social anxiety and its treatment. *Behaviour Research and Therapy, 26*(4), 297–302.

Moore, R., Ducheneaut, N., and Nickell, E. (2007). Doing virtually nothing: Awareness and accountability in massively multiplayer online worlds. *Computer Supported Cooperative Work, 16*(3), 265–305.

Morahan-Martin, J., and Schumacher, P. (2003). Loneliness and social uses of the Internet. *Computers in Human Behavior, 19,* 659–671.

Ng, B., and Wiemer-Hastings, P. (2005). Addiction to the Internet and online gaming. *CyberPsychology and Behavior, 8*(2), 110–113.

Nie, N. (2001). Sociability, Interpersonal relations, and the Internet: Reconciling conflicting findings. *American Behavioral Scientist, 45,* 420–435.

Nie, N., and Erbring, L. (2002). Internet and mass media: A preliminary report. *IT & Society, 1*(2), 134–141.

Novaco, R. W. (2003). *The Novaco Anger scale and Provocation Inventory.* Los Angeles, CA: Western Psychological Services.

Peters, C., and Malesky, A. (2008). Problematic usage among highly-engaged players of massively multiplayer online role playing games. *CyberPsychology and Behavior, 11*(4), 481–484.

Putnam, R. (2000). *Bowling alone: The collapse and revival of American community.* New York City, NY: Simon and Schuster.

Riggio, R. (1989). *Manual for the social skills inventory.* Palo Alto, CA: Consulting Psychologists Press.

Riggio, R. (2005). The Social Skills Inventory (SSI): Measuring nonverbal and social skills. In V. Manusov (Ed.), *The sourcebook of nonverbal measures: Going beyond words* (pp. 25–35). Mahwah, NJ: Lawrence Erlbaum Associates, Inc.

Riggio, R., and Riggio, H. (2001). Self-report measurement of interpersonal sensitivity. In J. Hall, and F. Bernieri (Eds.), *Interpersonal sensitivity: Theory and measurement* (pp. 127–142). Mahwah, NJ: Lawrence Erlbaum Associates.

Rogoff, B., Paradise, R., Arauz, R., Correa-Chávez, M., and Angelillo, C. (2003). Firsthand learning through intent participation. *Annual Review of Psychology, 54,* 175–203.

Rose-Kransor, L. (1997). Nature of social competence: A theoretical review. *Social Developmental Psychology, 6*(1), 111–135.

Segrin, C. (2000). Social skills deficits associated with depression. *Clinical Psychology Review, 20*(3), 379–403.

Senlow, G. (1984). Playing videogames: The electronic friend. *Journal of Communication, 34*(2), 148–156.

Shen, C., and Williams, D. (2010). Unpacking time online: Connecting Internet and massively multiplayer online game use with psychological well-being. *Communication Research,* [Epub ahead of print].

Smyth, J. (2007). Beyond self-selection in video game play: An experimental examination of the consequences of massively multiplayer online role-playing game play. *CyberPsychology and Behavior, 10*(5), 717–721.

Spence, S. (2003). Social skills training with children and young people: Theory evidence and practice. *Child and Adolescent Mental Health, 8*(2), 84–96.

Tse, W., and Bond, A. (2004). The impact of depression on social skills: A review. *Journal of Nervous and Mental Disease, 192*(4), 260–268.

Wierzbicki, M. (1984). Social skills deficits and subsequent depressed mood in students. *Personal and Social Psychology Bulletin, 10*(4), 605–610.

Williams, D. (2005, June). *A brief social history of game play.* Paper presented at the DiGRA 2005 Conference: Changing Views – Worlds in Play, Vancouver, Canada.

Williams, D. (2006). Groups and goblins: The social and civic impact of online games. *Journal of Broadcasting and Electronic Media, 50,* 651–681.

Williams, D., Ducheneaut, N., Xiong, L., Yee, N., and Nickell, E. (2006). From tree house to barracks. *Games and Culture, 1*(4), 338–361.

Williams, D., Yee, N., and Caplan, S. (2008). Who plays, how much, and why? Debunking the stereotypical gamer profile. *Journal of Computer-Mediated Communication Monographs, 13*(4), 993–1018.

Wu, J. (2010). *Global video game market forecast.* Retrieved from http://www.strategyanalytics.com/default.aspx?mod=ReportAbstractViewer&a0=5282.

Yee, N. (2002). *Befriending ogres and wood-elves – understanding relationship formation in MMORPGs.* Retrieved from http://www.nickyee.com/hub/relationships/home.html.

Yee, N. (2006). The demographics, motivations, and derived experiences of users of massively-multi-user online graphical environments. *Teleoperators and Virtual Environments, 15*(3), 309–329.

Games Cited

Blizzard Entertainment (2004), *World of Warcraft*, Vivendi Activision Blizzard.

9   "There Is No Place Like Home"

The Potential of Commercial Online Gaming Platforms to Become Third Places

Jeffrey Wimmer

Introduction: The Social Connectivity of Online Gaming Platforms

Digital games were traditionally seen as a new form of entertainment media that could involve considerably negative consequences. In contrast to these assumptions, recent studies show that digital gaming—because of its potential for interaction and interactivity—can be understood as a form of mediated communication having significant influence on everyday life and identity formation (e.g. Hand and Moore, 2006). Based on these findings, some authors claim that the mediatized "playgrounds" of massively multiplayer online role-playing games (MMORPGs) have the potential to establish social capital, and hence provide an opportunity for social involvement and participation (e.g. Steinkuehler and Williams, 2006; Ducheneaut, Moore, and Nickell, 2007). Following this approach, under specific circumstances, online games can be understood as a form of "social media," creating new socio-culturally and politically relevant spaces for interaction, which Oldenburg (1991) calls a third place.

Network-based multiplayer games feature an essential trait that distinguishes them from single-player games. They enable social interaction among the players in a virtual environment, as Manninen (2003) illustrates, "Multiplayer games enable players to communicate and collaborate in joint game sessions. Whether the activity is about shooting each other with rocket launchers or arranging virtual weddings, the underlying theme is about togetherness." The success of so-called social networking on platforms such as Facebook has increased the influence of network principles on the gaming industry and its game offers; also because network-based games have gained huge market growth within the industry during the last few years. Following this tendency, the video game-console manufacturers Microsoft and Sony set up the digital gaming platforms Xbox LIVE (XBL) and the PlayStation Network (PSN) to enhance the possibilities for distribution and consumption. Similar platforms exist for PCs, the most prominent being Valve's gaming network Steam. Online gaming platforms started appearing in 2002 and have since been increasing in their complexity and size.

This study starts with a short overview of current research findings regarding the potential of digital games in terms of a third place, which have been, up to this point, mostly focused on theoretical approaches and descriptions of game characteristics, and rarely on the gamers. In this field of study, research almost exclusively examined MMORPGs, while other manifestations of virtual gaming worlds were often neglected. Therefore, in a second step, selected results of an empirical case study on the usage and appreciation of online gaming platforms are presented in order to discuss whether the "semi-real" (Juul, 2005) communicative environment of online gaming networks, and the associated gaming culture, could constitute "third places," and, hence, assume important social functions for our mediatized society, beyond their intrinsic nature as entertainment media.

Digital Games as Virtual Manifestations of a Third Place

In his prominent analysis of contemporary American society, Putnam (2000) uncovers tendencies of social disintegration that are indicated (amongst other things) by an apparently rapid decrease of individual time spent in community with others, for example, in social activities in clubs or in church attendance. He illustrates this increasing trend of social disconnection with the striking metaphor of "bowling alone," the phenomenon of bowling individually outside a bowling league and/or without personal conversation. A central factor in this framework is his concept of social capital, which assumes that a system of self-regulating social associations and closely connected interpersonal networks generates trust, commitment, and participation. Interestingly, Putnam identifies television—especially its entertainment programs—and new media in general as the main causes for social isolation and separation. Their consumption, so his thesis states, reduces leisure activities to solitary pleasure, and absorbs time that could have been spent on social activities.

In this framework, a main factor for this development is the decline in public places or the so-called third places. As opposed to home as the "first place" and the workplace as the "second place," this normative term designates semi-public, informal meeting places that foster social interaction, and that thus serve an important social function aside from the actual purpose of their existence (Oldenburg, 1991, p. 16). In a way, they resemble medieval market places or Habermas' prominent example of coffeehouses and salons as the origins of democratic processes—in Oldenburg's words (1991, p. ix), "'homes away from home' where unrelated people relate."[1] Oldenburg (1991) ascribes the decline in public places in the USA to misguided, often auto-centered urban planning that allegedly disrupts public spirit and sociability (see also Whyte, 1988). Current studies show that nowadays an increasing number of public places are, or have become, private or commercial venues such as theme parks, sports facilities, shopping malls, etc., where an open socio-political debate could only be carried out under difficult conditions. Interestingly, Oldenburg (1991, p. 31) does not regard video arcades, which were very popular in the 1980s, as third places, because "not all games stimulate conversation and kibitzing; hence, not all games complement third place association. A room full of individuals intent upon video games is not a third place."[2]

However, new media calls for rethinking this perception of social capital and public space. Wellman, QuanHaase, Witte, and Hampton (2001) point out that even before the Internet age, community was no longer locally confined. The analytic consideration of new mediatized forms of community shows that new media do not provoke declining commitment or cause reduced time spent in community, but rather substantiate the transformation and integration of social capital and public space into digital networks. Depending on each specific context, we can expect both positive and negative contributions to social capital from the increasing social networking activities within digital media. Referring to this argument, Steinkuehler and Williams (2006) use the example of MMORPGs to show that digital games can provide access to new forms of socio-politically relevant spaces of interaction and participation. Based on a descriptive analysis of the specific communication structures and contexts of online games, the authors demonstrate that MMORPGs can satisfy Oldenburg's (1991) criteria to a certain extent, for example, by constituting a hierarchy-free sphere of communication ("neutral ground"), or by featuring only minor barriers for entry ("accessibility") (see Table 9.1). Moore, Gathman, and Ducheneaut (2009) argue that online games cannot be viewed as third places in their entirety because of their many different facets. Rather, specific "social public places" in these environments should be distinguished, such as virtual clubs in *Second Life* (Linden Lab, 2003), or virtual bars in *Star Wars Galaxies* (Verant Interactive / Sony Online Entertainment, 2003).

From a theoretical point of view, Steinkuehler and Williams (2006) suppose that novel places provided by online games could enrich the social capital of their users (see also Turkle, 1996; Ducheneaut et al., 2007): "Participation in such virtual 'third places' appears particularly well-suited to the formation of bridging social capital–social relationships that, while not usually providing deep emotional support, typically function to expose the individual to a diversity of worldviews." They pick up an argument that Rheingold (1993, p. 26) exemplified by the online community *The WELL*: Due to their special characteristics such as interactivity and intimacy, the various applications of computer-mediated communication, such as chats, discussion forums, and multi-user environments, facilitate different ways of forming relationships and communities, and, therefore, contribute considerably to the accumulation of social capital. Rheingold uses the term "virtual communities" for these new forms of community, which (can) act as third places on account of them functioning as communication spheres (see also Soukup, 2006).

An empirical pilot study involving a group of hardcore (clan) gamers could prove that computer gaming is able to contribute to a gain in social capital by establishing social contacts and resources (Reinecke and Trepte,

Table 9.1 Characteristics of a Third Place (Following Oldenburg, 1991, pp. 22 ff.; Steinkuehler and Williams, 2006, pp. 5 ff.)

Characteristic	Definition
Neutral ground	Third places are neutral grounds where individuals are free to come and go as they please, with little obligation to, and few entanglements with, other participants.
Leveler	Third places are spaces in which an individual's rank and status in the workplace or society at large are of no import. Acceptance and participation are not contingent on any prerequisites, requirements, roles, duties, or proof of membership.
Conversation is main activity	In third places, conversation is a main focus of activity in which playfulness and wit are collectively valued.
Accessibility and accommodation	Third places must be easy to access and are accommodating to those who frequent them.
The regulars	Third places include a cadre of regulars who attract newcomers and give the space its characteristic mood.
A low profile	Third places are characteristically homely and without pretension.
The mood is playful	The general mood in third places is playful and marked by frivolity, verbal word play, and wit.
A home away from home	Third places are home-like in terms of rootedness, feelings of possession, spiritual regeneration, feelings of being at ease, and warmth.

2009). The analysis shows that clan gamers use the shared gaming activity to extend their network of personal contacts and frequently form deep friendships with other gamers. Clan gamers experience a significantly higher level of real-life social support than other computer gamers, and develop a (basic) trust in social relationships built up in real life as well as in virtual communities (for similar findings see Ratan, Chung, Shen, Williams, and Poole, 2010; Wimmer, Quandt, and Vogel, 2010). However, further empirical evidence is necessary to answer the remaining question as to whether these findings also apply to other gaming cultures and to the majority of casual gamers. An analysis of online gaming networks will provide a further contribution to this matter.

Online Gaming Platforms as Social Places

Behind social networks, online games belong to the most important online activities. Steam with 30, XBL with 35, and the PSN with more than 77 million registered users are the world's largest online gaming platforms and are enjoying increasing popularity (Hryb, 2011; Klaß, 2010; Seidl, 2011). These new kinds of media offerings combine the core aspects of social networks as well as of online games with three of the currently most popular gaming platforms: PC, Xbox 360, and PlayStation 3.[3] Here, gamers are provided with an opportunity to follow their gaming pleasures in a social environment, which could go beyond the single-player gaming experience.

The study analyses both the applications and the use of online gaming platforms and draws conclusions regarding their suitability as third places. Following Steinkuehler and Williams' (2006) study, the networks' content is examined analytically with a questionnaire based on Oldenburg's (1991) eight characteristics. Because of the platforms' structures, some of Oldenburg's (1991) characteristics are hard or impossible to research with content analysis. Hence, a quantitative survey was conducted among German members of the online gaming platforms (N = 2,260) to examine their perception and evaluation of the provided virtual space.

Neutral Ground

None of the three gaming platforms can be considered entirely free of hierarchies because in each case a company provides the service. The aspects of the general terms and conditions, which are relevant for this research, proved to be very similar. Although the requirements for entry vary in regard to the users' age, the accounts are not strictly monitored. Because the Internet provides more anonymity than real-life communication spaces, specific network rules define the code of conduct so that certain people can be excluded in case of abuse. The enforcing of penalties indicates the control and authority exercised by the platform provider, but equivalent forms of control can, of course, be observed in real-life third places, such as the authority of a barkeeper in a pub.

The PSN has a few technical limitations, of which cross-game incompatibility stands out. The gamers have to use the same program or revert to the main PSN interface (also called XrossMediaBar). Steam and XBL are considerably more flexible in this aspect, although Microsoft requires a paid premium membership for this (and, of course, for other offerings). Each network has its limitations, yet they all have in common that users can subscribe and unsubscribe at will at any given time.

The lack of anonymity and the identification of shared interests between gamers boost personal and/or game-related commitment. This commitment can lead to friendships, but also brings further responsibilities and obligations (see Table 9.2). Consequently, 59.4% of the gamers are interested in knowing which of their gaming acquaintances are online and 33.1% consider regular contact with their friends in the network as rather/very important. However, only about a quarter of the respondents feel rather or very committed to the other players. These findings lead us to draw the conclusion that the majority of the relationships within the network are only casual contacts with only weak social bonds; nevertheless, the number of regular contacts with stronger social bonds should not be underestimated. Furthermore, the different ways of getting to know network friends have been collected on the basis of a five-step scale (5 = "a lot"; 1 = "none"). Thereby, two primary types of contact creation become apparent, of which one refers to the virtual space (multiplayer games in the network: 5 = "a lot": 40.9%; M = 3.64; SD = 1.45) and one to real life (school/university/job: 5 = "a lot": 33.4%; M = 3.50; SD = 1.42).

Leveler

Steam and XBL deliberately give users the option to specify their real-life profession and/or personal interests. For example, XBL lets its users state their name, motto, location, and a mini biography. Additionally, it is possible to design an avatar that can be used as a profile picture. The PSN only offers the choice of a username in combination with a selection of preset profile pictures. Steam allows users to upload an image of their choice, including photographs, provided that the terms of service are not violated.

Depending on the specific game, different conclusions on the users' personality can be drawn from game achievements.[4] Each online gaming platform provides similar, but in some aspects, exclusive features that let their users establish a specific status within the network. The wide range of functions and statistics in Steam makes it comparably difficult to get a clear picture of other users on this platform. However, conclusions on a user's real life can easily be drawn from the user status in the network, even though no information is actively divulged. For example, information such as the time of unlocking achievements can be used to determine the user's hours of work and his vacation days.

Table 9.2 Commitment of Platform Gamers

Neutral ground	Strongly disagree (1)	(2)	(3)	(4)	Strongly agree (5)	M	SD	n
I consider it important to get regularly in touch with my network friends.	22.0	19.7	25.2	19.8	13.3	2.83	1.33	1603
I have the feeling I might be missing something when I am not signed on to the network.	53.9	16.6	13.7	8.6	7.2	1.99	1.29	1646
I often check which of my friends are online.	10.0	12.3	18.3	24.6	34.8	3.62	1.33	1608
I feel committed towards other players.	27.1	18.6	26.5	20.6	7.3	2.62	1.28	1628

Almost 41% of the respondents are rather/very interested in the other gamers' real lives (see Table 9.3). A remarkable number of respondents would appreciate a connection to the first and second place. Almost two-thirds of the XBL and PSN gamers—in contrast to merely a third of the Steam gamers—hold an interest in the other players' trophies and gaming success. However, only a few of the respondents—only 8% of the Steam players—declare that they base their judgment of other players on these indicators of success. Apparently, these indicators of gaming success are not suitable for defining a user's network status within the network.

Conversation Is the Main Activity

A surprising 25.9% of the users rather, or even strongly agree with the statement that they spend most of their time in the network chatting with their friends (M = 2.59, SD = 1.31, n = 1606). Considering that these networks are primarily intended for gaming, interpersonal communication ranks significantly higher than expected. XBL surely has the most versatile offering of communication tools: voice chats of different kinds (individual or in groups), video chat, messages (text, tone, and image), and a connection to Windows Live Messenger (text chat), Facebook, and Twitter. However, all communication channels except one-on-one voice chat and text messaging require paid premium membership. Basic features can also be found in the PSN, but are technologically limited by the software. Cross-game chats and other communication activities are lacking. Steam offers a comparably small, but diversified range of communication tools.

Taking into account the fact that the networks were primarily created to play games, conversation takes on a more important role than expected. The differences could be evoked due to different basic requirements in the hard- and software. On the one hand, the Xbox 360—in contrast to the

Table 9.3 Appreciation of Status Within the Networks

Leveler	Strongly disagree (1)	(2)	(3)	(4)	Strongly agree (5)	M	SD	n
I am interested in what other players do in real life.	20.9	14.8	23.4	25.8	15.1	2.99	1.36	1641
I base my judgment of other players on their trophies.	47.3	17.1	17.7	11.5	6.5	2.13	1.30	1642
I am interested to know which trophies the other players have already achieved.	11.3	10.6	16.8	30.3	31.0	3.59	1.32	1650

PS3—has got a headset, and yet on the other hand, the communication via Steam or also via other programs on the computer is essentially easier and faster because of the keyboard. In the PSN, text messages are used almost equally as often as single-player and multiplayer games. In the case of Steam, the game activities distinctly predominate over functions such as the voice chat, profile comments, and text chat.

Accessibility and Accommodation

According to Oldenburg (1991), third places should be easily accessible at almost any given time. Online gaming networks are accessed through the World Wide Web and are thus generally more accessible than traditional third places. However, the PSN and XBL require additional hardware in order to unfold all their functions to their full potential. Steam can be accessed with most computers and thus holds a definite advantage, although the costs of hardware vary considerably. Another disadvantage of XBL in contrast to its competitors is that a paid premium membership is required to experience the full benefits of its offerings.

The Regulars

Third places command regular customers, who attract new customers and provide the characteristic mood for the place. In the case of the gaming networks, this concerns users, who are often online and signed into a network, plus those who have already been part of a network for a longer time.

Games are the main application used to meet new friends or long-term users. The list of previous game partners facilitates the initiation of contact and promotes socializing in all the networks. The acquaintance of hardcore gamers thus depends on contacts through the personal lists of friends, and, ultimately, on the particular usage behavior. The majority of the respondents mainly play together with gamers from their friend list (see Table 9.4). This confirms the assumption that contact with other users is primarily established and maintained via the friends' lists and underlying real-life networks. Only 9.7% of the responding PSN users access the PlayStation Home (PSH)[5] application several times per month or more frequently. Apparently, this program is of little importance to the users. Even though it was deliberately designed as a third place (slogan: "there is no place like home"),[6] the PSH is not a convincing argument for the PSN in general.

A Low Profile

The platforms—especially Steam—provide a wide range of functions. However, their simple design and limited possibilities for individualization reduce their complexity and make them attractive for casual gamers. Only a very small portion of the respondents had difficulty in finding their way

Table 9.4 Appreciation of Regular Gamers Within the Network

The regulars	Strongly disagree (1)	(2)	(3)	(4)	Strongly agree (5)	M	SD	n
I mainly play with gamers from my friend list.	10.0	12.0	19.1	24.3	34.6	3.62	1.33	1604
I center my attention on regular gamers.	22.7	14.8	24.5	25.6	12.3	2.90	1.34	1647

around in the network (see Table 9.5), the highest percentage being 7.1% of the Steam users, and just under half that percentage among the game-console users (XL: 3.5%; PSN: 2.8%). The greater complexity of Steam could originate from the basic differences between PC and game-console players.

The Mood Is Playful

Opening PlayStation 3 up to the Internet has established a fast-growing channel for additional information that can be obtained through the internal web browser. In comparison, Steam and XBL can be characterized as "closed" entertainment systems. However, individual options for config-uration and customization, such as the user profiles or comments, make genuine information available to the network. The mood is influenced partly by the operator's range of products and services, but also by the users inter-acting within the network. Altogether, only a small portion of the respond-ents consider the communication atmosphere in the networks as too serious or egoistic (see Table 9.6), which speaks in favor of the networks' suitability

Table 9.5 Profiles of the Online Gaming Platforms

A low profile	Strongly disagree (1)	(2)	(3)	(4)	Strongly agree (5)	M	SD	n
I can easily navigate through my online gaming network.	1.5	1.9	8.3	30.7	57.6	4.41	.84	1649
The platform's design appeals to me.	5.0	9.0	27.1	33.9	25.0	3.65	1.01	1639
I feel comfortable in my online gaming network.	2.3	4.3	21.4	39.0	33.1	3.96	.96	1620

as third places. The mood within the networks is also indicated by the topics of conversation and the frequency of their appearance in discussions. According to the respondents, specific and serious topics, such as politics, economics, or personal issues, are frequently discussed in all three networks.

A Home Away From Home

The customization of a platform's front end is a proper instrument to make users feel at home and welcome. However, the providers limit these options mainly to design aspects such as the choice of specific colors and the look of game avatars. Nevertheless, this at least represents a partially improved personalization as compared to real-life third places such as pubs or coffeehouses, which usually cannot be individually customized.

How much users look after each other depends strongly on their relationship. Hence, a group of virtual friends could be more attentive to each other than a group of regular pub goers. Accordingly, 72.1% of all respondents feel rather or very comfortable in their network (M = 3.96, SD = .96, n = 1620). This finding speaks in favor of the configuration, the design, and the atmosphere, and thus provides an additional argument for considering gaming networks as third places. However, the findings regarding the social relationships and commitment (see *Neutral Ground* above) do not comply with criteria that Oldenburg (1991) considers necessary for real-life third places.

Table 9.6 Evaluation of the Communication Atmosphere Within the Networks (Percentage of Users, n = 1749)

	(1)	(2)	(3)	(4)	(5)		M	SD
jovial	16.2	38.9	35.6	7.5	1.8	serious	2.40	0.91
aggressive	4.4	16.6	36.4	29.3	13.4	calm	3.31	1.04
offending	1.7	9.3	39.9	36.8	12.3	harmonious	3.49	0.89
tense	1.2	6.2	26.6	41.2	24.8	laid-back	3.82	0.92
playful	5.8	22.4	46.4	20.0	5.3	focused	2.97	0.94
cooperative	14.2	35.3	34.2	12.3	3.9	egoistic	2.57	1.01
closed	1.4	7.7	36.1	40.3	14.5	open	3.59	0.88
reserved	3.7	16.5	59.5	17.0	3.3	emotional	3.00	0.78
communicative	15.5	33.4	38.8	10.5	1.8	silent	2.50	0.94
cheery	20.9	47.3	28.2	3.0	0.6	grumpy	2.15	0.80
reclusive	1.1	5.8	32.9	42.5	17.7	sociable	3.70	0.87
profound	2.5	12.2	47.2	25.9	12.2	superficial	3.33	0.93
personal	5.4	19.8	41.7	25.1	8.0	anonymous	3.1046	0.99

Conclusion and Further Developments

The criteria established by Oldenburg (1991) to distinguish third places are used in this study to assess the suitability of online gaming platforms as social meeting points. The results of the study show that several characteristics of real-world third places can also be found in the virtual space of these gaming networks. However, this only applies fully to the criterion of a "low profile." Especially the appreciation of the communication atmosphere reveals room for improvement in several aspects. Steinkuehler and Williams' (2006) study provides points of reference on how gaming environments afford the potential to develop social relationships and how distinctive these relationships are. In real life, people maintain many weak relationships (bridging effects) and few strong relationships (bonding effects). This observation also shows up in the results of this research. The respondents establish social capital and, thereby, weak and strong relationships to other gamers in their gaming network. The number of friends and the used functions highlight that social interaction, right after gaming, is becoming highly significant as a preoccupation. Furthermore, the analysis of the conversational behavior makes clear that game-related topics have a distinct priority, yet private issues are not generally avoided. Due to the entertainment and profit orientation of the providers, online gaming platforms and their gamer networks can only be compared with real third places to a limited extent. Yet, they do support social interaction among their users and thereby provide a form of public value for the gaming community. For instance, 28.2% of all respondents rather, or strongly agree with the statement that they have already gotten to know other users in the network, who then helped them in real life (n = 1606).

The analysis concludes that XBL provides the best overall concept in combination with a paid premium membership. Steam, the platform operated by Valve, stands out with a number of unique functions. The PSN is quite similar to XBL in some aspects, but some of its functions are too strongly limited or inflexible, which is why the network failed to meet the requirements in the same way as its competitors did. However, the current developments of the gaming platforms signalize an increasing potential for becoming third places. Future studies should not only cover the main platforms, but also include the networks' Internet offers, and also current and future mobile devices in their research.

Notes

1   The strong normative character of this approach becomes evident when Oldenburg speaks of "great good places."
2   This diagnosis distinctly reveals the normative perspective of Oldenburg, because Huhh's (2008) analysis of South Korean video arcades—the so-called *PC Bang*—shows that video arcades can certainly provide media-cultural and social value in other contexts.
3   Wii is excluded from the analysis because of its very limited online services (Wii online) that currently cannot be considered as a genuine network.

4   The platform operators try to distinguish themselves from their competitors by adopting unique terms. Steam calls it "Steam achievement," XBL, "achievement," and the PSN, "trophy," but they all serve the same purpose. Depending on the game, they have different meanings and unlocking an achievement can indicate, for example, the difficulty, game progress, and the gaming style.

5   The PSH offers an environment that is highly evocative of the virtual world *Second Life* and fulfills similar purposes. Users are able to create their own avatar and to meet with others at different places. Among the users who are located in the public places, steady customers can also be perceived. However, since it concerns an additional program, and avatars are not directly connected to the online-ID of the PSN, PSH is not closely examined in this research.

6   Source: http://uk.playstation.com/pshome/.

References

Ducheneaut, N., Moore, R. J., and Nickell, E. (2007). Virtual third places: A case study of sociability in massively multiplayer games. *Computer Supported Cooperative Work, 16*(1–2), 129–166.

Hand, M., and Moore, K. (2006). Community, identity and digital games. In J. Bryce and J. Rutter (Eds.), *Understanding digital games* (pp. 241–266). London, United Kingdom: Sage.

Hryb, L. (2011). *A few stats before we head into E3.* Retrieved from http://major-nelson.com/2011/06/03/a-few-stats-before-we-head-into-e3/.

Huhh, J.-S. (2008). Culture and business of PC bangs in Korea. *Games and Culture, 3*, 26–37.

Juul, J. (2005). *Half-real: Video games between real rules and fictional worlds.* Cambridge, United Kingdom: MIT Press.

Klaß, C. (2010). *30 Millionen: Steam stellt einen neuen Mitgliederrekord auf.* Retrieved from http://www.golem.de/1010/78725.html.

Manninen, T. (2003). Interaction forms and communicative actions in multiplayer games. *Game Studies, 3*(1). Retrieved from http://www.gamestudies.org/0301/manninen/.

Moore, R. J., Gathman, E. C. H., and Ducheneaut, N. (2009). From 3D space to third place: The social life of small virtual spaces. *Human Organization, 68*, 230–240.

Oldenburg, R. (1991). *The great good place.* New York City, NY: Marlowe & Company.

Putnam, R. D. (2000). *Bowling alone: The collapse and revival of American community.* New York City, NY: Simon & Schuster.

Ratan, R. A., Chung, J. E., Shen, C., Williams, D., and Poole, M. S. (2010). Schmoozing and smiting: Trust, social institutions, and communication patterns in an MMOG. *Journal of Computer-Mediated Communication, 16*, 93–114.

Reinecke, L., and Trepte, S. (2009). *The social side of gaming: eSports und der Aufbau von Sozialkapital.* Unpublished research paper. Retrieved from http://www.hamburgmediaschool.com/download/medienmanagement/forschungsprojekte/ErgebniszusammenfassungESLStudie.pdf.

Rheingold, H. (1993). *The virtual community: Homesteading on the electronic frontier.* New York City, NY: Harper Collins.

Seidl, M. (2011). *PSN: Welches Land hat die meisten Accounts?* Retrieved from http://www.play3.de/2011/05/02/psn-welches-land-hat-die-meisten-accounts/.

Soukup, C. (2006). Computer-mediated communication as a virtual third place: Building Oldenburg's great good places on the World Wide Web. *New Media & Society, 8,* 421–440.

Steinkuehler, C. A., and Williams, D. (2006). Where everybody knows your (screen) name: Online games as 'third places.' *Journal of Computer-Mediated Communication, 11*(4), 885–909. Retrieved from http://jcmc.indiana.edu/vol11/issue4/steinkuehler.html.

Turkle, S. (1996). Virtuality and its discontents. Searching for community in cyberspace. *The American Prospect, 7*(24), 50–57.

Wellman, B., QuanHaase, A., Witte, J., and Hampton, K. (2001). Does the Internet increase, decrease, or supplement social capital? Social networks, participation, and community commitment. *American Behavioral Scientist, 45*(3), 437–456.

Whyte, W. H. (1988). *City: Rediscovering the center.* New York City, NY: Doubleday.

Wimmer, J., Quandt, T., and Vogel, K. (2010). The edge of virtual communities? An explorative analysis of clans and computer games. In K. Mitgutsch, C. Klimmt, and H. Rosenstingl (Eds.), *Exploring the edges of gaming: Proceedings of the Vienna Games Conference 2008–2009* (pp. 77–90). Vienna, Austria: Braumüller.

Games Cited

Linden Lab (2003). *Second Life.* San Francisco, CA: Linden Lab.

Verant Interactive / Sony Online Entertainment (2003). *Star Wars Galaxies.* San Francisco, CA: Lucas Arts.

10 It's a Quest(ion) of Timing[1]

Torill Elvira Mortensen

With its 2010 major installment of the multiplayer game *World of Warcraft* (*WoW*): *Cataclysm*, (Blizzard Entertainment, 2010) Blizzard builds further on the technology of *phasing*. This is a technology used to give the players a sense of progression and of playing in an environment where their progress makes an impact on the game environment. At the same time, it alters the perception of time and chronology for players when they try to create a consistent story from their gaming, as significant events may have taken place for one person in a group, but not for others. In group play, it causes interaction problems, as people need to be in the same *phase* in order to interact and cooperate, giving the rather confusing appearance of multiple "times" at the same time.

When playing a role-playing game (RPG), time adjusts to the technology and the players. In a live-action game, the time is fairly consistent with how long an act takes, whether it is walking a mile or (miming) chopping off a head. Tabletop games tend to treat time much more flexibly, as the game-masters and players of campaigns can, for instance, use narrative to compress travel time or extend the time it takes to describe actions. In digital multiplayer RPGs, the complaint used to be that the players made no impact on the unchanging game world: time was, basically, frozen. As Anders Drachen and Michael Hitchens[2] present their case:

> Some MMORPGs [massively multiplayer online role-playing games] permit players to cause permanent changes to the game world of minor game impact (Tychsen and Hitchens, 2006), for example, in the form of constructing structures (e.g., *A Tale in the Desert*) or the creation of in-game items. But for the most part, the players' progress and story occurs within a frozen moment (or very short recurring period) of the world time.
>
> Drachen and Hitchens, 2009, p. 194

The phasing technology solves the problem of the static, unchanging world in *WoW*. At the same time, it offers new challenges to playing roles in games, as it means players at different levels and at different points in quest lines cannot relate to the same events without making compromises with some of the tenets of role play brought over from other environments. In general, phasing creates problems related to co-play and makes social play increasingly difficult. This article is an exploration of what phasing does to the continuity of the environment players refer to—its challenges and rewards, from the perspective of both a game scholar and a player on a role-play server.

Lost in Time

In the multiplayer game *WoW* (Blizzard Entertainment, 2004), the main attraction is that you can play together with several other players. On the server where I spend most of my *WoW*-gaming time, there are approximately 22,000 characters. In 2010, the guild I played in had close to 200 characters. Still, when we played in *Wrath of the Lich King* (the *WoW* expansion released in 2008) and needed to find companions to play with in the game area Icecrown, we were only able to see a few of them. The game would tell us we were at the same location, and we could even sit next to each other and look at the other person's screen and see that we were at the correct virtual location—but we would not meet in the game.

These problems with connecting were caused by a choice the designers of *WoW* made when they introduced "phasing." J. Allen Brack, *WoW* producer, describes phasing in an interview in *Eurogamer* (Wesh, 2008): "What we do is we have different world states, and depending on what quests you've completed, it changes what world state you're seeing." For the gamers, this meant they could be at the exact same spot without meeting, because they were in different world states. In a way, they were there at different "times."

Game Time

José P. Zagal and Michael Mateas wrote an article in 2010, looking at studies of in-game time, in order to see if "time" would be a relevant concept to use in computer games at all (Zagal and Mateas, 2010). They cite, among others, Drachen and Hitchens (2009), which will be discussed further in this article, but not Lindley (2005), which is also discussed here. Their main point (Zagal and Mateas, 2010) is that different authors have different approaches and different conclusions as to how game time functions, leaving this a ripe field for academic discussion. None of the articles they cite discusses phasing, but as we will see from the discussion on Drachen and Hitchens (2009), phasing changes the progression of in-game time.

In most mediated situations, we are dealing with more than one "time" at the same time. Even as unmediated events unfold, we may be dealing with two or three simultaneous "times": We can see something happen and predict what it will lead to, or we can see it happen and suddenly understand how it came to be. Both the past and the future can, in this manner, be present in the same instance of *now*. Knowing that even in so-called real time, the experience of time can be fluid; it is no surprise that games play with time. Lindley (2005) has written about the semiotics of time in *Gamestudies.org*:

> For any particular ludic system, such as a computer game, time structure can be considered in terms of a number of distinct layers of meaning analogous to the levels of encoding identified in structuralist narrative theory: a generation level, a simulation level, a performance level and a discourse level.

Lindley discusses time in ludic systems, or games, on four levels. In this discussion, the player experiences the *discourse* level, while the game events are revealed to the player in the *performance* level. The progression of events as they are being made available to the players is addressed as the *simulation* level, and the *generation* level is in the universe of the code: "the system of functions, rules and constraints constituting a space of possible worlds of experience created by the designers of the game" (Lindley, 2005).

Now for some gaming examples. In one of the first clearly phased quests mentioned above, my response was first a lack of understanding, frustration that I could not help, or be helped by others in this multiplayer environment, as assisting friends is one of the most important tools for progress in *WoW*, and then relief when I saw that the quest line was manageable alone. I was astounded by the way in which the quest revealed a plot in the game story and this gave me background for further interaction with the narrative of the game. This personal experience was the *discourse* level. On the *performance* level, I took part in a battle in Icecrown, where the non-player characters (NPCs)—who were most important in the story and in several previous quests—played out a tragedy where my game character fought with them in a battle, went to speak to the Horde Warchief in Undercity, and then fought another battle together with these NPCs, to finally return and find that the areas were then very different from when I started the quest.

On the *simulation* level, the game had made certain that I got the events in the correct order by chaining the quest, but also by playing the videos, and through checking my character files to check on my quest progress. This process of checking and unveiling was controlled by the code or the *generation* level: the invisible level where the pixels and sounds are put together, making the three levels that are mentioned above possible.

Lindley (2005) goes on to try to build a description of the different states of time in a game, and summarizes his discussion in a model where game, narrative, and simulation are points in a triangle. Within this, he positions different games and media experiences. In this triangle, RPGs are positioned in the center between the three points.

The RPGs are positioned somewhere between strategy games and action games. At the extreme end of the simulation point, we find the so-called avatar worlds. *WoW* is perhaps a little closer to this: It is an avatar world, it has a degree of role play in it, and it contains and opens up for the creation of narratives. It even contains several small movies, or cut-scenes, which are closer to the multipath narratives in the narrative point of the triangle. We also find adventure game-type challenges from the NPCs in the game, mainly in player-versus-environment (PvE) multiplayer adventures. It has strong action and strategy aspects, and contains references to other game types, integrating these within the game. It has some areas and modes of play that make it a first-person fighter, with strong player-versus-player (PvP) interaction, while it also allows for avatar development and pure socializing.

This means that the ludic time of *WoW* is literally all over the place: The game embraces all the different positions of Lindley's (2005) model. The game even has little games within the game, such as the quest in Ogri'la in Outland, where the players have to solve a riddle that is basically the memory game *Simon* (MB Games, 1978) designed by Ralph H. Baer and Howard J. Morrison, launched in 1978 at Studio 54. This is a simple game of the same game family as *Tetris*, which shows that *WoW* also embraces the upper-left end of Lindley's triangle. While Lindley gives us some concepts and alternative viewpoints on time, the model cannot be used for *WoW* as a whole. It is only useful when limited to single game events, quests, or special game modes or areas, such as battlefields or instances.

Logical and Chronological Time

We see a similar collapse of carefully constructed models happen when we apply Drachen and Hitchens' (2009, p. 175) model of layers of game time to *WoW*. They use their model to discuss different digital games, and also to expand their argument to pen and paper (PnP) or tabletop games and live-action role-play games (LARPs). In their 2009 article in *Games and Culture*, Hitchens presents a model of layers of time. Drachen and Hitchens develop and discuss this model based on experiments with players, observation, and participation in different types of games, both online and offline. The layers are *play* time, *engine* time, *game progress* time, and *game world* time.

Not all of their time layers are equally relevant to this example, such as, for instance, engine time. Zagal and Mateas (Zagal and Mateas, 2010, p. 862) define engine time as the execution of the game, and claim that "Engine time and playing time are typically identical, although subtle differences can be found. For example, when a player saves a game, a break occurs in playing time but engine time continues."

However, the "engine" of *WoW* is linear, as *WoW* does not so much progress, as exist in multiple states of individual progression depending on the progress of the avatar. In addition, the player cannot save and reload, at best, the player can resurrect and retry. Drachen and Hitchens' (2009) discussion about time is still a lot more relevant to understanding phasing than Lindley's (2005), since their model embraces player-created and player-perceived progression. However, I claim that the phasing technology of *Cataclysm* changes what Drachen and Hitchens call game progress time, and addresses the different layers of progress: game progress and story progress. The way phasing is used in *Cataclysm* impacts both: As the game world changes, the player's progress through the game is influenced by it, and the story changes.

Drachen and Hitchens (2009, p. 171) also distinguish between *logical* and *chronological* time in their exploration of game time both in digital and analogue games: "In nondigital games, overall game time is often logical, specifying the ordering of events, whereas in digital games, time is often used in a chronological fashion, notably as a balancing tool in multi-player and massively multiplayer games."

Logical time means in this case that time progresses one act after the other, while chronological time means that time progresses by the clock, by measurable bits. Where logical time tends to be extremely flexible and depend on the player (a good player can do what has to be done quickly), chronological time is a common control element in digital games, where the designers limit tasks by the clock by ensuring that a monster will only appear (respawn) at intervals for every player's allotted time for killing it. In *WoW*, the game time is both logical in the sense of it being ordered and organized by the events and acts of the players, and chronological, as play is controlled through time.

Game Progress

WoW is also a game hybrid in terms of how the role-play servers (RP servers) strive to break down the distinctions between PnP games, LARPs, and digital games. Since the early text-based multi-user games or multi-user dimension (MUD) games, gamers have used digital games to explore free-form role play (Mortensen, 2003). *WoW* has kept several of the properties of the MUDs (Mortensen, 2006), and from among those, some strong tools for role play.

This means that the layers of time that Drachen and Hitchens (2009) mainly claim are used in LARPs also, to a certain extent, belong to *WoW*, particularly *game progress*: in the sense of avatars changing with time. Phasing permits this, but at the same time, it disrupts free-form RP, because it controls the direction of the change for the avatars to a large extent. Phasing forces a certain history on the player rather than leaving it totally open to the players' imagination.

In digital games where a vital part of the pleasure of the game belongs to mimesis, make-believe, there are as many stories as there are players. They connect through the fictitious frame and the story potential it offers. Let us look at a quest from *WoW: Wrath of the Lich King*. The quest concerns Angrathar the Wrathgate, the first explicitly phased quest in *WoW*. Angrathar the Wrathgate is a gate into the stronghold of the arch-enemy that was introduced and fought in the expansion *Wrath of the Lich*

King. At Angrathar, the opposing factions are about to make a joint attack on the archenemy of them all. They are betrayed at the last moment, and two of their youngest commanders and heroes are killed. This throws both factions back into fighting each other. Several major game areas change permanently for the players who finish this quest line.

There were earlier examples of players being in different phases, despite being on the same level; the most powerful and visible example was quite heavy-handed in the way certain new areas, particularly new instances, were unlocked. The most spectacular example of the opening of a new area in *WoW* through the use of keys was opening the gates for the new raid instances in the desert of Silithus, when the players had to work in order to gain the status and objects that would let them open the gates on their server. Game scholar René Glas describes how this event progressed, and how gaining the key objects and the power it gave to a few players created immense tension among the players and guilds (Glas, 2010, pp. 191–195). An interesting point raised by this example is how strongly the players felt about the event and their ability to influence the progress of the server, and through that, the virtual world, and the progress of the story.

However, I claim that the original, most experienced phasing-type technique in *WoW* is a very common phase, and that everybody experienced it sooner or later: death, with its subsequent release of the spirit from the body and the infamous corpse run, when the player steers the spirit of the avatar back to the body.

How to Ignore Your Death

One fiercely debated topic in digital RPGs is permanent death. Permanent death (PD) is quite common in arcade-type games, where you have a number of chances in which to finish the game, after which you return to the very beginning and start over. In RPGs, PD is still debated, mainly in discussions about risk and structure. Two scholars and designers who have argued for PD are Gonzalo Frasca and Richard Bartle.

One of Gonzalo Frasca's early papers on games was "Don't Play It Again, Sam: One-Session and Serial Games of Narration" (Frasca, 1998). This paper discussed the higher stakes in a game that could be played only once. There are such games available, mainly independent (indie) games, such as the tongue-in-cheek flash game *You Only Live Once* by Marcus Richert (Richert, 2009). From the comments on the Kongregate website where the game can be found (Kongregate, 2009–2011), one player noted: "I played this game on Newgrounds a few years back. When I saw it here on Kongregate, I figured I could cheat and play again. I was wrong. This guy was serious about living only once." While several of the players were impressed with this kind of dedication and also shared information that might offer a second chance, some were angry, and raged against the game structure with exactly the same arguments as in the 1998 discussion with Frasca: The stakes are too high, with no room for error.

Game designer and scholar Richard Bartle is not as drastic in his call for PD. He offers several different versions of what he consistently calls PD, and suggests how they can be implemented in the game (Bartle, 2004, pp. 416–420). He still argues for it: "Virtual worlds are about identity: if you can't lose something, you don't value it; therefore, you can never value your identity in a non-PD world as much as you can in a PD world" (Bartle, 2004, p. 433).

Despite this, PD is rare. The stakes are too high, it enrages the less-than-hardcore gamers, and a PD game would be very hard to sell. In addition, the examples from both Frasca and Bartle include games where the players lose from a few hours or minutes of effort up to a few months. In a game such as *WoW*, the player might lose years of investment. Hence, *WoW* is played as a succession of deaths; in the lower levels, it is mainly fight–die–run to corpse–resurrect–fight–die.

There is a certain absurdity to the situation: You fight and lose, and are dead. Then you are offered the chance to release your spirit, so you can, in spirit form, run back to the corpse, resurrect, and then heal up and go back into the fight.

The corpse-run phase is designed to introduce some kind of mild consequence to *WoW*. It is very annoying "down time"; you cannot do anything, not even rearrange your armor, exchange weapons, or trade objects with other players, all typical down-time activities. All you can do is run up to your virtual corpse, find a safe spot, and then hit the "resurrect now" button. During the corpse run, everything is blue and misty, and you cannot see any NPCs or monsters until you are very close to where you fell. You can see the spirits of other players, as during that time you are in the same phase as the other dead player characters. When you approach your body, you can see misty images of your enemies, a feature that may lead you to pick a safer place to resurrect. This is a very sophisticated aspect of this particular version of phasing: You are not entirely in another world. You can see just enough to take some evasive measures, but not enough so that you can interact or do much exploration on your own.

Being the most common example of phasing in the game, it has, of course, been exploited in many ways, and changed in response. The early exploits were graveyard runs and corpse hopping, which allowed players to explore areas they could otherwise not enter. Most of the time death has no benefits. However, where it is really annoying is in role play. Most serious RP groups in *WoW* have reinterpreted in-game death as defeat or severe damage, where the character is helpless and unconscious.

Subverting the Story Versus Being an Official Hero

On December 15, 2005, a group of players on the European RP server Argent Dawn defeated the enemy faction leader Fandral Staghelm. They were the first group on that server to succeed with such plans, and knew it would take both a large effort, secrecy, and the help of 35 friends to do it.

The raid was well executed, nobody died, and everybody was there for the victory screenshot in front of the gates to Orgrimmar. However, Staghelm soon respawned, walking around as if nothing had happened, and so the guild had to rewrite the *WoW* story line to legitimize their kill, claiming the respawned Staghelm was a Horde agent (Mortensen, 2006, p. 407). This was a good fix for the first kill of an enemy faction leader, but as the practice became increasingly popular as a way to show off the organization and PvP skills of guilds and groups, it became absurd. How many spies in the Alliance or Horde camp were really needed? In addition, who was controlling the current spy?

In the previously discussed quest line of the battle at Angrathar the Wrathgate, at one point the avatar participates in a battle in Undercity and kills not the leader of the Forsaken, but her second in command, Varimathras (Blizzard Entertainment, 2008). This quest line is different depending on the perspective of the participants, Horde or Alliance.

While Varimathras is not a faction leader, he was a prominent figure who had by then been killed uncountable times during Alliance raids on the Undercity aiming to kill Sylvanas. What makes the Battle of the Undercity instance of his death so different from all the others is that in this case, he stays dead! During the early period of the *WoW* expansion *Wrath of the Lich King*, if a character, who was still in the early phase, arrived in Undercity, there was nothing special to direct attention toward the quest. After having finished the quest, the game world was permanently changed.

Permanent Change and Differentiated Stories

With *Cataclysm,* permanent change became the norm rather than the exception. The starter areas changed, and each area told new stories, leading new characters through a more story-driven rather than level-driven introduction. This served several goals: shorter leveling time, more protected leveling on PvP servers, and more uniform equipment after leveling.

The two new races in *WoW*, the worgen and goblins, were fully designed for *Cataclysm*. To use the worgen as an example, the new player quests start out in a new area, and depend heavily on phasing. In order to gain the abilities and skills, they need to be fully aware of what the races offer; the new avatars need to follow the story line. Where it used to be possible to run over to other areas to "level" together with a friend, having to go through the unfolding story restricts the activities of the new player.

At the same time, phasing offers interesting and surprising events, and leads new players very clearly through the initial steps of creating a character and learning to play. Each new skill needs to be used in order to solve the next quests, and each finished quest line unlocks a new area where new skills are needed. In the case of learning areas, phasing created new views and new stories, and led to a craze of "alts"—alternative characters, as opposed to the main character, into which players put the most effort, and that they are known as within the game.

For the largest group of *WoW* players, the most obvious change of the phasing technology in *Cataclysm* was not in the starting areas, but in the changes in the old, and the introduction of the new areas. The new area of Hyjal opened up in the middle of Kalimdor, the western continent on the *WoW* map. It is connected to a volcano, and fire elementals were burning the once green area down to ashes. The quest lines in Hyjal lead the players into a process of changing Hyjal back to being green.

This became a very powerful and touching experience, as the players were not used to being able to actually do any good. *WoW* has a dystopic story line, and whenever one evil has been defeated, another rises. In this world of constant defeat, to see that the world can be made green and beautiful again made an impression. When I asked players in-game about examples of phasing that they remembered and that had impressed them, the answer was always this: How Hyjal flowered after they had finished the story line.

Playing in Different Times

For players, the elaborate change in how to experience the game led to problems with playing together. Players were not just affected by having made different impacts on the world; they were also affected by being in different "times." While the different aspects of time up until this point had made very little impact on the play, now it suddenly created a difference on what Lindley (2005) calls the *generation level*.

The many other layers of time constructed by the players, either as parts of their role play or as the different guilds' mutual progression, were disrupted and put aside by the code, proving in this limited instance, at least, Lessig's claim that code is law (2006).

By introducing phasing, Blizzard Entertainment brought single-user modes into a multi-user game. One of the aspects of virtual worlds is that they make us experience a sense of being independent of space and time, able to meet and interact with others despite being so far apart that we would otherwise never connect. Breaking up time was surprisingly frustrating to the players, surprising because everybody was still in the same game, on the same server. However, when we think about how it influenced the time flow of the game, and made players dependent on a type of time they had no influence over, the frustrations of the players make sense. Having to spend play time not connecting, meant spending "real" time not connecting, and led, in many ways, to a waste of time for those whose main goal with the game was to spend time with their friends.

Notes

1   This article is based on a presentation at the University of Hohenheim, Germany, July 2011, and a paper presented at the NorMedia Conference on Akureyri, Iceland, August 2011.

2   Anders Drachen, author of Drachen and Hitchens (2009), and Anders Tychsen, mentioned in the quotes from this article, is the same person.

References

Bartle, R. (2004). *Designing virtual worlds*. London, UK: New Riders.

Drachen, A., and Hitchens, M. (2009). Game Time: Modeling and analyzing time in multiplayer and massively multiplayer games. *Games and Culture, 1*(2), 170–201.

Frasca, G. (1998). *Don't play it again, Sam: One-session and serial games of narration*. Paper presented at the Digital Arts and Culture Conference 1998, Bergen, Norway. Retrieved from http://cmc.uib.no/dac98/papers/frasca.html.

Glas, R. (2010). *Games of stake; control, agency and ownership in World of Warcraft* (Doctoral thesis). University of Amsterdam, Amsterdam, The Netherlands.

Lessig, L. (2006). *Code: Version 2.0* (2nd ed.). New York City, NY: BasicBooks.

Lindley, C. A. (2005). The semiotics of time structure in ludic space as a foundation for analysis and design. *Gamestudies.org, 5*(1), Retrieved from http://www.gamestudies.org/0501/lindley/?pagewanted=all.

Mortensen, T. E. (2003). *Pleasures of the player: Flow and control in online games* (Doctoral thesis). Volda University College, Volda, Norway.

Mortensen, T. E. (2006). *WoW* is the new MUD: Social gaming from text to video. *Games and Culture, 1*(4), 397–413.

Wesh, O. (2008). *World of Warcraft: Wrath of the Lich King*. Retrieved from http://www.eurogamer.net/articles/world-of-warcraft-wrath-of-the-lich-king_9.

Zagal, J. P., and Mateas, M. (2010). Time in video games: A survey and analysis. *Simulation Gaming December, 41*(6), 844–868.

Games Cited

Blizzard Entertainment (2004), *World of Warcraft*, Vivendi Activision Blizzard.

Blizzard Entertainment (2008), *World of Warcraft: Wrath of the Lich King*, Blizzard Entertainment Inc.

Blizzard Entertainment (2010), *World of Warcraft: Cataclysm*, Blizzard Entertainment Inc.

Gamestop Corporation (2006), *You Only Live Once*, Retrieved from http://www.kongregate.com/games/raitendo/you-only-live-once.

MB Games (1978), *Simon*, MB Games.

Richert, M. (2009), *You Only Live Once*, http://www.marcusrichert.com/. Retrieved from http://www.kongregate.com/games/raitendo/you-only-live-once.

11 Social Interaction Design in MMOs

Nelson Zagalo and Aníbal Gonçalves

Introduction

Games are inherently of a social nature. Chess or checkers were designed to be experienced not only with the game itself, but also with others. On the other hand, video games are inherently of a solitary nature. Since the beginning, the story of games was attached to the specificity of putting the machine in the place of the opponent. A.S. Douglas' (1954) PhD thesis on human–machine interaction from the University of Cambridge was to prove that an algorithm could be built that would be able to respond in a similar manner to human-to-human play.[1] Even with *Pong*, the beauty of it was that we could be alone at home and still play the game against the machine.

The question raised is what is more rewarding to the user? We have seen from the current trends in video games that the social aspect has never vanished, and more than ever, video games use the social element as a selling point. Starting with multi-user dimension games (MUDs), then MMOs, and more recently social games, online games have brought the social into the equation again—even more so than before.

Therefore, studying MMOs means studying social aspects of games, aspects such as "human attachment" (Bowlby, 1969, p. 39), or in a broader sense, how communities are built. Mammalian babies would not survive without strong attachments to their parents, who feel, in return, the need to protect and take care of their offspring; a process of basic bonding. As most studies in positive psychology demonstrate, it took millennia of evolution for us to feel the most rewarded through doing good to others (Sheldon and Lyubomirsky, 2004). This leads us to the main question about what generates groups and communities, and why they stay together. The answers are in survival: The group is a survival factor for mammalians, and we can say that the energy to propel grouping comes from the actions of interdependence between members of a group.

Consequently, interdependence must be the main reason for action, and thus the main design concern in any social game. On the other hand, social relations created from interdependent actions are mostly purposeful and are not strong enough to create in-depth socialization. Designers need to convince players to invest in social relations, because game success is dependent not on interdependency, but on the interest of players in coming back to continue playing with others. Hence, why should people have to socialize with other players, and deal with all the human complexities and problems, only to be able to progress in a game? The answer is in MMO game design, which uses, as its core design, basic techniques of social persuasion. To define these techniques, we have used the work done by Cialdini (2001) on influence. He argues that humans use shortcuts to analyze the world around them, to help in coping with relationships, and that some of these shortcuts can be traced as patterns. These human behavioral patterns are able to evoke in each of us, non-conscious, automatic responses. These automatic responses are the fruit of millennia of evolution, created by real causes with real impacts on us, and so they have generated in our brains a strong framework for action toward others in our socializing brain.

Interdependency

> Without community, you simply have a bunch of independent players running around the same environment. Players won't be drawn in and there won't be anything there to bind them. The key to creating community, therefore, is interdependence.
>
> Braid McQuaid, *EverQuest* designer, quoted according to Aihoshi, 2000

Research has defended that social interaction is the main driving force for gamers to continue playing MMOs (Griffiths, Davies, and Chappell, 2003) or social games (Zagalo, 2012). In games such as *Chess* or *Pong*, social interaction introduces the emotions of a second person into the game and raises sentiments toward the game that are not achievable against a machine. However, we are playing against the other person, so there is no cooperation or collaboration; hence, the design only needs to take into account one person's needs at a time. On the other hand, there are multi-player games with cooperative goals, such as MMOs and social games.

Interdependence is a relationship in which each member is mutually dependent on the other; thus, we can say that it represents a vital condition for the creation of cooperative action. Players perceive game missions and goals as only reachable when helping and when being helped by others. Situations of helping/being helped are then responsible for generating the greatest moments of social interaction in-game, and this is why we need to first understand what interdependence is, why it occurs, and how it is represented in-game. Kelley and Thibaut (1978) devised theories on interdependence describing the process as a relation between reward and costs, where rewards would be gratification and pleasure, while costs would be loss and punishment. Rewards and costs can be seen as the positive and negative impacts from an interdependent relation. Kelley and Thibaut then defined four specific types of rewards and costs: emotional, social, instrumental, and opportunity. We will focus on the example of the massively multiplayer online role-playing game (MMORPG) *World of Warcraft (WoW)* (Blizzard Entertainment, 2004), since it is one of the biggest and best-known MMO games on the market. We will also focus our attention more on the most dedicated and faithful part of the community, which refers to players on the maximum level: raiders and PvPers.[2]

Starting with the "emotional" type, we get the positive and negative feelings resulting from a relationship, which affect us more the closer the relationship is. Any social game is more than just a game; it is a community, with all the human relationships and emotions that come with it—respect, dislike, jealousy, compassion, admiration, and so on. In MMO games, players normally have several circles of friendships within the game community. It is true that most of the relationships are based on functional and instrumental interests, the 25-man raiding group, the player who exchanges materials with us for a certain profession, or the person who organizes groups in trade chat on Sundays. However, as in every social space, we form emotional bonds with the ones who interact and relate more. The reward that comes from an emotional link in an MMO is not much different from a real-life relationship. The joy of helping a friend against a common threat, or just sharing everyday experiences on voice chat, thus building trust, is the main pillar of friendship. It comes with costs as well, and if losing a friend that we only casually play with can be hard, losing a close friend because he is leaving the game, for example, can be like having a "real" friend leaving the country.

In the "social" type, we have a person's social appearance and their ability to interact in social environments. Rewards come from the positive aspect of a person's social appearance and the enjoyable social situations in which he can engage. In fantasy MMOs such as *WoW*, the social appearance of a player is defined by his avatar. This includes things such as genre and race, but most importantly, the equipment, titles, and visible guild tab. Having the best equipment or the best title represents status within the game world, and high status is rewarding by nature. By looking at someone's appearance, a player can have a clear idea of someone's skill and experience with the game.

In *WoW*, there are several objectives to tackle that require cooperative play; some of them require the participation of up to 25 players at the same time, and across various game sessions. To support this, the game features a system to form organized groups known as guilds. Designers also introduced a system to support these groups, by allowing guild leaders to search for suitable recruits in-game, and for a solo player to find a guild that meets his interests. Usually, the most successful guilds have very tough criteria for accepting new members, and through the achievement system,[3] a guild leader can easily confirm a character's experience in the game. This makes working on social appearance one of the first priorities for players who wish to try out real end-game content and to apply to a better guild. A player is also expected to behave according to the group rules, especially in a guild, and especially during a trial period.[4] Being polite and willing to learn will often improve the chances of permanent membership and will also increase the opportunity to be part of guild-made groups. Even if the player is not particularly skillful in the game, being able to interact properly in this social environment can improve his status within it.

On the costs side, like in every role-playing game (RPG), equipment is essential in *WoW*. The very game system is designed to cut off players from some content if they do not have the required global item level. Additionally, even in groups formed by strangers (PUGs[5]), players often ask for the item level value of others, and tend to neglect the ones that have poor equipment.

For the "instrumental" type, rewards and costs deal with activities and tasks in a relationship. Rewards are obtained when a person's partner is skillful in conducting tasks, such as taking good care of the children, or earning enough money to pay the bills. On the other hand, costs occur when a partner causes unnecessary work, or the partner impedes the other's progress in a task. There are several reward systems in *WoW*; some require time dedication, and others depend on the individual skill with the game. Whatever the kind of reward, the best ones are only obtainable with the help of others. In a raid group, a group quest, or in a battleground, it is not only the group that needs enough numbers to succeed, but the game also features a variety of mechanics where the player needs to fulfill his task properly or there is a chance of failure for the group as a whole. This is known as synchronous gameplay, where interactions occur simultaneously in real time between various players.

The very core of the combat system in *WoW*, known as Trinity, is also the most interdependent structure in the game. Trinity is a group of player classes, where each one performs a different role—tanks, healers, and damage dealers—tanks can mitigate incoming damage from enemies, healers restore damage done to team members, and damage dealer classes do damage to enemies. Depending on the fight and how the damage is handled, being able to properly conduct his task and role will reward a player with a spot in good groups.

There is something crucial for a guild dedicated to player-versus-environment (PvE) within an MMO—the progress. It is the main factor for competition in *WoW*, both on a global scale, server level, and individual level. Progress is measured by which bosses were defeated by a guild, and by who defeated them first. This makes group leaders tend to favor the best players for a spot in a group, despite the fact that it might be another player that deserves a chance by behaving perfectly.

This way, the skill of a player in conducting tasks is more important once he reaches a certain level of the game. Costs can occur both when a player is skillful or non-skillful at a particular task. Let us take the example of a fight, where only three players of a guild are capable of conducting a certain task in that fight. There is a cost to others that are not able to do it, because they will not even be given a chance to try and do so, and there is also a cost for the three players, because they will be destined to do it over and over again, even if they do not need any of the rewards from that fight.

Finally, "opportunity" rewards are those gains that come from being together in a relationship with a partner. Costs occur when a person must give up something that they normally would not for the sake of the relationship. Being a member of a good guild allows a player to access a certain kind of content that would be inaccessible otherwise. Being a friend with a member of a good guild can also get a player to experience content that he otherwise would not be able to experience. If a guild group is short on numbers, it is typical to fill out the group with a friend of one of the members. By doing so, the group and the invited friend can defeat stronger bosses and gain the respective rewards and achievements.

Costs refer to what is expected from players within the guild. Members are requested to respect a schedule, to be available on certain days of the week, and even to contribute with materials the guild needs every week. Usually, the responsibilities correspond to the rank within the guild, which grants a member different types of permission, from talking in the chat room, to even being able to remove another member from the guild.

To conclude, interdependence results in quantifying outcomes and these are determined to be positive when the rewards outweigh the costs in a relationship, and vice versa.

Persuasion

Interdependency is really the main factor that obliges players to interact and cooperate; however, it is not sufficient to keep players engaged throughout playing. Interdependency in MMOs acts more strongly upon the instrumental level, as we have seen, but we need to dig deeper to understand what happens at the psychological level to keep gamers attached to the game. For that, we have analyzed MMO persuasion, making use of Cialdini's (2001) six influence factors: reciprocity, commitment and consistency, social proof, liking, scarcity, and authority. Before presenting our analysis, we present an element of significant importance related to the basic works of human perception, which is commonly defined as the principle of contrast (Whitney, Hubin, and Murphy, 1965). This principle states that our perception is affected when we have to see the difference between two things that are presented one after the other.

Reciprocity

We know that our survival as a species depends on our experience as a group; we compare ourselves to others, we often rely on others for a number of tasks, and in the process, we shape our bonds (Bowlby, 1969). It is only natural that the feedback (Watzlawick, Beavin, and Jackson, 1967) element of communication systems is seen as vital for us as members of a community. This way, the concept of reciprocity presented by Cialdini

(2001), which is referent to the way people tend to return favors, is justified. This is embedded into who we are in such a way that our response comes as an automated process and without doubts. Our response is, in fact, so strong that "by first doing us a favor, strange, disliked, or unwelcome others can enhance the chance that we will comply with one of their requests" (Cialdini, 2001, p. 30).

The design of reciprocity in MMOs is not as obvious as we see, for example, in social games, but it is supported by the same basic concepts. WoW has several features that require players to search for the assistance of others, the character profession being an essential design system for reciprocity. Players have a limit of two professions per character, but the game guarantees that players will need materials or pieces only available from other professions than their own.

Reciprocity is also a very strong persuasion factor when someone considers stopping playing. Players often go through so-called burnout time,[6] especially during periods of intense gaming, after the release of new content, for example. The problem here is not just the one-to-one reciprocity, but also the group's interests versus the individual's interests. Let us take, for example, a situation where the group gives an important piece of equipment to a specific player during a successful raid. This reward also comes with the responsibility of the player using that piece, and for the player to be available during future runs so that everyone can also be rewarded. This is not something that is designed within the system, and it does not even work as a guild rule in most cases; however, it is something designers take into account—the need to correspond to what the group has given to the individual.

Commitment and Consistency

Without commitment and consistency, basic elements such as trust, respect, or dignity would not be possible. It is in assuming the consistency of daily actions that a child knows that its mother will never abandon it. The child can feel safe, grow, and develop its creative thinking. This applies throughout life, from birth until death. Therefore, what is crucial is to understand how we can create the foundation for trust. The evolutionary process led this commitment even further. Knox and Inkster (1968) presented a study in which it was verified that subjects who were betting on horse races were much more confident in a particular horse immediately following the placing of the bet: "Once we make a choice or take a stand, we will encounter personal and interpersonal pressures to behave consistently with that commitment" (Cialdini, 2001, p. 53).

WoW is one of the last-standing, large MMOs supported by a monthly subscription fee. In a time where free-to-play is in vogue, and where the financial models of MMOs are turning to micro-transactions, there are still millions of people that keep playing and paying for WoW. Our intention is not to argue that consumers value a product that they pay for more highly, but there is an internal pressure to justify the subscription value with game time. This commitment is also mutual: MMOs need to be updated regularly with new content, and the design promotes a series of mechanics that incentivize players to log in every day to fulfill a certain number of tasks, so there is always something new to see and do for the players.

Social Proof

The logic of social proof is something that comes from within, something that works in the perceptual and cognitive fields. A contagion affects us when we are made to feel or do something to resemble another person. One of the areas where this contagion is most effective is the emotional field.

> A practical case of this process is the known laughter clubs, in vogue in India. Another case (...) [is] the sound effects of laughter in movies and comic series in the 40s–60s, still present in contemporary comic series like *Seinfeld* (1990–1998) and *Friends* (1994–2004).
>
> Zagalo, 2009, p. 39

Also in the 1950s, Asch (1951) held the so-called experiments of compliance. He showed that even when we know the correct answer, if the group in which we operate gives the wrong answer, we tend to follow the wrong answer in order to belong to the group. Compliance with the group functions as something that infects and takes over the decision-making capacity of the subject. Thus, the concept of social proof turns out to be linked intrinsically to the functioning of the logic for the previous two factors: reciprocity and consistency. Consequently, social proof becomes the basic metric we use to gauge our behavior in social situations.

WoW uses its own platform for the continuous production of messages and to record players' actions. A global system based on achievements clearly stratifies players by considering what they have and have not done within the game. When a player moves up a level, there is an animation; when he completes a particular goal, he gets an achievement notice; and if his team is the first on a server to defeat the main threat of the expansion, the guild gets a server-wide achievement notification that all players see in real time. This model is not new, even without the existence of online and real-time systems; the basis of any "collective game" always had this logic with leaderboards, championships, cups, and prizes. The collective nature of MMORPGs motivates players to keep up with the progress of their peers and also incentivizes new players to reach the skill level of the most experienced members.

Liking

> Few of us would be surprised to learn that, as a rule, we most prefer to say yes to the requests of people we know and like.
>
> Cialdini, 2001, p. 144

In a simpler form, attraction is the main ingredient that enhances the social-proof factor discussed above. If people tend to follow the group, they have an even greater tendency to follow someone they like or admire within that group.

This liking factor plays a crucial role in keeping players in the game. MMOs are designed to consume almost all the free time of their players. This makes playing two of these games at the same time close to impossible, so unless groups migrate *en masse* for a different MMO, it is very unlikely that they will just leave their micro-communities behind and move on to something different on their own.

Beyond all that, *WoW* features two specific services designed around the liking factor: "recruit a friend" and "resurrect a friend." These programs allow players to bring new people to the game and also to bring back friends that have stopped playing. This mechanic eases the promotion work for the game, because new players will arrive directly via friends, just in exchange for some game benefits. It is a way of using the existing community as a marketing tool, giving incentives that mean nothing to those who are invited, but since they can be important for the friend who plays, they might agree to comply and try out the game.

Scarcity

The supply and demand together with the "just-in-time" production systems lead to an organic system that is mutable in space and time. Demand for today, once satisfied, no longer exists tomorrow. Therefore, it becomes necessary to adjust the supply. One of the techniques created was designated by shortage. Knowing that the low supply may induce greater demand, the best way to ensure the maintenance of the demand is to create the idea that there is scarcity: "People seem to be more motivated by the thought of losing something than by the thought of gaining something of equal value" (Cialdini, 2001, p. 205).

Many products from various industries use this strategy. Examples include chocolates that are only sold during the winter, the Disney classics in DVD/Blu-ray that are sold for a limited amount of time, alongside several other products that launch limited editions. In the case of *WoW*, we are talking about a product that is already on the market, a product that is not going to vanish, or start having problems in terms of physical supply. Thus, on the supplier's side there is only one requirement—to keep the player base active to maintain players' interest in the game.

Playing online games can feel too much like playing with borrowed toys that are never in our possession. As Furby's (1991) study demonstrated, possession gives people a "sense of personal competence or control," and players need to fulfill their control over the game, and their control over the money they have spent. In some way, this is how "virtual goods" were created in online games. In *WoW*, virtual goods are equipment pieces, weapons, mounts, pets, or even just cosmetic objects, such as a picnic table or a perfume. Being a subscription model, these objects are usually available within the game and do not cost additional money to get; however, some are rare, some are very rare, others are limited, or are only available on certain occasions (such as special holidays). Designers define the levels of scarcity, determining the rarity of virtual goods and how hard they are to get, to keep players involved with the game, persuading them to continue in the name of their competence and control over the game.

Authority

Human beings have a natural tendency to obey when authority factors are present. In the 1960s, social experiments performed by Milgram (1963) measured the willingness to obey an authority figure who instructed the subjects to perform actions that conflicted with their personal ideas. Subjects exhibited blind obedience, being available to comply, even when the act was morally against their most profound beliefs. Cialdini summarizes the importance of this obedience within groups and communities:

> Whenever we are faced with a potent motivator of human action, it is natural to expect that good reasons exist for the motivation. In the case of obedience to authority, even a brief consideration of human social organization offers justification aplenty. A multilayered and widely accepted system of authority confers an immense advantage upon a society. It allows the development of sophisticated structures for production of resources, trade, defense, expansion, and social control that would otherwise be impossible.
>
> Cialdini, 2001, p. 195

In WoW, authority has not been directly built into the game rules, but the presence of authority stirs up players through the constant comparison of game accomplishments, making authority emerge naturally in the relationships. A player can be recognized as an authority by his title, his equipment, or his guild position. The structure of a guild in WoW consists of several ranks, but only one person rules all, the guild master, the player who created the guild in the first place. Despite this totalitarian figure, the structure of power in a guild is normally divided between the guild master and several other officers,[7] sort of like a general and his colonels.

Guild leaders can enforce more or less authority depending on the guild's objectives, and top-end game guilds are very strict with their rules and the obedience of their members. In addition, as we have seen, to overcome the greatest challenges in the game demands synchronous and symmetrical types of cooperative gameplay, requiring careful planning, strategy, and sometimes flawless execution for victory to be achieved, and that means total obedience to the guild master and the officers who work on the strategies for those fights. We can say that game design does not enforce authority, but it surely encourages it, designing rewards for the fiercer authoritarian groups. Consequently, authority becomes a game goal.

Conclusion

The research presented here is not exhaustive and excludes many other situations in the game where we can see the same strategies in use, for example, in the expanding development of social messaging, both instant and asynchronous, with several layers of relationships and interconnectivity with social networks. Blizzard Entertainment's Real ID and Battle Tag systems allow a multiplatform approach to chat—a smartphone application that allows players to access the auction house, their bank, and even the guild chat in real time anywhere. These tools might become crucial as publishers move to a multi-MMO/game approach, to encourage players to stick with a particular network of games, building their commitment to it, and improving the chances that they will invest time in building up friends on that network, thus increasing game revenues from subscriptions or microtransactions in the process.

From this analysis, we can reach the conclusion that game design for social interaction is deeply rooted in evolutionary influential factors for the maintenance of communities. Interdependency is, in fact, the root for all networking systems in nature. At the same time, MMO social strategies are being designed according to very well-known marketing techniques from the middle of the 20th century. In part, this can result in the conclusion that the essential objective of MMOs is to guarantee sales and returns, but more important than that is for an MMO to guarantee its own survival.

Notes

1   The project output from this PhD was the first known computer game in history, *Noughts and Crosses* (1952), which ran in the Britannic electronic computer EDSAC.
2   Raiding is a type of mission in which a very large number of players get together to fight against AI-controlled monsters (or Bosses) that require coordination, strategic planning, and execution to defeat. PvP is a gaming term that refers to "player-versus-player" modes. In the case of MMOs, the PvP works as "groups versus groups," and can vary between small teams in an arena, to 40-man battles in a huge battleground.
3   Achievements are rewards in the form of points, granted each time a player finishes an objective.
4   Before being accepted as full members, players usually need to go through a trial period when they need to prove their value as a player.
5   PUG is an abbreviation for a pickup group; a term used commonly in MMORPGs to identify groups that are not formed by people that know each other.
6   This refers to when a player is tired of the current content and asks for time off from his guild leaders.
7   An officer is the second rank held in a guild. Usually each officer is responsible for a different aspect of a guild's management.

References

Aihoshi, R. (2000). *Brad McQuaid interview*. Retrieved from http://rpgvaul-tarchive.ign.com/features/interviews/bmcquaid_a.shtml.

Asch, S. E. (1951). Effects of group pressure upon the modification and distortion of judgment. In H. Guetzkow (Ed.), *Groups, leadership and men*. Pittsburgh, PA: Carnegie Press.

Bowlby, J. (1969). *Attachment and loss: Volume 3: Loss: Sadness and depression*. New York City, NY: Basic Books.

Cialdini, R. B. (2001). *Influence: Science and practice* (4th ed.). Boston, MA: Allyn & Bacon.

Douglas, A. S. (1954). *Some computations in theoretical physics*. PhD Dissertation, University of Cambridge, UK.

Furby, L. (1991). Understanding the psychology of possession and ownership: A personal memoir and an appraisal of our progress. *Journal of Social Behavior and Personality*, 6(6), 457–463.

Griffiths, M. D., Davies, M. N. O., and Chappell, D., (2003). Breaking the stereotype: The case of online gaming. *CyberPsychology and Behavior, 6*, 81–91.

Kelley, H. H., and Thibaut, J. W. (1978). *Interpersonal relations: A theory of interdependence*. New York City, NY: Wiley.

Knox, R. E., and Inkster, J. A. (1968). Postdecisional dissonance at post time. *Journal of Personality and Social Psychology, 8*, 319–323.

Milgram, S. (1963). Behavioral study of obedience. *Journal of Abnormal and Social Psychology, 67*(4), 371–378.

Sheldon, K. M., and Lyubomirsky, S. (2004). Achieving sustainable new happiness: Prospects, practices, and prescriptions. In A. Linley and S. Joseph (Eds.), *Positive psychology in practice* (pp. 127–145). Hoboken, NJ: John Wiley & Sons.

Watzlawick, P., Beavin, J., and Jackson, D. (1967). *Pragmatics of human communication: A study of interactional patterns, pathologies, and paradoxes*. New York City, NY: W.W. Norton & Company.

Whitney, R. A., Hubin, T., and Murphy, J. D. (1965). *The new psychology of persuasion and motivation in selling*. Englewood Cliffs, NJ: Prentice-Hall.

Zagalo, N. (2009). *Emoções Interactivas, do Cinema para os Videojogos* [Interactive emotions, from film to videogames]. Coimbra, Portugal: Gracio Editor.

Zagalo, N. (2012). Communication and design in social games. In L. Andrade and T. Falcão (Eds.), *Realidade Sintética: jogos eletrônicos, comunicação e experiência social* (pp. 57–72). São Paulo, Brazil: Scortecci Editora.

Games Cited

Atari Inc. (1972). *Pong*. Sunnyvale, CA: Atari Inc.

Blizzard Entertainment (2004), *World of Warcraft*, Vivendi Activision Blizzard.

Verant Interactive (1999). *EverQuest*. Sony Online Entertainment.

Part IV

Co-Located and Console Gaming

12 Get Together

Console Playing as a Group Experience

Sonja Kröger and Thorsten Quandt

Introduction

According to Nielsen's annual US gaming survey, 56% of US households own at least one current-generation gaming console (Nielsen, 2012). Console gaming is the most relevant area in the games industry nowadays—economically, console gaming has greatly surpassed traditional PC gaming, and for many games, consoles also serve as the lead platforms for development. The acceptance of gaming outside the group of traditional core gamers can be attributed to the success of easy-to-use technological platforms and more casual console systems that are promoted for use in the living room. Furthermore, console games have been especially designed to allow for playing in mixed groups on relatively equal terms; that is, young people with advanced gaming skills and seniors without any gaming experience.

As previously mentioned by Voida and Greenberg (2009), and despite its relevance, console gaming has not received much in the way of academic attention, at least with regard to its specific features and qualities. The discussion in the social sciences is still centered on a number of key research topics that are strongly traditional in the sense that they follow well-known disciplinary research paths that were previously applied to other "new media" and formats. Therefore, the literature highlights how there has been much research on online gaming and on the harmful effects of digital (solitary) gaming. These harmful aspects include, for example, excessive game play, aggressive attitudes and behavior, and social isolation (e.g., Festl, Scharkow, and Quandt, 2012; Kim and Kim, 2010; Griffiths, 2010). However, we already know from other studies that the positive aspects of virtual worlds hold more appeal and outweigh the presumed negative effects of such worlds. It is frequently argued that digital games have the potential to support physical activity, that they can encourage cooperative and competitive behavior, and that they can positively influence cognitive skills (e.g., Ducheneaut, and Moore, 2004; Kolo and Baur, 2004; Nardi and Harris, 2006; Shie and Cheng, 2007; Yee, 2006). From the perspective of social sciences, some researchers focus on the integration of digital games into our daily life, and the individual as well as the social implications of such integration. Digital games provide numerous opportunities for users to come together and interact with each other. In this context, several studies illustrate (Chen and Lei, 2006; Hsu and Lu, 2004; Jansz and Tanis, 2007; Jansz and Martens, 2005) that social interaction is one of the most important motivational factors for playing digital games.

Forms of Co-Located Gaming

The public and academic dialogue about digital games often relates to traditional computer games where one person sits in front of a computer playing. Yet, regarding the continuous development of gaming software and hardware in recent years, it seems to be appropriate to enlarge the perspective of digital game settings: New kinds of entertainment systems have been established, and they have totally changed the game settings following the release of consoles such as Nintendo's Wii, Microsoft's Xbox 360, and Sony's PlayStation 3 (consoles that include various forms of motion controllers). Besides the academic attention on solitary play, recent fieldwork has already analyzed players' experiences during special forms of digital game play such as massively multiplayer online games (MMOs) (e.g., Clarke and Duimering, 2006; Cole and Griffiths, 2007) or local-area network (LAN) parties (e.g., Vogelgesang, 2003). In both game settings, MMOs and LAN parties, hundreds and up to a thousand people meet (in real and/or virtual life) to play together. The findings from these studies provide important insights into how digital game environments offer different opportunities for users to interact.

Nevertheless, they are different from console game settings. Compared to research in online gaming, the specific features and qualities of home-based console gaming seem to be understudied and will be systematized and covered below.

In the first step, to give a better understanding of the practices surrounding console gaming, we emphasize its characteristics. Consequently, it seems to be necessary to be able to differentiate between the ways in which gamers are present in different game settings. Gajadhar (2012, pp. 21–22) describes three forms of co-located digital game settings: (a) artificial, (b) mediated, and (c) co-located scenarios.

a   In this context, Gajadhar (2012) describes artificial co-players as non-human opponents or collaborators who are controlled by the computer. A typical game setting is, for instance, a chess game, played by one person (sitting in front of the computer) against the artificial intelligence of the chess program.

b   Contrary to the artificial co-player, mediated co-players are defined as humans. Specific for this type of co-located game setting is that the gamers interact via the Internet. Consequently, the behaviors of the persons are represented through digital avatars (Gajadhar,

2012) and the gamers do not interact face-to-face with each other. MMOs, such as *World of Warcraft* (*WoW*) (Blizzard Entertainment, 2004), are based on the principle of groups of gamers fulfilling quests together.

c The co-located game setting refers to a game setting where the gamers are located in the same room, playing the same digital game together or against each other. Just as in mediated game settings, the gamers interact in the game through their digital avatars. In addition to this virtual interaction, these settings offer the opportunity for players to interact directly in the real world (Gajadhar, 2012) because they are standing or sitting next to each other. This game setting is, for instance, exemplified by a karaoke game, such as *SingStar* (Sony Computer Entertainment, 2004), where two people sing songs side-by-side.

As outlined above, digital game play environments can have an influence on the social interactions of gamers. In this context, Salen and Zimmerman (2003) point out that digital game play can be surrounded by so-called *internal* or *external* social interactions. According to the authors, the former refer to interactions of the game characters within the game, whereas external social interactions stem from players' activities outside the game (e.g., the exchange of information, sharing experiences).

Therefore, it seems to be evident that artificial and mediated co-play settings do not offer gamers a good environment for external social interactions. Even if a gamer of an MMO knows that there is another human playing with him somewhere in the world (or maybe they use a headset to talk to each other), these settings still afford less room for social interaction, which would produce a strong feeling of being together with another person.

Only co-located game settings provide many forms of internal and external social interactions such as face-to-face communication, identification from facial expressions and gestures, or behavioral engagement. Consequently, console games, especially, might give gamers a strong sense of being together with others and promote sociability.

Overview of Console Gaming Research

As this article offers an overview of studies that were published in more than one research discipline, the authors had to ensure that the search had been wide enough to find all the relevant material. Therefore, the authors decided to search relevant studies via the search engine Google Scholar, which provides access to relevant literature across different research fields. Related literature was identified from October 1 until October 10, 2012, by using the following keyword search terms: *console gaming/games, co-located gaming/games, collocated gaming/games, exergaming/exergames, digital games and health* as well as *social interaction and games*. In addition to this, the bibliographies of the literature identified by the electronic search through Google Scholar were reviewed to identify further studies. All types of methodological study were eligible for inclusion in the review, but they needed to include a co-located game setting (as described above), and they needed to be published in English.

Overall, the authors found 45 studies corresponding to the above criteria. They can be classified into six key subjects, which will be described below (for an overview: see Table 12.1).

Health

Nearly half (20) of the studies identified here fall into the *games and health* category. According to the literature in this field, it has been suggested that high levels of screen time (e.g., television and digital gaming) are responsible for people's sedentary lifestyles. Especially young people were criticized for being antisocial, and it is presumed that their media use results in physical inactivity (for an overview, see Daley, 2009). Yet despite the negative effects, console systems such as Nintendo's Wii offer opportunities for directed movement of the whole body. Many researchers see the opportunity for positive effects of console gaming from these technical innovations. In this context, it has been proposed that new-generation console games may contribute to people's well-being. Most of the studies identified investigate research experiments on the health benefits for children. Positive effects of playing active console games on body weight were assumed by Maddison et al. (2007). Additionally, the results by Graves, Stratton, Ridgers, and Cable (2007) reveal that children who play console games such as tennis, bowling, or boxing use significantly more energy compared to the children in the non-gaming control group. Moreover, several studies even posited that playing console games provides children with psychosocial and emotional health (for an overview, see Ekeland, 2005). Nevertheless, even if the studies in this field show that exergaming can develop children's fitness, they also emphasize that console gaming is not a feasible substitute for real sports or activities.

Other age groups were analyzed by Harley, Fitzpatrick, Axelrod, White, and McAllister (2010) as well as Aarhus, Grönvall, Larsen, and Wollsen (2011). Both studies analyzed the psychological and physical benefits of seniors due to co-located gaming with the Nintendo Wii. Results show positive effects as players learned new technical literacies, made new social connections with peers in sheltered housing (Harley et al., 2010), and they showed that the Nintendo Wii Fit could be used as a supplement to physiotherapy exercises to increase seniors' fitness (Aarhus et al., 2010). Additionally, Younbo, Koay, Ng, Wong, and Kwan (2009) postulated that playing co-located games had a positive impact on the overall well-being of the elderly compared to playing traditional board games.

Table 12.1 Overview of the Research Fields of Console Gaming

Focus	Method	Sample	Platform(s)/ Game(s)	Author(s)
Health				
Psychological and Physical Well-Being	Rehabilitation Session, Observation, Physiotherapeutic Test, Interview	Seniors	Nintendo Wii	Aarhus et al. (2011)
Energy Costs	–	–	Nintendo Wii, Intellivision Video Game Console	Brown et al. (2008)
Physical Activity and Well-Being, Competence in Sports	Experiment	Children (9–12 years)	-	Chin et al. (2008)
Energy Expenditure of (Non-)Obese Children	Experiment	Children (8–12 years)	PlayStation 2	Epstein et al. (2007)
Energy Expenditure	Experiment	Children (10–13 years)	PlayStation 2, Nintendo Wii	Graf et al. (2009)
Energy Expenditure	Experiment, Anthropometric Measures	Children (13–15 years)	Nintendo Wii, Xbox 360	Graves et al. (2007)
Physical and Social Activity	Observation, Interview, Video Analysis	Seniors (60–94 years)	Nintendo Wii	Harley et al. (2010)
Energy Expenditure and Heart Rate	–	–	PlayStation 2	Kemble et al. (2007)
Energy Expenditure	Experiment	Children (8–12 years)	PlayStation 2, Xbox	Lanningham-Foster et al. (2006)
Physical Activity	Physical Tests	Children (10–14 years)	Sony PlayStation 2	Maddison et al. (2007)
Energy Expenditure and Heart Rate	Experiment	Children (6–12 years)	Xavix	Mellecker, McManus (2008)
Physical Activity, BMI and Waist Circumference	Experiment	Children (10–14 years)	PlayStation 2	Ni Mhurchu et al. (2008)
Physical Gaming in Households	Interview, Home Tour, Game Log	Adults	Different Console Systems	Sall, Grinter (2007)
Energy Expenditure	Experiment, Physiological Measures	Children (7–14 years)	–	Seigel et al. (2008)
Physical, Psychological, Cognitive Benefits	Literature Review	Children	–	Staiano, Calvert (2011)
Energy Demands, Cardiorespiratory Response	Experiment	Children	Dance Dance Revolution 3rd Mix	Tan et al. (2002)

Continued overleaf

Focus	Method	Sample	Platform(s)/ Game(s)	Author(s)
Energy Expenditure of (Non-)Obese Children	Experiment, Questionnaire, Anthropometric and Physiological Measures	Children and adolescents	Dance Dance Revolution	Unnithan et al. (2006)
Cardiovascular Fitness, Bone Health	Experiment, Physiological Measures	Children	Dance Dance Revolution	Wetzsteon et al. (2006)
Physical and Psychosocial Effects	–	Older Women	Nintendo Wii	Wollersheim et al. (2010)
Psychological and Physical Well-Being	Interview, Questionnaire	Seniors (56–92 years)	Nintendo Wii	Younbo et al. (2009)

Social Interaction/Social Presence

Focus	Method	Sample	Platform(s)/ Game(s)	Author(s)
Engagement, Social Interaction	Experiment, Questionnaire	Adults (22–32 years)	Nintendo Wii	Boguslawski (2007)
Social Processes, Social Play Experience	Theoretical Framework	–	–	de Kort et al. (2007a)
Engagement, Involvement	Experiment	Adults (16–34 years)	PC	Gajadhar et al. (2009a)
Player Enjoyment	Experiment, Questionnaire, Self-Report	Adults (16–34 years)	PC	Gajadhar et al. (2008b)
Social Presence	Experiment, Self-Report	Adults (20–34 years)	PC	Gajadhar et al. (2008a)
Social Presence	Experiment, Questionnaire	Adults (23–32 years)	PC	Hayley (2010)
Social Context	Focus Group, Interview	Adolescents	–	Kaye, Bryce (2012a)
Social Interaction and Fun	Questionnaire, Group Gaming	Adults (20–30 years)	Nintendo GameCube	Klastrup (2003)
Social Presence	Questionnaire, Experiment, Self-report	Adults (19–23 years)	Sony PlayStation 2	Mandryk, Inkpen (2004)
Spatial Presence and Emotion	Experiment, Questionnaire, Self-Report	Adults (19–34 years)	Game Boy Advance	Ravaja et al. (2006)
Group Interaction	Video Recording	Children	Different Console Systems	Schott, Kambouri (2003)
Social Use of Handheld Devices	Interview, Observation	Adults (18–34 years)	Nintendo DS	Szentgyorgy et al. (2008)
Intergenerational Interactions	Questionnaire, Group Gaming, Focus Group	Wide Range, Children to Adults (3–84 years)	Different Console Systems	Voida, Greenberg (2012)
Social and Physical Interaction	Experiment, Observation, Questionnaire	Adults	Handheld Augmented Reality	Xu et al. (2008)

Focus	Method	Sample	Platform(S)/ Games(s)	Author(s)
Communication				
Communication Between Gamers	Experiment, Self-Report	Adults (16–33 years)	PC	Gajadhar et al. (2009b)
Social Communication	Experiment, Questionnaire	–	Nokia N97, Sony PlayStation 3	Kauko, Häkkilä (2010)
Social Communication	Experiment, Questionnaire	Adults (21–53 years)	Mobile Devices	Li, Counts (2007)
Family				
Parent–Child Connectedness	Questionnaire	Adolescents and Their Parents	–	Coyne et al. (2011)
Family Life and Digital Games	Focus Group, Interview	Adolescents and Their Family	PC, Console	Eklund (2013)
Game Playing at Home	Interview	Adolescents and Adults (17+)	PC, Different Console Systems	Randall (2011)
Motivation				
Motivation, Gaming Experiences	Online-Questionnaire	Adults	–	Kaye et al. (2012b)
Motivation and Perception	Questionnaire, Group Gaming, Focus Group	Wide Range, Children to Adults (3–84 years)	Different Console Systems	Voida, Greenberg (2009)
Game Dynamics				
Measurement for Social Interaction	Biometric Measurement, Questionnaire, Self-Evaluation	Adolescents	Sony PlayStation 2	Bromley et al. (2013)
Movement Control Strategies	Interviews, Questionnaires, Video Observation	Experienced Gamers	Nintendo Wii	Pasch et al. (2009)
Gaming Practice, Game Mechanics, Interaction Design	Questionnaire, Group Gaming, Focus Group	Wide Range, Children to Adults (3–84 years)	Different Console Systems	Voida et al. (2010)

Social Interaction/Social Presence

Research within this section is multifaceted in terms of the methodological approaches and the size of the selected samples. Most of the studies follow an experimental design and focus on adults' social interactions during co-located gaming. Only one study that was identified focused on children (Schott and Kambouri, 2003).

Social presence has been defined by Biocca, Harms, and Burgoon (2003, p. 459) as "the sense of being together with another." They identified three key dimensions that describe the multidimensional construct of social presence: awareness, psychological involvement, and behavioral engagement. Based on these assumptions, and to measure the feelings of being together in digital games, de Kort and colleagues (de Kort, IJsselsteijn, and Poels (2007; see also de Kort, IJsselsteijn, and Gajadhar 2007) developed a "Social Presence in Gaming Questionnaire". The investigation by Ravaja et al. (2006) showed that the nature of the opponent (computer, friend, or stranger) had an influence on spatial presence during game play. The authors found that compared to playing against a computer, playing against another human "elicited higher spatial presence, engagement, anticipated threat, post-game challenge appraisals, and physiological arousal" (p. 327). In this context, Mandryk and Inkpen (2004) presented research testing the efficacy of physiological measures, and uncovered different physiological responses in the body when playing against an artificial intelligence source versus playing against a friend. Consistent with these results, Gajadhar, de Kort, and IJsselsteijn (2008a) employed physiological measurements to explore the influence of the social setting on player experience. The results of the study reveal that playing against a human brings more enjoyment than playing against a computer.

Communication

Communication is considered a central part of social interaction, and it is an essential element of digital co-located gaming. Overall, three studies were identified that focused on communication during digital game play. All age groups of adolescents were studied, with a preference for experimental research design. From recent literature in this field, we know that face-to-face communication provides a degree of social richness. However, the experiment by Gajadhar et al. (2009b) showed that the sense of social presence also increased through computer-mediated communication. The *video and audio* setting in this study demonstrated a higher involvement of the gamer than in the *none* (no video and no audio communication during game play) condition. The experimental study by Kauko and Häkkilä (2010) provided a better understanding of the social game experience during co-located mobile gaming. The results revealed that oral communication had a major role in co-located game play, and that the player's social interaction and presence were significantly higher in co-located, face-to-face game settings than in settings where players were seated side-by-side.

Family

Since the rise of digital games, these new media technologies have been primarily associated with young male gamers, sitting alone in front of a computer and playing excessively. Even though increased efforts were made by digital game companies to advertise digital games as family-based entertainment, only when Nintendo's Wii console system had been released did digital games make the breakthrough to be considered as "family-friendly" (Chambers, 2012, p. 70). Surprisingly, only three studies were identified with a focus on *family and console games*. Two studies followed qualitative approaches and referred to interview data to explore the role of digital games within the family's everyday lives (Eklund, 2013, see Chapter 13; Randall, 2011). The other study took a quantitative approach and aimed to assess the relationship between parental co-play of video games and behavioral and family outcomes (Coyne et al., 2011). All studies showed positive associations for console co-playing within the family.

Motivation

Motivations for media use in this context for digital games have been traditionally studied from the viewpoint of the uses and gratification approach. A result of these studies is that there is not a unique reason why people play games, but rather that the reasons differ across genres, sex, age, etc. In general, many reasons have already been identified for digital game playing, such as structural coupling to the player's environment, competition, identity formation, escapism, anger management, or the exercise of power (Ganguin, 2010, pp. 237 ff.). So far, much research has been undertaken on all types of digital games, but without a focus on co-located console gaming.

Only two studies deal with "motivations for, perceptions of, and practices surrounding the shared use of console games" (Voida and Greenberg, 2009, p. 1559). The results show that not the games themselves, but the social interactions enabled by the co-located game play are an essential motivation for console gaming. The study revealed that social interactions such as teamwork, common goals, and shared successes were the main motivations for the participants.

Additionally, Kaye, Bryce, and Pollard (2012b) demonstrated that playing with others rather than alone enhanced gaming enjoyment, particularly for console games such as Nintendo's Wii.

Game Dynamics

Three explanatory approaches were identified within this section, focusing on how to better understand interaction in co-located game settings to design the future generation of movement-based console games.

Voida, Carpendale, and Greenberg (2010) conducted a study of co-located group console gaming to determine the relationships between console game design and group interactions. They examined six key types of behavior displayed in the observed co-located gaming sessions: *constructing shared awareness, reinforcing, shared history, sharing in success and failure, engaging in interdependence,* and *self-sacrifice*. Their findings highlight how competition-related games basically do not engender individual-oriented gaming practices, and how cooperative-oriented games principally do not always facilitate group-oriented gaming practices: Social interactions are rather influenced by the mechanics of the game play, the setup, and the scoring design. Bromley, Mirza-Babaei, McAllister, and Napier (see Chapter 14) adapted the categories by Voida et al. (2010), and referred to Bartle's four player types (1996; see also Chapter 2) to describe a practical methodology for measuring social interaction. The results of this experiment showed that players who shared the same categories (e.g., killers or achievers) had stronger correlations between the social interactions and biometric results. For instance, game sessions that involved the player type of *killer* had a higher degree of *trash-talk* interaction than observed game sessions without killers.

Additionally, data obtained by Pasch, Bianchi-Berthouze, van Dijk, and Nijholt (2009) revealed that movement-specific items, such as *natural control, mimicry of movements, proprioceptive feedback*, and *physical challenge,* influence immersion in movement-based interaction. Solely focusing on Nintendo's Wii *Boxing* game, the researchers provided a better understanding of how body movement may affect gamers' experiences in movement video games. The researchers suggested that a game controller that leaves more space for user-experience appropriation might motivate physical activity and emotional well-being.

Conclusion

Console gaming is different to "traditional" PC-based gaming: It allows for direct interactions within a physical space, and with motion controllers and movement-detection systems (e.g., Xbox Kinect), the interaction becomes physical as well. The games themselves are primarily designed for gaming groups and not for solitary play. Therefore, console games are often designed to give gamers a strong sense of "being together," and as such, they are inherently "social."

The literature review illustrates that there are multiple studies on console gaming. However, they do not cover a wider range of research in an exhaustive way. There are just a few key areas that have received most of the academic interest so far. A considerable number of studies focused on *health and gaming*, providing deep insights into the positive effects of console gaming, and on how it can improve people's well-being. Other key areas included *social interaction, communication, family*, and *motivation* and *game dynamics*, but they drew much less attention.

Needless to say, a deeper understanding of the special features of console gaming is needed. Important matters for future research include whether and how console gaming improves social and educational skills. Additionally, more research is needed on console gaming in varying social contexts; that is, peer-group playing or family playing. There are many more open questions and this article has only given a rough outline of the current research, its findings, and some of its shortcomings.

References

Aarhus, R., Grönvall, E., Larsen, S. B., and Wollsen, S. (2011). Turning training into play: Embodied gaming, seniors, physical training and motivation. *Gerontechnology, 10*(2), 110–120.

Bartle, R. A. (1996). Hearts, clubs, diamonds, spades: Players who suit MUDs. *Journal of MUD Research, 1*(1), 19.

Biocca, F., Harms, C., and Burgoon, J. K. (2003). Toward a more robust theory and measure of social presence: Review and suggested criteria. *Presence, 12*(5), 456–480.

Boguslawski, G. (2007). *Body movement, social interaction and engagement in video game play: It's a different game all together.* London, United Kingdom: Citeseer.

Brown, G. A., Holoubeck, M., Nylander, B., et al. (2008). Energy expenditure of physically active video gaming: Wii boxing, Wii tennis, and Dance Dance Revolution. *Medicine and Science in Sports and Exercise, 40*(5), 460.

Chambers, D. (2012). "Wii play as a family": The rise in family-centred video gaming, *Leisure Studies, 31*(1), 69–82

Chen, K. T., and Lei, C. L. (2006). Design implications of social interaction in online games. *Entertainment Computing-ICEC 2006* (pp. 318–321). Cambridge, UK: Springer.

Chin, A., Paw, M. J., Jacobs, W. M., Vaessen, E. P., Titze, S., and van Mechelen, W. (2008). The motivation of children to play an active video game. *Journal of Science and Medicine in Sport, 11*(2), 163–166.

Clarke, D., and Duimering, P. R. (2006). How computer gamers experience the game situation: A behavioral study. *Computers in Entertainment, 4*(3) 1–23.

Cole, H., and Griffiths, M. (2007). Social interactions in massively multiplayer online role-playing gamers. *CyberPsychology and Behavior, 10*(4), 575–583.

Coyne, S. M., Padilla-Walker, L. M., Stockdale, L., and Day, R. D. (2011). Game on ... girls: Associations between co-playing video games and adolescent behavioral and family outcomes. *Journal of Adolescent Health, 49*(2), 160–165.

Daley, A. J. (2009). Can exergaming contribute to improving physical activity levels and health outcomes in children? *Pediatrics, 124*(2), 763–771.

de Kort, Y. A. W., Ijsselsteijn, W. A., and Gajadhar, B. J. (2007). People, places, and play: A research framework for digital game experience in a socio-spatial context. *Conference proceedings of the DiGRA Conference "Situated Play"* (pp. 823–830). New York, NY: ACM Press.

de Kort, Y. A. W., IJsselsteijn, W. A., and Poels, K. (2007). Digital games as social presence technology: Development of the Social Presence in Gaming Questionnaire, Proceedings of PRESENCE: The 10th International Workshop on Presence (pp. 195–203).

Ducheneaut, N., and Moore, R. J. (2004). The social side of gaming: A study of interaction patterns in a massively multiplayer online game. *Proceedings of the ACM Conference on Computer Supported Cooperative Work* (pp. 360–369). New York, NY: ACM Press.

Ekeland, E., Heian, F., and Hagen, K. B. (2005). Can exercise improve self-esteem in children and young people? A systematic review of randomised controlled trials. *Br J Sports Med, 39*(11), 792–798.

Eklund, L. (2013). Family and games: Digital game playing in the social context of the family. In T. Quandt and S. Kröger (Eds.), *Multiplayer: The Social Aspects of Digital Gaming* (pp. 162–171), Abingdon: Routledge.

Epstein, L. H., Beecher, M. D., Graf, J. L., and Roemmich J. N. (2007). Choice of interactive dance and bicycle games in overweight and nonoverweight youth. *Annals of Behavioral Medicine, 33*(2), 124–131.

Festl, R., Scharkow, M., and Quandt, T. (2012). Problematic computer game use among adolescents, younger and older adults. *Addiction, 108*(3), 592–599.

Gajadhar, B. J. (2012). Understanding player experience in social digital games: The role of social presence. Retrieved from http://alexandria.tue.nl/extra2/731192.pdf.

Gajadhar, B. J., de Kort, Y. A. W., and IJsselsteijn, W. A. (2008a). Influence of social setting on player experience of digital games. *Proceedings of the CHI 2008 "Works in progress" Conference* (pp. 3099–3104). New York, NY: ACM Press.

Gajadhar, B. J., de Kort, Y. A. W., and IJsselsteijn, W. A. (2008b). Shared fun is doubled fun: Player enjoyment as a function of social setting. In P. Markopoulos, B. de Ruyter, W. IJsselsteijn, and D. Rowland (Eds.), *Fun and games* (pp. 106–117), New York, NY: Springer.

Gajadhar, B. J., de Kort, Y. A. W., and IJsselsteijn, W. A. (2009a). Rules of engagement: Influence of co-player presence on player involvement in digital games. *International Journal of Gaming and Computer-Mediated Simulations, 1*(3), 14–27.

Gajadhar, B. J., de Kort, Y. A. W., and IJsselsteijn, W. A. (2009b). See no rival, hear no rival: The role of social cues in digital game settings. In F. J. Verbeek, D. Lenior, and M. Steen (Eds.), *Proceedings of CHI Nederland Conference "Change!"* (pp. 25–31), Leiden, Netherlands.

Ganguin, S. (2010). *Computerspiele und lebenslanges Lernen: Eine Synthese von Gegensätzen*. Wiesbaden: VS Verlag.

Graf, D. L., Pratt, L. V., Hester, C. N., and Short, K. R. (2009). Playing active video games increases energy expenditure in children. *Pediatrics, 124*(2), 534–540.

Graves, L., Stratton, G., Ridgers, N. D., and Cable, N.T. (2007). Comparison of energy expenditure in adolescents playing new generation and sedentary computer games: Cross sectional study. *BMJ, 335*(7633), 1282–1284.

Griffiths, M. D. (2010). The role of context in online gaming excess and addiction: Some case study evidence. *International Journal of Mental Health and Addiction, 8*(1), 119–125.

Harley, D., Fitzpatrick, G., Axelrod, L., White, G., and McAllister, G. (2010). Making the Wii at home: Game play by older people in sheltered housing. *Lecture Notes in Computer Science, 6389*(2010), 156–176.

Hayley, M. (2010). *How social context affects levels of immersion: Does physical presence matter?* Project Report for the Degree of Master of Science, University College, London, United Kingdom.

Hsu, C. L., and Lu, H. P. (2004). Why do people play on-line games? An extended TAM with social influences and flow experience. *Information and Management, 41*(7), 853–868.

Jansz, J., and Martens, L. (2005). Gaming at a LAN event: The social context of playing video games. *New Media & Society, 7*(3), 333–355.

Jansz, J., and Tanis, M. (2007). Appeal of playing online first person shooter games. *CyberPsychology and Behavior, 10*(1), 133–136.

Kauko, J., and Häkkilä, J. (2010). Shared-screen social gaming with portable devices. *Proceedings of the MobileHCI 2010* (pp. 317–325). New York, NY: ACM Press.

Kaye, L. K., and Bryce, J. (2012a). Putting the "fun factor" into gaming: The influence of social contexts on experiences of playing videogames. *International Journal of Internet Science, 7*(1), 23–37.

Kaye, L. K., Bryce, J., and Pollard, P. (2012b). "I need a Wii": Motivations and experiences of playing videogames. *Leisure Studies, 31*(1), 69–82.

Kemble, C. D., Mahar, M., Rowe, D., Murray, N., and Cooper, N. (2008). Energy expenditure during rest, traditional video game play and interactive video game play in adolescent boys. *Medicine and Science in Sports and Exercise, 40*(5), 88.

Kim, M. G., and Kim, J. (2010). Cross-validation of reliability, convergent and discriminant validity for the problematic online game use scale. *Computers in Human Behavior, 26*(3), 389–398.

Klastrup, L. (2003). "You can't help shouting and yelling": Fun and social interaction in *Super Monkey Ball. Level up conference proceedings* (pp. 382–390). Utrecht, The Netherlands: University of Utrecht.

Kolo, C., and Baur, T. (2004). Living a virtual life: Social dynamics of online gaming. *GameStudies, 4*(1). Retrieved from http://www.gamestudies.org/0401/kolo/.

Lanningham-Foster, L., Jensen, T. B., Foster, R. C., Redmond, A. B., Walker, B. A., Heinz, D., and Levine, J. A. (2006). Energy expenditure of sedentary screen time compared with active screen time for children. *Pediatrics, 118*(6), 1831–1835.

Li, K. A., and Counts, S. (2007). Exploring social interactions and attributes of casual multiplayer mobile gaming. *Mobility '07 Proceedings of the 4th international conference on mobile technology, applications, and systems and the 1st international symposium on computer human interaction in mobile technology* (pp. 696–703). New York, NY: ACM Press.

Maddison, R., Mhurchu, C. N., Jull, A., Jiang, Y., Prapavessis, H., and Rodgers, A. (2007). Energy expended playing video console games: An opportunity to increase children's physical activity? *Pediatric Exercise Science, 19*(3), 334.

Mandryk, R. L., and Inkpen, K. M. (2004). Physiological indicators for the evaluation of co-located collaborative play. *Proceedings of the ACM Conference on Computer Supported Cooperative Work* (pp. 102–111). New York, NY: ACM Press.

Mellecker, R. R., and McManus, A. M. (2008). Energy expenditure and cardiovascular responses to seated and active gaming in children. *Archives of Pediatrics and Adolescent Medicine, 162*(9), 886–891.

Nardi, B., and Harris, J. (2006). Strangers and friends: Collaborative play in *World of Warcraft. Proceedings of the 2006 20th Anniversary Conference on Computer Supported Cooperative Work* (pp. 149–158). New York, NY: ACM Press.

Ni Mhurchu, C., Maddison, R., Jiang, Y., Jull, A., Prapavessis, H., and Rodgers, A. (2008). Couch potatoes to jumping beans: A pilot study of the effects of active video games on physical activity in children. *International Journal of Behavioral Nutrition and Physical Activity, 5*(1), 8.

Nielsen (2012). *Trends in U.S. video gaming – The rise of cross-platform.* Retrieved from http://www.nielsen.com/us/en/newswire/2012/the-latest-trends-in-us-video-gaming.html.

Pasch, M., Bianchi-Berthouze, N., van Dijk, B., and Nijholt, A. (2009). Movement-based sports video games: Investigating motivation and gaming experience. *Entertainment Computing, 1*(2), 49–61.

Randall, D. (2011). All in the game: Families, peer groups and game playing in the home. In R. Harper (Ed.), *The connected home: The future of domestic life* (pp. 111–131), London, United Kingdom: Springer.

Ravaja, N., Saari, T., Turpeinen, M., Laarni, J., Slaminen, M., and Kivikangas, M. (2006). Spatial presence and emotions during video game playing: Does it matter with whom you play? *Presence, 15*(4), 327–333.

Salen, K. and Zimmerman, E. (2003). *Rules of play: Game design fundamentals.* Cambridge, MA: MIT Press.

Sall, A., and Grinter, A. E. (2007). Let's get physical! In, out and around the gaming circle of physical gaming at home. *Computer Supported Cooperative Work, 16*(1–2), 199–229.

Schott, G., and Kambouri, M. (2003). Moving between the spectral and material plane: Interactivity in social play with computer games. *Convergence, 9*(3), 41–55.

Seigel, S., Haddock, B. L., Wikin, L. D., and Brock, J. A. (2008). Energy expenditure in overweight youth using active video games versus a straight stationary bike protocol. *Medicine and Science in Sports and Exercise, 40*(5) Supplement, S460.

Shie, K.-F., and Cheng, M.-S. (2007). An empirical study of experiential value and lifestyles and their effects on satisfaction in adolescents: An example using online gaming. *Adolescence, 52*(165), 199–216.

Staiano, A. E., and Calvert, S. L. (2011). Exergames for physical education courses: Physical, social, and cognitive benefits. *Child Development Perspectives, 5*(2), 93–98.

Szentgyorgy, C., Terry, M., and Lank, E. (2008). Renegade gaming: Practices surrounding social use of the Nintendo DS handheld gaming system. *Proceedings of the CHI 2008 "Works in Progress" Conference* (pp. 1463–1472). New York, NY: ACM Press.

Tan, B., Aziz, A. R., Chua, K., and Teh, K. C. (2002). Aerobic demands of the dance simulation game. *International Journal of Sports Medicine, 23*(2), 125–129.

Unnithan, V. B., Houser, W., and Fernhall, B. (2006). Evaluation of the energy cost of playing a dance simulation video game in overweight and non-overweight children and adolescents. *International Journal of Sports Medicine, 27*(10), 804–809.

Vogelgesang, W. (2003). LAN-Partys: Jugendkulturelle Erlebnisräume zwischen Off- und Online. *Medien und Erziehung, 47*(5), 65–75.

Voida, A., Carpendale, S., and Greenberg, S. (2010). The individual and the group in console gaming. *Proceedings of the 2010 ACM Conference on Computer Supported Cooperative Work* (pp. 371–380). New York, NY: ACM Press.

Voida, A., and Greenberg, S. (2009). Wii all play: The console game as a computational meeting place. *Proceedings of the 27th International Conference on Human Factors in Computing Systems* (pp. 371–380). New York, NY: ACM Press.

Voida, A., and Greenberg, S. (2012). Console gaming across generations: Exploring intergenerational interactions in collocated console gaming. *Universal Access in the Information Society, 11*(1), 45–56.

Wetzsteon, R. J., Swanson, K. S., Pickett, K., Golner, S., Stovitz, S. D., and Petit, M. A. (2006). Energy expenditure and ground reaction forces of an active video game, *Dance Dance Revolution*, in healthy weight and overweight children. *Medicine and Science in Sports and Exercise, 38*(5) Supplement, S255.

Wollersheim, D., Merkes, M., Shields, N., Liamputtong, P., Wallis, L., Reynolds, F., and Koh, L. (2010). Physical and psychosocial effects of Wii video game use among older women. *International Journal of Emerging Technologies and Society, 8*(2), 85–98.

Xu, Y., Gandy, M., Deen, S., Schrank, B., Spreen, K., Gorbsky, M., White, T., Barba, E., Radu, J., Bolter, J., and MacIntyre, B. (2008). BragFish: Exploring physical and social interaction in co-located handheld augmented reality games. *Proceedings of the 2008 International Conference on Advances in Computer Entertainment Technology* (pp. 238–276). New York, NY: ACM Press.

Yee, N. (2006). The psychology of massively multi-user online role-playing games: Motivations, emotional investment, relationships and problematic usage. In R. Schroeder and A.-S. Axelsson (Eds.), *Avatars at work and play: Collaboration and interaction in shared virtual environments* (pp. 187–207), Dordrecht, The Netherlands: Springer.

Younbo, J., Koay, J. L., Ng, S. J., Wong, L. C. G., and Kwan, M. L. (2009). Games for a better life: Effects of playing Wii games on the well-being of seniors in a long-term care facility. *Proceedings of the Sixth Australasian Conference on Interactive Entertainment* (pp. 1–6). New York, NY: ACM Press.

Games Cited

Blizzard Entertainment (2004), *World of Warcraft*, Vivendi Activision Blizzard.
Sony Computer Entertainment (2004). *SingStar*, SCE London Studio.

13 Family and Games

Digital Game Playing in the Social Context of the Family

Lina Eklund

Introduction

In the information age (Castells, 1996) of today, we see a restructuring of social structures and identities (Giddens, 1990). The family is one such changing social context, and even though changing family structures are one of the hallmarks of contemporary life, we still rely on the family for emotionally satisfactory lives. Family is still the most important social context we have for support and psychosocial well-being (Cherlin, 1999). In the public debate on digital games, the focus is often placed on the problems that they pose for family life (Bergmark and Bergmark, 2009). In Sweden, parents worry about digital games (Brun, 2005) and tend to heavily control this activity for adolescents in the home (Eklund and Bergmark, 2013), but at the same time the understanding of the activity is low (ibid.; Linderoth and Bennerstedt, 2007). This chapter aims to examine the patterns of social play and experiences when gaming with family members. The focus is on people who play games, therefore offering a new perspective on family life and digital games. The main research question concerns what the role of digital gaming in family interaction and relationships is for people engaged in gaming.

Computer and video games form a part of our technologically mediated culture. These digital games have gone from being a marginal pastime to being part of our general culture (Shaw, 2010), and gaming is spreading to new age groups and social groups (Juul, 2010). In the past, as new culture forms spread they changed our lives; books, TV, video, and the Internet, all of these affected the ways in which we live and interact with one another (Castells, 1996). Since the mid-1990s, digital games have grown exponentially and today we have passed a benchmark where more than 50% of the population in the Western world plays these games; therefore, our idea of who plays digital games has been revised (Juul, 2010). For example, statistics from the American market show that the average gamer is 34 years old and that "Women age 18 or older represent a significantly greater portion of the game-playing population (37%) than boys age 17 or younger (13%)" (ESA, 2011, p. 3). Previous research on gaming has shown that social aspects of both online and offline digital gaming are important for players. Many play with family or with friends that they know from outside the game (Cole and Griffiths, 2007) and gaming can strengthen social bonds within families (Durkin and Barber, 2002). In a study by Shen and Williams (2011), families playing online games together were shown to increase the amount of time spent together. At the same time, digital gaming is said to both hamper offline social relations due to time displacement and lead to conflicts in families over time usage (Brun, 2005).

This study builds on data consisting of face-to-face focus group, pair, and single interviews carried out in Sweden between 2009 and 2011. The interviews were held to investigate social gaming habits, and in analyzing the material, it soon became apparent that gaming with family members was an important aspect of social gaming. A comparative sampling method was used, as interviewing several groups (men, women, older/younger adults, couples, parents, and adult children) offers more detailed insight (Glaser and Strauss, 1967). While the samples aimed at capturing a broad selection of game users, the purpose is not to generalize the results, but rather to give insight into the subject at hand. Questions were put to a total of 33 participants in interviews lasting from 45 minutes up to 1 hour 30 minutes. Sampling was done in the sixth form (ages 17–20) of an upper secondary school in the Stockholm area. Participants were made up of people who responded to two advertisements: one was posted at Stockholm University (ages 24–39), and the other on the project website, yielding one pair for the interview (aged 17 and 49).

All interviews—group, pair, and individual—followed the same setup and theme, and the same questions were asked; broad and open questions about social digital-gaming experiences and habits were asked in the style of in-depth interviewing or open-structure interviewing (Hayes, 2000). In conjunction with all interviews, a short questionnaire was handed out to gather additional information, as an extended focus group (Berg, 2009). Interviews were recorded and transcribed in full and all quotes were translated by the author. Data were analyzed using thematic qualitative analysis (Boyatzis, 1998). The data were structured around themes emerging from the interview transcriptions—here, the respondents' experiences of family-based gaming.

Playing Games With Family

Playing digital games with family members varies in both context and scope; however, the importance of digital gaming for family social life is consistent within this group. For some of the informants, gaming is a way of spending time with siblings, a joint interest, and an activity shared while growing up, which has continued even after moving away from home. For others it is a way for the entire family to spend time together.

Among the interviewees, gaming functions as a shared hobby, a common interest bringing family members together. As an example, Veronika (17) and Lotta (49), mother and daughter, play the online game *World of Warcraft* (Blizzard Entertainment, 2004, *WoW*) together. On a normal evening, they spend at least a couple of hours playing the game and they have done so for several years. This joint activity is a way for them to spend time together and share the same frame of reference. Furthermore, they participate in offline events; in 2008, they went to Paris on a "World Wide Invitation" to spend several days doing game-related activities. When describing the significance gaming has had for them, they say:

LOTTA (49): Yes of course we spend a lot more time together than we
    would have done otherwise {Veronika: yes} I'm sure about that.
VERONIKA (17): The same with talking, too.

The game has an important role in Lotta and Veronika's relationship, a common interest that brings them closer together.

Gaming is often an activity shared with siblings when growing up. Helen (19) plays games together with her brothers and gaming has always been important in her family, from watching her father and uncle play as a child, to visiting gaming cafés with her brothers before they had a computer at home. Stefan (17) and Peter (17), two twin brothers still living with their parents, tell me they often play the same game on a console, together, but also play the same game on different computers and then compare their playing experiences, both in a competitive way and to provide mutual assistance. To talk about games is an important part of the gaming experience for all of the informants; the experience of the game becomes heightened when telling others about it. Discussing it is part of the pleasure, as Peter explains:

PETER (17): For example, telling someone "oh shit, I did the
    coolest thing in *Age of Empires* [Ensemble Studios, 1997]" that
    might not be the first thing I thought at the moment but that's
    what's important in the end.
STEFAN (17): Yeah, it fills a social function.

For Maria (18) games are important for her relationship with her parents and foremost with her mother, who recently passed away.

MARIA (18): I feel that I have a very close relationship with both
    my parents. They are in fact two of my best friends.

They have played a multitude of games over the years, especially during the period before Maria's mother passed away when games were very important. Each day they played *WoW* (Blizzard Entertainment, 2004); the game was a way for them to spend time together and do something together, even though Maria's mother was ill; a collaborative escapism during a very emotionally taxing time. Today she still uses one of her mother's old game characters. Doing so keeps the memory of their joint experiences alive.

Playing games together creates a shared space for the family members to interact around a joint activity and this aspect is persistent in all of the interviews.

Gaming as Doing

Sara (36) and Ulf (39) are a married couple living together with their daughter and Sara's son from a previous marriage. They play an online game together on a daily basis; it is a shared activity for them. They explain that they value an active life, and are engaged in both political and union activities. Playing games in their free time is a way of doing something together in the family; watching TV, for example, they see as too pacifying. Gaming together is a way for them to share everyday life within the family. The informants in general push for the specific character of games in relation to other media; the recurring word used is *active*.

MATTHIAS (25): [Gaming is] a different kind of culture and escapism
    like watching a movie or reading a book or something, but
    more active, you are more there.

Although games are compared to other entertainment media, such as TV, digital games have their own specific characteristics. You cannot passively consume the games, as without input actions from the gamer, the game will not progress, and the story will not be told, as the gamer needs to control the situation; games are interactive (Salen and Zimmerman, 2004). This is something that gamers are aware of and discuss, as in the quote below.

TYRA (24): Games, unlike films, are something where you have
    performed, you have completed a game.
NINA (18): Maybe you could replace some of it with books but it
    is not as involving, there aren't as strong emotions involved
    "Yeah, I killed the boss!"
HELEN (19): Exactly.

After completing a game or overcoming a challenge, gamers are proud of what they have accomplished. Games are rewarding; challenges encourage gamers to invest in the situation and to relish victories over these challenges (Juul, 2005). The interactive aspects of games make them enjoyable and linked to the specific aspects of digital games as *games*.

The "social design" of games makes it possible and fun to play them with others and therein lies some of the charm of the activity. Gaming, for many of the informants, is foremost a social activity; some never play alone. The social aspects of gaming also transcend the actual gaming moment. Once a gaming session, single or multiplayer, is over, you talk, evaluate, brag, and compare your experiences, and this is an important part of gaming. Jonas (25) explains that games are bonding experiences and that is why it is fun to talk about games:

JONAS (25): You do something active yourself so it ends up a
    little in the same category as an experience you have had in

```
your everyday life, IRL [in real life] experiences, but at the
same time there are others who have had the same experiences.
But it's a very special shared experience and it matters, you
can bond quite a lot over it.
```

Offering shared points of reference is something other media types do; see, for example, tabloid reading (Johansson, 2006). However, gaming is something you actively participate in together with others. In social gaming, you *do* something *together* with others.

Gaming Online, Keeping Family Close

The informants claim that one reason digital games are well suited for social play is that online gaming, in particular, makes performing a joint activity easy. Time constraints in ordinary life are a prominent factor, and a perceived lack of time is worked around through the use of computer-mediated communication (CMC). In an interview, Matthias (25) discusses how it is easy to meet with your friends by playing a game online; instead of trying to get everyone together, you can log onto a game and turn on a voice chat program. A group of friends and partners, playing WoW (Blizzard Entertainment, 2004), agree that without the game they would not have been friends today; even though they met through contexts unconnected to the game. The game has been the factor that kept them together.

```
RITA (26):  I don't think we would be sitting here today without
    World of Warcraft.
LOUISE (23): No, I do not think so either.
LUKE (27):  Probably not.
```

Even though they all live within walking distance and regularly meet each other physically, the game is a central point of focus. The game is a common reference, and through a voice chat program they "hang out," talking on a daily basis; often they use the game and chat channel to organize spontaneous eating out. However, they all believe that it had not been enough just to chat; the game in itself is important. For this group, the game functions as a socially cohesive marker, keeping them in contact and in the same frame of reference. Playing online is easy and provides a shared social setting for the involved, something which gives a ground for sociality.

Helen (19), whose parents separated recently, now lives with her mother. She plays backgammon with her father over the Internet during weekdays as a way to spend time together when they do not have time to meet face-to-face.

```
HELEN (19): Now that we're not living together it is a great way
    to socialize, to play some backgammon through the net.
```

NINA (18): Yeah, in your case, it's easier to find the time to play
    some backgammon, than "Hey let's get together and have dinner
    or a coffee". "No I can't that day." And so on. You can always
    squeeze in something like that.
ANNIKA (19): Just sit down in front of the computer.

When time is limited, CMC in games facilitates continuous interaction, a continuity of association. Something leisure activities in general can provide following divorce (Kelly, 1983). Other informants also participate in these types of games over the Internet. Nina (18) plays *Betapet* (Betapet, 2003), an online version of Scrabble, with her boyfriend in the evenings, since they do not live together. They normally talk on the phone at the same time but the game offers them something to do as they talk. Another informant, Kristoffer (34), plays over the Internet with his two brothers.

KRISTOFFER (34): I play a lot with my brothers, I mean I see them
    normally anyway but it is very fun to sit with your headset
    and talk with them and you talk about all sorts of things as
    well [besides the game].

Playing over the Internet is easy to set up and offers the participants a joint activity at the same time as them being able to spend time with each other.

Gaming as a Marginalized Activity

Games can, on the other hand, also be a source for conflict in a family. As gaming often takes up a considerable amount of time, parents or siblings not playing themselves can object to the activity. The time gaming takes and the "newness" of the media are prominent features in this. Games in their very form are difficult to understand if you do not participate in them, whereas other more established media, such as TV, are more immediately accessible just by observing.

MIKE (17): Often it's older people that complain about computer
    games because they aren't informed, it can be sports jocks
    at school, or parents, or even grandparents, but it feels
    like it's always like this when something new comes, people
    complained about comics for making you stupid.

Playing games is still perceived as a marginal activity by many and is therefore hard to relate to, especially when gamers play online and create alternative social networks. Seeking online social contact can, however, be the result of existing conflicts within the family rather than the cause of conflict. Diana (25) is the only one of the informants to have experienced a serious conflict over gaming in the family. When she was a teenager, her father had problems with alcohol and the family in general could be described as dysfunctional, at that time. In the interview, Diana (25) discussed the fact that, at this point, she did not have many friends and so spent a lot of time playing an online game, *Ragnarok Online* (Gravity Co., 2002). Her best online friend was from Australia so she spent her nights playing with him. Her father disapproved of this activity and this in the end led to her being thrown out of her home. She explains that this was resolved and now she lives with her parents again, although she is looking for a place of her own. She still plays games and her family has reconciled themselves with her interest, as she now works with digital games. For Diana, gaming was a way of creating a space of her own in a stressful situation, though this also became something that aggravated the situation.

The relative novelty of the media results in informants engaging in situations where they have to defend their activity to people who do not play. Every now and then, groups, activities, conditions, and so on crystallize in society and media as deviant. Gaming is by far neither the first nor the last activity to be treated as a threat to societal values and interests, but rather follows a long tradition of what have been called moral panics (Cohen, 1980). As gaming permeates media awareness in a more general sense, which is definitely happening, we should expect the understanding of this activity to increase. What is worth pointing out is also the immense changes this medium is still undergoing as it finds its form; an example of one such change over the last ten years is the support most games today have for social play.

Concluding Discussion

For most of these informants, playing games with family members is an important part of their gaming habits. The support for CMC offers opportunities for joint activities over time/space boundaries, and gaming can function as a mutual interest and/or hobby for the gamers, creating shared frames of reference. Digital games facilitate spending time together in some instances and also increase the perceived quality of the family members' relationships. Games, as a shared activity, can also support families in difficult times, offering the opportunity for "collaborative escapism." At the same time, the informants say that gaming is often considered as a "strange" and anti-social leisure activity, even though digital gaming is an activity that is becoming part of our mainstream culture, seeping into a "general" consciousness.

For the informants, gaming is a multifaceted activity where the social aspect plays a major role. Gaming experiences improve when playing with others; this is something the informants agree upon, or as Stefan (17) expresses it: "So like they say: A shared pleasure is a double pleasure." However, it is not just that they can play together; the social experience of the game transcends the actual game situation and creates a common ground of experience and contexts for the gamers.

```
LUKE (28):  It's this that you do something together [while playing].
   It is not just talking, then I might as well phone someone.
LOUISE (23):  But then maybe it is to have shared frames of refer-
   ence. Like have a common language.
```

In the sample, gamers share the idea of what constitutes "good" gaming, where playing games with your family comes first, friends second, then Internet friends, and last comes strangers you meet online. Gaming is placed in a discourse where it is more highly valued when performed together with others, and the closer the relationship with these others, the better. Oldenburg claims that social interaction in general benefits from two components: sociality and activity (1999, p. 47); this is clear in the case of gaming. We enhance the activities by increasing activity or social involvement. Gaming in this light has much in common with "traditional" leisure activities, where the focus is on *doing* something *together* with significant others.

The informants emphasize digital games as social facilitators, offering arenas for joint activity, while adding continuity to relationships with family members, those both close and geographically separated. In a study of family leisure, the authors conclude that leisure activities that are unique, shared, interactive, purposive, challenging, and requiring sacrifice have the capacity to deepen family relationships and cohesiveness (Palmer, Freeman, and Zabriskie, 2007). Common in the gamers' stories is how gaming is used to extend time together with family members who they meet often in other settings. Gaming is not performed *instead of* other activities, but rather to *complement* them. Gaming together with family members is about a creation of shared experiences, of a sense of belonging together. Moreover, digital gaming makes this play community wider in both time and space, re-embedding both activity and relationships in new space/time constellations. We can share this feeling of togetherness with loved ones not present, or with people we have never, and will never meet face-to-face. Today, due to new relationships across time and space, we are more spread out geographically (Giddens, 1990); we often live apart from family and friends. By using games and CMC, people find ways of linking these new time and space combinations. Online games have been said to overcome spatial and temporal constraints, thereby becoming "third places," places for informal social interaction (Ducheneaut, Moore, and Nickell, 2007; Steinkuehler and Williams, 2006).

The form of the medium (McLuhan, 1964) says more about its societal influence than the content of the medium. It was the form of TV as a mass communication medium that changed how we accessed information, not foremost the content of different programs—as McLuhan expressed it, "the medium is the message." While research on digital gaming often focuses on the content of different games, this study shows how the form of the medium offers certain opportunities to the users. As social gaming combines doing with socializing, the shape and opportunities of this particular medium become clear. The fact that games entail aspects of activity, the pleasure of participating in something together with others, and that sometimes support CMC gives games the unique position which these gamers ascribe to them, is undoubtedly responsible, in part, for the success of digital games in recent years. Gaming with family members might share many of the same functions/roles that other leisure activities do; however, starting up a game takes little time and does not require vast amounts of space, although certain economic resources are needed. Gaming is an activity that can be performed together while occupying different physical locations; this gives digital games a unique form. As the informants describe their gaming, the image of a multifaceted activity emerges with different meanings depending on the social context of use.

References

Berg, B. L. (2009). *Qualitative research methods for the social sciences* (6th ed.). Boston, MA: Pearson Education.

Bergmark, K. H., and Bergmark, A. (2009). The diffusion of addiction to the field of MMORPGs. *Nordisk Alkohol- och Narkotikatidskrift*, 26(4), 415–426.

Boyatzis, R. E. (1998). *Transforming qualitative information: Thematic analysis and code development.* Thousand Oaks, CA: SAGE Publications.

Brun, M. (2005). *När livet blir ett spel och andra utmaningar för den digitala generationens föräldrar* [When life becomes a game and other challenges for the digital generation of parents]. Lidingö, Sweden: Langenskiöld.

Castells, M. (1996). *The information age: Economy, society and culture. Volume 1. The rise of the network society.* Oxford, UK: Blackwell Publisher.

Cherlin, A. J. (1999). *Public and private families: An introduction* (2nd ed.). Boston, MA: McGraw-Hill.

Cohen, S. (1980). *Folk devils and moral panics: The creation of the mods and rockers.* Oxford: Basil Blackwell.

Cole, H., and Griffiths, M. D. (2007). Social interactions in massively multiplayer online role-playing gamers. *CyberPsychology and Behavior*, 10(4), 575–583.

Ducheneaut, N., Moore, R. J., and Nickell E. (2007). Virtual "third places": A case study of sociability in massively multiplayer games. *Computer Supported Cooperative Work*, 16(1–2), 129–166.

Durkin, K., and Barber, B. (2002). Not so doomed: Computer game play and positive adolescent development. *Journal of Applied Developmental Psychology*, 23(4), 373–92.

Eklund, L., and Helmersson Bergmark, K. (2013). Parental mediation of digital gaming and internet use. In *FDG 2013: The 8th International Conference on the Foundations of Digital Games* (pp. 63–70). Retrieved from http://www.fdg2013.org/program/papers/paper09_eklund_bergmark.pdf

Entertainment Software Association (Ed.). (2011). *2011 Sales, demographic and usage data: Essential facts about the computer and video games industry.* Retrieved from www.theesa.com.

Giddens, A. (1990). *The consequences of modernity.* Palo Alto, CA: Stanford University Press.

Glaser, B. G., and Strauss, A. L. (1967). In N. K. Denzin (Ed.), *Sociological methods. A sourcebook* (pp. 105–114). Chicago, IL: Aldine.

Hayes, N. (2000). *Doing psychological research.* Maidenhead, UK: Open University Press.

Johansson, S. (2006). "Sometimes you wanna hate celebrities": Tabloid readers and celebrity coverage. In S. Holmes and S. Redmond (Eds.), *Framing celebrity: New directions in celebrity culture* (pp. 343–358). New York City, NY: Routledge.

Juul, J. (2005). *Half-real: Video games between real rules and fictional worlds.* Cambridge, MA: MIT Press.

Juul, J. (2010). *A casual revolution: Reinventing video games and their players.* London, UK: MIT Press.

Kelly, J. R. (1983). *Leisure, identities and interactions.* London, UK: George Allen & Unwin Publishers.

Linderoth, J., and Bennerstedt, U. (2007). *Living in World of Warcraft – the thoughts and experiences of ten young people.* Stockholm, Sweden: The Swedish Media Council.

McLuhan, M. (1964). *Understanding media: The extensions of man.* New York City, NY: McGraw Hill.

Oldenburg, R. (1999). *The great good place: Cafés, coffee shops, bookstores, bars, hair salons and other hangouts at the heart of a community.* Philadelphia, PA: Da Capo Press.

Palmer, A. A., Freeman, P. A., and Zabriskie, R. B. (2007). Family deepening: A qualitative inquiry into the experience of families who participate in service expeditions. *Journal of Leisure Research, 39*(3), 438–458.

Salen, K., and Zimmerman, E. (2004). *Rules of play: Game design fundamentals.* Cambridge, MA: MIT Press.

Shaw, A. (2010). What is video game culture? Cultural studies and game studies. *Games and Culture, 5*(4), 403–424.

Shen, C., and Williams, D. (2011). Unpacking time online: Connecting Internet and massively multiplayer online game use with psychosocial well-being. *Communication Research, 38*(1), 123–149.

Steinkuehler, C. A., and Williams, D. (2006). Where everybody knows your (screen) name: Online games as "third places". *Journal of Computer-Mediated Communication, 11*(4), 1–26.

Games Cited

Betapet (2003), *Betapet*, ValuSoft, Inc.

Blizzard Entertainment (2004), *World of Warcraft*, Vivendi Activision Blizzard.

Ensemble Studios (1997), *Age of Empires*, Microsoft.

Gravity Co. Ltd (2002), *Ragnarok Online*, Burda:ic GmbH.

14 Playing to Win?

Measuring the Correlation Between Biometric Responses and Social Interaction in Co-Located Social Gaming

Steve Bromley, Pejman Mirza-Babaei,
Graham McAllister, and Jonathan Napier

Introduction

The importance of defining and measuring social interaction is fundamental to current games research, as has been demonstrated by the prominence of conferences and publications in this field, and the continued success of casual "co-located" games.

Voida et al. presented the definition for six key types of behavior that emerged during social gaming sessions (Voida, Carpendale, and Greenberg, 2010), and we note that their work paves the way for future research to examine the causal relationship between game dynamics and social interaction. Hence, there is the potential to develop the research of Voida et al. in defining social interaction in co-located gamers, and to identify which behaviors cause positive reactions in gamers in order to optimize these gameplay experiences.

This chapter presents two contributions. It demonstrates an iteration of pre-existing work on defining social interaction, tailored to a specific genre of interest, that of commercial games development. The second aim of this chapter is to utilize this iteration of social-interaction research and demonstrate a practical methodology that is useful for industry.

In order to give this study relevance to industry, prior to conducting this study, interviews were conducted with eight employees of Relentless Software (a game development company specializing in co-located social games). These interviews focused on play testing during development, the limitations of existing methodologies, and the aspects of player behavior that Relentless Software wanted to increase their understanding of through-play testing.

The interviews and an iterative development process gave insight into how social interaction is of interest to games development, which influenced the adaption of Voida et al.'s behaviors for this study. The revised categories are displayed in Table 14.1.

This chapter details a practical methodology, useful for industry in measuring social interaction and its effect during gameplay. This approach concurrently records biometric responses alongside a chronological record of verbal interaction, and applies this to a social gaming setting. This achieves a greater understanding of how a player's inherent motivations are linked to social interaction during co-located, multiplayer gaming.

This chapter develops the work by Voida et al. on social interaction among various player types, and also provides a greater understanding of a player's intrinsic motivations, aligning with those discussed by Bartle (Bartle, 2004). The method described in this research allows a greater degree of insight into the reception of a game from the earliest possible play sessions, and allows developers to tailor their games to meet the desires of specific demographics.

Existing Research

Social Interaction

Voida et al. (2010) made significant advances in defining six key types of behavior displayed in co-located gaming sessions, through a review of player behavior during multiplayer games such as *Guitar Hero* (Harmonix, 2005) and *Mario Party* (Hudson Soft, 1998). Through running a number of co-located gaming sessions, they identified behaviors that related to, or altered the social dynamics of the group. These key forms of interaction were utilized for this study, as the basis for coding social interaction.

Based on an iterative test and evaluation process performed with Relentless Software and the interviews with the development team, Voida et al.'s categories were revised, and are described in Table 14.1. In addition to these categories, a pilot study implied that a final category would be required, "off topic," to capture any interaction that was non-game-related.

Biometrics

Biometrics (physiological measurements) is the practice of using sensors attached to the user's body to monitor bodily data including arousal and valence. Biometrics are now being integrated into game research (Drachen, Nacke, Yannakakis, and Pedersen, 2010; Nacke, 2011; Mirza-Babaei et al., 2012) and game development in the game industry (Ambinder, 2011). Common physiological measures include galvanic skin response (GSR), facial muscle measures, cardiac interbeat intervals, and electroencephalography (Kivikangas et al., 2011). Common approaches distinguish physiological analysis on a temporal dimension: studying phasic psychophysiological and behavioral responses at game events (points in time) (Ravaja, Turpeinen, Saari, Puttonen, and Keltikangas-Järvinen, 2008) and studying tonic responses to variations in the in-game variables (time span) (Mandryk and Atkins, 2007).

Table 14.1   Voida et al.'s Categories of Social Interaction Behavior and the Adapted Categories Used in This Study

Category by Voida et al.	Revised social interaction category	Description
Constructing shared awareness	Shared awareness	• Building a shared awareness of the game state • Collaborative problem solving • Reporting own status
	Requesting information	• Querying game or player status
Reinforcing shared history	Shared history	• Discussing prior game events
Sharing in success and failure	Shared success	• Celebrating group or individual success
	Shared failure	• Recognizing group responsibility for failure • Commiseration with a player
Engaging in interdependence and self-sacrifice	Team optimization	• Discussing group dynamics, roles or contributions
Talking trash	Trash talk	• Celebration of one's own success • Mocking another player's failure
Falling prey to the computer's holding power	Self-indulgence	• Not observing the game's rules • Distracted by objectives not recognized by the team

Generally, researchers using biometric approaches may find it difficult to match the data to the player's emotional experience. The many-to-one relationship between psychological processing and physiological response makes it difficult to interpret change in a player's biometric reaction to a particular emotion (Cacioppo, Tassinary, and Berntson, 2007); therefore, researchers utilize biometric measures in conjunction with other user-research methods to assist in the interpretation of the measures. For example, researchers have developed techniques for effective, post-session interview video playback, the benefits and challenges of which have been discussed by Mirza-Babaei, Long, Foley, and McAllister (2011).

In this chapter, we follow a similar approach to the analysis of a player's biometric measurements at game events (points in time) with post-session interviews to interpret the physiological measurements.

Player Profiling

An initial series of pilot studies, prior to the research, demonstrated that a player's reactions to events were not uniform. Hence, we required a method of classifying players to generalize their reactions.

Bartle's Test of Gamer Psychology was created by Erwin Andreasen and Brandon Downey (Andreasen and Downey, 2003) based on Bartle's (Bartle, 2004) research. The test presents 30 dichotomous questions centered on each player's intrinsic motivation in online games, and aims to categorize players into four groups, as below:

- Killers (Clubs)
  Killers are interested in combat/competition with other human players, and prefer this over interaction with non-player characters.

- Achievers (Diamonds)
  Achievers are most interested in gaining points or alternative in-game measurements of success. These players will often go out of their way to gain items that have no in-game benefit besides prestige, such as "achievements."

- Explorers (Spades)
  These players are interested in discovering the breadth of a game, and will explore new areas or take non-optimal routes to explore.

- Socializers (Hearts)
  These players are interested in the social aspect of gameplay, rather than the game itself. They enjoy interacting with other players, and use the game primarily as a means of communication.

Through analyzing players based on their type, this study captured and represented players' motivations while playing games, and discovered how this affected the types of social interaction evident during gameplay.

Methodology Development

The two-year iterative prototyping process with Relentless Software allowed for the creation of a methodology to reflect the industry's require-ments. The data for the final study was collected over a two-week period, comprising eight paired play sessions, with 16 participants in total. Each play session lasted up to 30 minutes, and consisted of a round of gameplay.

The Tool

In order to effectively capture verbal-interaction data, a custom tool was created to record social interaction noted during play sessions (Bromley, 2012).

The tool combines timer controls with the ability to turn on and off each form of verbal interaction, and it exports timelines detailing when each form of social interaction occurred during the play session (Figure 14.1). During play sessions, the researcher was able to note any verbal interaction between the players and classified it within the revised categories using this tool.

The Games

Buzz! Quiz World (Relentless Software, 2009) was chosen as the game for the final study, as the game is designed based on provoking social interaction. The game takes the form of a multiplayer trivia quiz, lasting up to 30 minutes, where each player is given multiple-choice questions to answer, using a custom controller that allows for the quick selection of the player's choice. One player is declared as the winner.

By putting the players into direct competition, the pilot study implied that *Buzz! Quiz World* would create a diverse range of interaction, and would allow a qualitative evaluation of the differences between different player types. As a trivia game, it also relied little on manual dexterity, and hence would minimize any bias as a result of a player's previous experience with the game, reducing variables in the study. The simple game controller allows gameplay to be performed with only one hand, ensuring that the GSR signal suffered minimal disruption from the player's hand movement.

Figure 14.1   The Social-Interaction Recording Tool. (Redrawn from author's original.)

The Study

Players

In order to ensure that the study recreated authentic social interaction, as would be found in a typical co-located gaming session, pairs of players from pre-existing social groups were recruited.

Prior to each session, each player undertook an online adaption of the Bartle test, with their player "type" being noted. This was performed independently of the researchers, who were unaware of each player's assigned type during the sessions and while categorizing the social interaction, to prevent bias.

Study Design

The players (Table 14.2) were required to play one game of *Buzz! Quiz World*, which comprised six rounds, lasting up to 30 minutes.

The game footage, the camera recording of the player's face, and the screen containing the physiological data (GSR in this study) were synchronized into a single screen recorded for analysis. GSRs were gathered using the BIOPAC hardware system, sensors, and software from BIOPAC Systems by using two passive SS3LA BIOPAC electrodes.

During the play session, the researcher noted any verbal interaction between the players and categorized it within the revised categories, using the tool described earlier.

After the gameplay session, participants were asked to perform an unguided review of the "player experience" of the session. To evaluate this, they were given graph paper with the x-axis indicated as time, and the y-axis as "player experience." Participants were then asked to plot their experience over time and their own recollection of their feelings, as demonstrated in Figure 14.2.

Table 14.2 Session Data Showing the Players in Each Session

Alias Player 1	Category Player 1	Alias Player 2	Category Player 2
Adrian	Achiever	Brian	Killer
Gertrude	Achiever	Harold	Explorer
Ian	Achiever	James	Socializer
Edward	Explorer	Francesca	Explorer
Charlie	Killer	Dylan	Killer
Kieran	Killer	Lauren	Achiever
Matthew	Killer	Norbert	Explorer
Olga	Killer	Patrick	Socializer

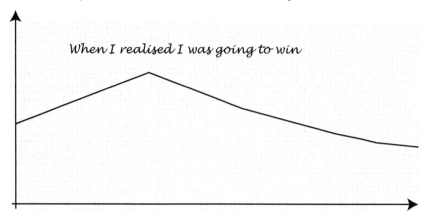

Figure 14.2 A Killer's Self-Assessment Graph (Dylan). (Redrawn from author's original.)

In this study, a lightweight biometric method was applied, which did not attempt to interpret player emotion. This used measures of a player's phasic GSR purely to identify "events" with a stronger effect on a player's feelings on a per-individual basis. After plotting their experience, the video footage related to the players' gameplay was played back to the participants, who were asked to recall these specific moments and inform the experimenter of their thoughts.

There were a number of reasons for choosing this methodology as an appropriate way to gain insight into the player's experiences while playing the game. Players were required to watch the entire session to give them the context in which these events happened, and allow them to verbally feed-back a truer understanding of what they were thinking at that time.

After the sessions, the social-interaction data was analyzed quantitatively to gain an understanding of the characteristics of each player type. This was then triangulated with qualitative data, gained through the user's self-evaluation, and the biometric-led, post-session interviews to give a depth of understanding to the data, and explain *why* players acted the way they did.

Results

As implied by the pilot study, it was found that the player's behavior fell into four main categories. Within each of these groups, it was noted that the player's self-expressed motivation, biometric "peaks," and social inter-action closely aligned, implying that players within each category shared characteristics during social gaming sessions.

Table 14.3 shows the extent to which each form of interaction was noted during the gameplay. By triangulating these quantitative studies with the qualitative data, it is possible to see patterns in the biometric and interaction data when the players are divided into their player "type" categories.

Table 14.3 Table Showing the Percentage of the Session's Total Interactions in Which Each Type of Social Interaction Was Noted

Session	Player 1	Player 2	Percentage of total interaction in the session							
			Shared awareness	Shared history	Shared failure	Requesting information	Trash talk	Shared success	Off topic	Self-indulgence
1	Achiever	Killer	13	28	13	9	23	8	2	4
2	Achiever	Explorer	26	24	15	19	11	5	–	–
3	Achiever	Socializer	28	15	15	10	6	26	–	–
4	Explorer	Explorer	7	34	15	20	13	10	2	–
5	Killer	Killer	4	24	18	16	27	9	2	–
6	Killer	Achiever	45	15	23	15	–	–	4	–
7	Killer	Explorer	60	5	18	3	5	9	–	–
8	Killer	Socializer	42	18	15	10	10	5	–	–
Total percentage of each interaction			28	20	18	13	12	9	1	0.5

Killers

As is evident in Table 14.3, games that involved killers showed a much higher degree of "trash talk" interaction than games without killers. This trend is particularly evident in the game with two killers playing one another, which was the game with the highest degree of trash talk.

These games had the highest occurrence of "shared failure," behavior that indicated discussing and taking shared responsibility for failure in a round, or getting questions wrong.

This data was supplemented by an understanding of the in-game actions and interactions that led to strong GSR peaks. It was noted that killer arousal was highest when the game was competitive, and against opponents who were perceived as being of equal skill. When killers became aware that they were going to win, or that the opponent showed little competition, their levels of GSR arousal dropped rapidly.

Achievers

"Shared-history" interactions were most prevalent among groups that included achievers. It was apparent through the achievers' interaction that they were more likely to share their answers in the sessions when they believed they had the correct answer. Despite the advantage this potentially gave to the other players, achievers continued to demonstrate that they knew the correct answers throughout the session. Engagement for achievers was also highest during the explanation of rounds and in-game instructions. The reasons for this are discussed in the concluding section.

Socializers

Games that involved socializers displayed the highest level of shared awareness, where the players would discuss what was happening within the game. Socializers were also the primary cause of the "shared success" behavior type, where successfully answering questions, or winning rounds, resulted in congratulations and joint celebration, even if the player had not personally won.

Like achievers, it was common for socializers to share answers during social gaming sessions. However, it was noted that the nature of this interaction focused on collaboratively working out an answer, rather than on displaying the player's own knowledge.

The use of biometrics and user interviews revealed that during these sessions, socializers did not display strong intrinsic reactions to the progress of the game, whether successful or not. This is distinct from the other player types, where success in a round would typically show a significant biometric reading.

Explorers

Games that featured explorers displayed a greater degree of requesting information. They also displayed the highest degree of the shared-history behavior type, with this behavior being equally prevalent in games featuring explorers and achievers.

Throughout the sessions, explorers displayed minor reactions to events, with slight biometric peaks when being asked challenging questions, or when exploring new topics.

In-game events that led to significant responses involved an increased arousal when players were selecting the round themselves, or when they were being asked new questions on an unfamiliar topic. Unlike players from the other groups, they also displayed an interest in the animations of the player's avatars, and the aesthetics of the game environment.

The concluding section provides some depth on the behavior observed and offers potential explanations for why this is the case.

What Does This Mean for Game Developers?

The results show a correlation between the interactions and biometric results emerging among players who share categories. By combining this with an understanding of player motivation gained from user interviews, profiles have been developed for each "type" of player. This can be applied independently of this method by Relentless Software to develop future games in the same genre.

For killers, it was seen that GSR arousal was highest during these sessions when the competition was perceived as "worthy," and when opponents were close in skill level or points. Arousal sharply dropped when it became obvious that the killer was going to win, and this is very closely reflected in the player's self-assessment graphs, such as in Figure 14.2. Hence, the primary recommendation for targeting games development toward killers would be to use mechanics to ensure that both players always have the chance to win.

The emphasis on trash talk among killers could be developed by in-game mechanics, such as the ability to taunt, as found in other multiplayer games.

Among the achievers who were studied, increased arousal was noted in rounds where there was a visible indication of progress. Achievers requested additional visual displays of progress or ability levels, as evident through Ian's comments suggesting that the audience should be shown to support the players by "shouting their name when players are doing well." Game designers can therefore target achievers by increasing the degree to which progress or success can be displayed during the game, and allow players to display their skill through badges or trophies.

Achievers, such as Adrian and Gertrude, were frequently seen to be answering questions aloud, despite the advantage this gave their opponent. It can be concluded that displaying the breadth of their knowledge is a more important priority to achievers than winning the game.

Socializers were noted as having a low level of arousal toward the progress of the game, and did not show GSR peaks as a result of in-game success. Instead, it was obvious through their interaction data that they were most interested in shared experiences, and hence showed prominent "shared success" interactions.

As noted in the results section, shared awareness was also evident with socializers; however, unlike achievers, the nature of this interaction seemed more collaborative than simply "showing off." As such, it can be recommended that games should give players opportunities to discuss in-game events—this was particularly noted during *Buzz! Quiz World* at the end of the rounds. Additional "down time" to discuss the game would aid in targeting players who display socializer characteristics.

In contrast to other player types, interaction among explorers was largely noted to be cooperative and inquisitive, such as in them describing the animations displayed by the in-game avatars. Their verbal interactions involved them discussing the question's topics or the game's mechanics. As such, the recommendation can be made to target games toward explorers through offering a non-repetitive gaming experience, with a range of forms of interactions and avenues for exploration, such as a variety in the rounds and topics.

The adaption of Voida et al.'s categories into a practical methodology provides the industry with an increased understanding of interaction in their games, which can then be used to inform future iterations of development. In particular, this would be of use for targeting specific player demographics, and reviewing potential game ideas' resonance with these player types.

References

Ambinder, M. (2011). *Biofeedback in gameplay: How valve measures physiology to enhance gaming experience.* Game Developers Conference 2011, San Francisco, CA.

Andreasen, E. S., and Downey, B. A. (2003). *Measuring Bartle-quotient.* Retrieved from http://www.andreasen.org/mud.shtml.

Bartle, R. A. (2004). *Designing virtual worlds.* UK: New Riders.

Bromley, S. (2012). *Capturing fun: Creating a tool to measure social interaction during play testing.* Conference proceedings of the Game User Research Workshop at the CHI 2012, Austin, TX.

Cacioppo, J. T., Tassinary, L. G., and Berntson, G. (2007). *Handbook of psychophysiology* (3rd ed.). New York City, NY: Cambridge University Press.

Drachen, A., Nacke, L. E., Yannakakis, G., and Pedersen, A. L. (2010). *Correlation between heart rate, electrodermal activity and player experience in first-person shooter games.* Presented at the Sandbox 2010.

Kivikangas, J. M., Chanel, G., Cowley, B., Ekman, I., Salminen, M., Jarvela, S., and Ravaja, N. (2011). A review of the use of psychophysiological methods in game research. *Journal of Gaming and Virtual Worlds, 3*(3), 181–199.

Mandryk, R. L., and Atkins, M. S. (2007). A fuzzy physiological approach for continuously modeling emotion during interaction with play technologies. *International Journal of Human-Computer Studies, 65*(4), 329–347.

Mirza-Babaei, P., Long, S., Foley, E., and McAllister, G. (2011). *Understanding the contribution of biometrics to games user research.* Paper presented at the DiGRA 2011, Hilversum, The Netherlands.

Mirza-Babaei, P., Nacke, L. E., Fitzpatrick, G., White, G., McAllister, G., and Collins, N. (2012). *Biometric storyboards: Visualising game user research data.* CHI EA 2012, Austin, TX.

Nacke, L. E. (2011). Proceedings of BBI Workshop at CHI 2011: *Directions in physiological game evaluation and interaction.* Vancouver, Canada.

Ravaja, N., Turpeinen, M., Saari, T., Puttonen, S., and Keltikangas-Järvinen, L. (2008). The psychophysiology of James Bond: Phasic emotional responses to violent video game events. *Emotion, 8*(1), 114–120.

Voida, A., Carpendale, M. S. T., and Greenberg, S. (2010). The individual and the group in console gaming. In: *Proceedings of the 2010 ACM Conference on Computer Supported Cooperative Work* (pp. 371–380). Savannah, Georgia, USA.

Games Cited

Harmonix (2005), *Guitar Hero*, RedOctane.

Hudson Soft (1998), *Mario Party*, Nintendo.

Relentless Software (2009), *Buzz! Quiz World*, Sony.

15 Anything But Speechless

Face-to-Face-Communication During Co-Located Gaming

Judith Ackermann

Introduction

The first digital game, *Tennis for Two*, was designed for two persons, who could navigate it by using separate input controllers. With the technical evolution, the possibilities of playing computer games together have multiplied. They include the shared use of a single-player game, engaging in a multiplayer game using one single technical device (e.g. a games console), participating in co-located multiplayer games realized on many technical devices (e.g. at local-area network (LAN) parties), and engaging in an online multiplayer game, which does not rely on the co-presence of the players, and offers the possibility of playing with people all over the planet. "Video gaming is increasingly a social pastime and social interaction has become an important motive for many players" (Ruggles, Wadley, and Gibbs, 2005, p. 114). The diverse forms of community gaming allow various numbers of possible players and, in combination with that, require different dimensions of organizational effort. While it is rather easy to come together for a dyadic games console match, it is very complicated to find a location and a time and space to gather thousands of gamers and their computers in one place to start a huge LAN event. In addition, the technical affordances of the different multiplayer constellations vary. While the players only have to set up the console and the TV to have a game round with this technical device, a LAN event requires the installation of a LAN, in which all the participating computers are integrated properly, preceding the actual gaming event. As the number of players who participate in the digital game(s) increases, the communication required to coordinate their gaming experience becomes more important and more complex as well.

Communication and Games

Communication is an essential element of gaming—this counts as true for classic, non-media play as well as for digital games. It ensures that the players know that they are part of a game. This is very important as "play behaviors resemble 'serious' behaviors but they do not serve their intended purpose" (Pellegrini and Smith, 2003, p. 277). Play does not come up with innovative actions, but integrates already established ones into the gaming context by disconnecting them from their former goals and meanings. The gaming situation establishes a kind of a quasi-reality (Heckhausen, 1963, p. 226), which allows for the adoption of activities and objects from reality in order to make them playable (Oerter, 1999, p. 9). Even though the players are still part of their surrounding reality, they enter a second, shared reality dimension at the same time. In that way, a game can be seen as a separated activity (Caillois, 1960, p. 16), which takes place in a special frame of time and space that needs to be established by the players. They take part in a fictional activity, but are, at the same time, aware of the fact that they are acting inside a quasi-reality (ibid.).

According to Bateson (1955, p. 184), the participants of a certain game open up a psychological frame, which consists of specific rules, by stating "This is a game." Knowing about the existence of that frame is inevitable to interpret utterances inside the frame in the right way. For example, if two children establish the scenario of "eating a cake" and "eat" their "cake" from empty plates, an utterance such as "this cake is delicious" can only be understood by knowing about the existence of the game frame.

Different from a dream, in which the dreamer is not aware that he/she is dreaming, the players of a game have to be reminded frequently by others or themselves that they are acting inside the game frame to maintain the shared frame (ibid., p. 185). This is done by meta-communication, a type of communication that contains information about how to interpret other verbal and nonverbal messages. According to Bateson (1955, p. 180), meta-communication tells people that the actions in which they "engage do not denote what these actions for which they stand would denote" (ibid.). In this sense, meta-communication helps to establish and maintain the existence of the shared game frame as well as to terminate it at the end. "[A] good deal of talk is directed to creating, clarifying, maintaining, or negotiating the social pretend experience. In order to pretend you must know who your partner is, what he thinks he's doing or intends to do, where he thinks he is, and what it is he is handling or using; he must have similar information about you" (Garvey and Berndt, 1977, p. 7).

According to Griffin (1984, pp. 79–88), meta-communication happens between the poles "within frame" and "out-of-frame," by allowing many in-between forms. Griffin differentiates seven forms of meta-communication according to the extent to which they can be located verbally and/or nonverbally within and out-of-frame respectively.

The form of meta-communication, which is verbally and nonverbally located within a frame, is called *enactment*. It is present when the players completely act out their roles, which is only possible when "each action automatically and implicitly metacommunicates the appropriate response" (ibid., p. 81). This can be the case when the players have agreed on the imported activities and objects from reality in advance of the game sequence in question.

The type most out-of-frame is called *overt proposals to pretend* (ibid., pp. 87–88), and signifies that the players act outside the game frame, verbally as well as nonverbally. Typical examples of that category are discussions about what to play in the future—often accompanied by phrases such as "Let's pretend." The *implicit pretend structuring* (ibid., pp. 86–87) is quite similar, but leaves out phrases such as "let's say." A typical utterance would be "I am the mother, now." Both types of meta-communication are very important for real-life play.

> [They] release players from the constraints of the play definition. Because they are outside the frame of play they can collectively and radically re-structure that frame if they wish. They can move ahead in time; they can replay past events in different ways. They can adapt the script to be more compatible with their needs or to resolve differences among collaborators. They can abandon one script and try another. The ability to move collectively outside of the play frame through the use of overtly out-of-frame metacommunication enables players to control the make-believe world.
>
> ibid., pp. 87–88

On the contrary, *prompting* (ibid., pp. 85–86) only means a short break from the game action in order to give commentaries that directly refer to the game story. A child might explain what it is doing in the game, while simultaneously acting nonverbally inside the frame. Utterances in this category are very short and come together with a change in the voice tone. After the prompting, the player reenters the frame directly. Another form of meta-communication happening in-between is *storytelling* (ibid., pp. 84–85), which describes a development in the game action, without performing these actions. This is often the case with scenes that are too hard to perform. When *underscoring* (ibid., pp. 82–84), the child acts nonverbally inside the chosen role, but verbally leaves it to emphasize his/ her actions through voice, which "points to the representation [...] and thus tends towards the out-of-frame position" (ibid., p. 83).

Even more located within the frame is the *ulterior conversation* (ibid., pp. 81–82), which helps in constituting the game's rules and plot without leaving the scenario. Conversations inside this category resemble enactment in the way that they take place inside the frame verbally as well as nonverbally. Still "[u]lterior conversation differs from enactment because it is used intentionally to propose transformations and develop the action of the play in ways that have not been previously conjointly established" (ibid., pp. 81–82). An example would be to suggest new actions from the point of view of the game character.

Specifics of Meta-Communication During Digital Gaming

Different from classic non-media play, computer or video games separate the as-if action from the player. The player navigates the avatar, who then handles the as-if action. That is why digital gaming can be much more easily identified than non-media play. For example, it is not the player him-/

herself who "shoots" at the enemy, but the avatar. The player only pushes the buttons to tell him what to do. In that way, there is much more distance between the player and the action than in real-life play.

This also has consequences for the communication taking place. The player can talk and (partially also) act out-of-frame while still being part of the game. This is especially the case with round-based games, where the player initiates an action at one time, and after that, the avatar performs it. This leaves room for talk that not only fulfills ludic functions but also fulfills social functions (Thon, 2009, pp. 33–34). Neitzel (2007, p. 250) refers to the "manifold shifts between communication, meta-communication, and self-referential communication" that happen during computer games.

The forms of communication appearing in digital games vary as the different ways of using computer and console games together offer various communication channels for the inter-individual exchange. Using a single device for a group game only allows face-to-face communication (FTF), while online gaming only operates with computer-mediated communication (CMC). Co-located gaming with connected technical devices supports FTF and CMC at the same time, which is seen as a huge advantage over online games (e.g. by Manninen, 2003), and points to the complexity of the communication taking place. As long as it is possible, players prefer direct talk over CMC to interact with their teammates (Ackermann, 2010, p. 113). Depending on the size of a co-located group gaming event, this cannot always be realized: A LAN event can be attended by thousands of participants, while a private LAN only has very few participants, and LAN parties can be located in the middle (Vogelgesang, 2003, pp. 68–73). CMC accordingly is more frequent at LAN events than at LAN parties or private LANs. This makes the research of verbal processes during rather small LANs especially interesting. To analyze the direct talk at LAN parties, three LANs with eight to twelve participants each and various gender constellations were organized by the author. The duration of the events was limited to six hours, and included the construction and the dismantling of the LAN party setting as well as the actual gaming processes. For the method, a non-participative observation was chosen. All actions were recorded audio-visually and the 18 hours of data were analyzed quantitatively by way of a theme-frequency analysis following grounded theory, and qualitatively with an ethnomethodologic approach using conversation analysis (for more details see Ackermann, 2011).

Types of Meta-Communication at LAN Parties

By looking at the distribution of the communication themes at LAN parties (Figure 15.1), one can see that only 1% of the time the participants spend at the sessions was not filled with utterances. This accounts for 13 minutes and 20 seconds of 18 hours of the data material.

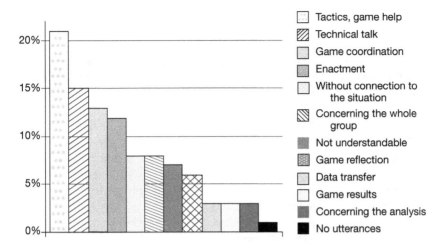

Figure 15.1 Theme-Frequency Analysis of LAN Parties.

When looking for utterances reflecting total game immersion, it can be seen that only 12% of the utterances exhibit game enactment statements—a relatively small part of the observed communication. The biggest portion of the communication (21%) was used for explanations concerning the games in use. This included narrative information, tactical advice, and help with the game handling. In addition, there was a lot of talk concerning computer techniques (15%). This covers explanations and tips for the network installation, but also verbalizations and comparisons of computer features. As a LAN party can only be realized after having installed the LAN properly, there is a lot of technical work to be done in advance of the chance to play together, which explains the high level of technical talk. The next field is occupied by the inter-individual coordination of the community game (13%). This again makes sense, as the organizational effort increases with the rising number of participants. In that dimension, it is much more complicated to coordinate a group of 12 people bringing their own computers to play together, than a group of two people playing at a single console. The participants not only have to agree on the game that will be played, they also have to make sure that everyone possesses that game, that the teams are built equally, and that there is consensus according to individual group rules added to the in-game rules.

In addition, there are dialogues that do not stand in relationship to the event itself, such as talking about school or holidays (8%). There is a lot of talk focusing on the group situation, such as discussing when some pizza should be ordered, or asking if anyone knows where the toilets are, how to open the windows, etc. (8%). Critical reflections about computer games and gaming in general, such as explaining the likes and dislikes of specific game genres also occurred (6%). Three percent of the time was filled with utterances concerning the data exchange of films, music, games, etc. Another

3% was covered by reflections on the game results, such as in comparing who was the best in the team, 3% was concerned with the analysis itself, and 7% was too quietly realized to be categorized.

Remembering the two-pole scale on which meta-communication, according to Griffin (1984), happens during game play, the different communication themes found at LAN parties can be located on that scale (Figure 15.2).

By leaving out the 8%, which could not be classified or have not been filled with utterances, the remaining 12% take place totally within frame. These are those statements in which the players act out according to the game script, and correspond to the enactment category in Figure 15.1.

One example for this type of meta-communication is the following set of utterances found at the male LAN party:

```
Transcript 1, male LAN party:
01 M.ExpA1:    E:Y (--) who's KILLing there, (.) doctor remix,
02             piss off,¹
```

By asking who is killing inside the game at the moment, the boy is talking from the point of view of his avatar being attacked. In addition, by vituperating doctor remix to leave the field, he is acting out according to the game plot. This becomes clear by the fact that he addresses his colleague with the name of his avatar and not with his real name. In addition, he does not stop

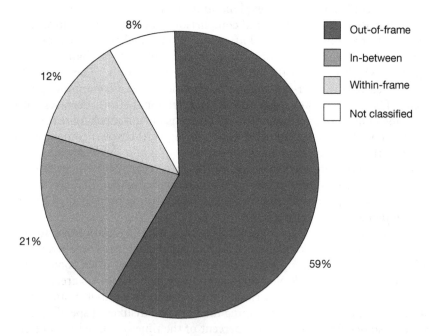

Figure 15.2 Types of Meta-Communication.

to navigate his own avatar through the virtual world, which shows that he is also nonverbally acting inside the game.

Similar utterances can be found in the other gender constellations. One more example is taken from the female LAN party.

```
Transcript 2, female LAN party:
01 F.LayA1: ((breathing in abruptly, then to herself))
02          YOU pigs (--) <<f> you PIIGS, get out of there>
03 ((some girls start laughing))
```

The girl, who is on her first visit to a LAN party, is enacting when she scolds the others as pigs, and demands that they leave a certain place. She, in that case, is in no way addressing her companions' real identities as pigs, but is shouting out within the frame from the point of view of her character being attacked by the others.

What is interesting to see is the other girls' reaction to her utterances: They start laughing, which shows that at that point the other players are acting less within the frame. Otherwise, they would have reacted to the affront in a different way. In addition, the girls' laughter gives potential to the thesis that the rather violent language appearing in digital games is not intended to be taken seriously, but serves for entertainment purposes (Thon, 2007, p. 176). Furthermore, the laughter gets the talking girl out-of-frame. What this shows is that not necessarily all the players are in the same state of meta-communication at the same time. From that perspective, it is not surprising that moments of enactment are quite hard to find, as the reactions of the co-players can terminate the immersion immediately.

Dialogues that can be located between the two poles of meta-communication account for 21% of the time spent at the LAN parties. These are the utterances in which the players help each other inside the game while playing it. They correspond to the category tactics/game help (see Figure 15.1).

An example for this in-between type is the following:

```
Transcript 3, mixed-sex LAN party:
01 F.LayA1: do i then just have to go to the little field in the
02          middle
03 M.ExpA2: for example or [YOU could]
04 W.LayA1:                [THAT one] ((she shows it))
05 M.ExpA2: or you use the corners [of course]
06 F.LayA1:                        [<<all> i just>] wanted to
07          say either the corners or?
08 M.ExpA2: right either you use the corners [here]
09 W.LayA1:                                  [yes] or else I
10          [would]
11 M.ExpA2: [or] the fields here in the [middle] (--) or
12 W.LayA1:                             [right]
13 M.ExpA2: maybe possibly even also e:h the PATH up there
```

The example taken from the mixed-sex group illustrates how the participants comment on the game *Warcraft 3* while playing it. They are nonverbally inside the frame, but verbally out of it. In this dialogue, a lay girl is asking a boy, who frequently visits LAN parties, about the next steps inside the game. While talking, the two youths continue to play. Still, there are also moments when they leave the frame nonverbally. In line 4, for example, the girl underlines her idea of what to do next by showing it with her finger pointing at the screen. She, in that moment, stops navigating the game character with her hand, and has left the frame nonverbally for a short break. Still, the two players do not pause the game action as a whole, and thus they do not completely exit the frame. Similar dialogues take place in all the observed constellations.

However, this leaves a very high proportion of the communication out-of-frame (59%). This includes all the coordination activities, the technical discussions, and the reflections about the game while not playing it. An example of that form of meta-communication can be found in the next transcript taken from the female LAN party.

```
Transcript 4, female LAN party:
01 F.ExpA1:  so what would you say? Do you want to play
02           the newer version or this CD? (--) What do
03           you think?
04 F.LaiB2:  then let's play the new one, yes?
06 F.ExpA3:  [yes]
07 F.ExpI4:  [yes] THAT one I would say, too
08 F.ExpA1:  good
```

The example shows an out-of-frame conversation. The girls from the female LAN are coordinating their community game by deciding which version of a certain game they want to use. As this type of meta-communication is the most common at LAN parties, this reveals that co-located gaming can hardly be seen as a game-only event. On the contrary, the (immersive) gaming action only occupies a very small part of the whole event.

Conclusion

The research shows that co-located gaming in various constellations is accompanied by a lot of face-to-face talk, which goes far beyond game-enactment statements. As in real-life play, meta-communication is needed to arrange agreements between the players concerning the communal entering of the game world, and the guarantee that every participant knows that he/she is still part of the game. As in real-life play, the communication during computer gaming can be located on a scale between "within-frame" and "out-of-frame." Applying Griffin's two-pole scale of meta-communication during play to the direct talk at LAN parties impressively reveals that co-located gaming is not only highly communicative, but that it also contains a lot of direct talk that cannot be reduced to immersive game-enactment statements. On the contrary, out-of-frame utterances are much more frequent than those totally within the frame or in-between the two poles. This emphasizes the thesis that gaming itself is by far not the only activity taking place at LAN parties, but is outweighed by coordination activities, technical work, dialogues concerning the group situation, utterances with no relation to the setting, and many more out-of-frame themes.

The study shows the high potential of observing communication during digital gaming sessions to get a deeper insight into what is actually happening in and between the players and the game. By regarding authentic gaming sessions as a whole, researchers get a very realistic insight into gaming that is less influenced by memory effects or social desirability than by questioning gamers about their gaming experiences. Despite these advantages, the communicative aspects of digital gaming are still not often the main focus of digital games research. This can be seen as a serious research gap that should be filled by future studies.

Note

1   All transcripts are translated from German by the author.

References

Ackermann, J. (2010). The edge of communication? Examining communicative challenges of LAN-Parties. In K. Mitgutsch, C. Klimmt, and H. Rosenstingl (Eds.), *Edges of gaming. Conference proceedings of the Vienna Games Conference 2008–2009* (pp. 103–118). Vienna, Austria: Braumüller Verlag.

Ackermann, J. (2011). *Gemeinschaftliches Computerspielen auf LAN-Partys. Kommunikation, Medienaneignung, Gruppendynamiken*. Münster, Germany: Lit.

Bateson, G. (1955). A theory of play and fantasy. In G. Bateson (Ed.) (1987), *Steps to an ecology of mind. Collected essays in anthropology, psychiatry, evolution, and epistemology* (pp. 177–193). Northvale, New Jersey, London: Jason Aronson Inc..

Caillois, R. (1960). *Die Spiele und die Menschen. Maske und Rausch*. Munich, Vienna: Albert Langen Georg Müller Verlag.

Garvey, C., and Berndt, R. (1977). Organization of pretend play. *American Psychological Association. JSAS Catalog of Selected Documents in Psychology*, 7(4), 1–23.

Griffin, H. (1984). The coordination of meaning in the creation of a shared make-believe reality. In I. Bretherton (Ed.), *Symbolic play: The development of social understanding* (pp. 73–100). Orlando, FL: Academic Press.

Heckhausen, H. (1963). Entwurf einer Psychologie des Spielens. *Psychologische Forschung, 27*, 225–243.

Manninen, T. (2003). Interaction forms and communicative actions in multiplayer games. *The International Journal of Computer Game Research, 3*(1). Retrieved from http://www.gamestudies.org/0301/manninen/.

Neitzel, B. (2007). Metacommunication in play and in (computer) games. In W. Nöth and N. Bishara (Eds.), *Self-reference in the media* (pp. 237–252). Berlin, Germany: De Gruyter.

Oerter, R. (1999). *Psychologie des Spiels. Ein handlungstheoretischer Ansatz* (2nd ed.). Weinheim, Basel: Beltz.

Pellegrini, A. D., and Smith, P. (2003). Development of play. In J. Valsiner and K. J. Connolly (Eds.), *Handbook of developmental psychology* (pp. 276–291). London, Thousand Oaks, New Delhi: Sage Publications.

Ruggles, C., Wadley, G., and Gibbs, M. R. (2005). Online community building techniques used by video game developers. In F. Kishino, Y. Kitamura, H. Kato, and N. Nagata (Eds.), *Entertainment computing—ICEC 2005: Proceedings from the 4th International Conference Sanda, Japan, September 19–21, 2005 Proceedings. Lecture Notes in Computer Science, Volume 3711* (pp. 114–125). Berlin, Heidelberg, New York: Springer.

Thon, J.-N. (2007). Kommunikation im Computerspiel. In S. Kimpeler, M. Mangold, and W. Schweiger (Eds.), *Die digitale Herausforderung: Zehn Jahre Forschung zur computervermittelten Kommunikation* (pp. 171–180). Wiesbaden, Germany: VS Verlag.

Thon, J.-N. (2009). Zur Struktur des Egoshooters. In M. Bopp, R. F. Nohr and S. Wiemer (Eds.), *Shooter: Eine multidisziplinäre Einführung* (pp. 21–41). Münster, Germany: Lit.

Vogelgesang, W. (2003). LAN-Partys: Jugendkulturelle Erlebnisräume zwischen Off- und Online. *Merz, Medien + Erziehung, 47*(5), 65–75.

Part V

Risks and Challenges of Social Gaming

16 An Overview of Online Gaming Addiction

Mark D. Griffiths

An Overview of Online Gaming Addiction

Online gaming has become a topic of increasing research interest. Over the last decade there has been a significant increase in the number of empirical studies examining various aspects of online gaming compared to the preceding decade. This has resulted in a wide-ranging selection of papers focusing on different aspects of the topic including many on problematic and addictive play (Kuss and Griffiths, 2012) and gaming addiction treatment (King, Delfabbro, and Griffiths, 2012; King, Delfabbro, Griffiths, and Gradisar, 2011).

Given the lack of consensus as to whether gaming addiction exists and/or whether the term 'addiction' is the most appropriate to use, some researchers have instead used terminology such as 'excessive' or 'problematic' to denote the harmful use of video games (Yellowlees and Marks, 2007; Festl, Scharkow, and Quandt, 2013). Terminology for what appears to be for the same disorder and/or its consequences include problem video game playing (King, Delfabbro, and Zajac, 2011), problematic online game use (Kim and Kim, 2010), video game addiction (Griffiths and Davies, 2005; Skoric, Teo, and Neo, 2009), online gaming addiction (Charlton and Danforth, 2007; Griffiths, 2010), Internet gaming addiction (Kuss and Griffiths, 2012), and compulsive Internet use (van Rooij, Schoenmakers, van de Eijnden, and van de Mheen, 2010). This chapter briefly examines a number of key areas in the study of problematic online gaming (e.g., history, prevalence, negative consequences, factors associated with online gaming addiction, treatment).

A Brief History of Gaming Addiction

Following the release of the first commercial video games in the early 1970s, it took until the 1980s for the first reports of gaming addiction to appear in the psychological and psychiatric literature (e.g., Ross, Finestone, and Lavin, 1982; Soper and Miller, 1983). The 1990s saw a small but significant increase of research into gaming addiction with almost all of these studies being carried out in the UK and on adolescents, typically surveying children in school settings (e.g., Griffiths,

1997; Griffiths and Hunt, 1998; Phillips, Rolls, Rouse, and Griffiths, 1995). The 2000s saw a substantial growth in the number of studies on gaming addiction, particularly as gaming expanded into the new online medium where games could be played as part of a gaming community (i.e., massively multiplayer online role-playing games [MMORPGs], such as *World of Warcraft* (Blizzard Entertainment, 2004) and *EverQuest* (Verant Interactive (1999)). The impact of online gaming has been large and has led not only to an increase in the number of gamers but has turned gaming into a 24/7 activity in which gamers can play along with or against other gamers all over the world. Consequently, it has provided new elements to gaming that did not previously exist (e.g., gamer interaction, the formation of online social relationships, cooperative learning experiences, etc.). Approximately 60 studies were published on gaming addiction between 2000 and 2010 (Kuss and Griffiths, 2012) and a vast majority of these examined MMORPG addiction and were not limited to the study of adolescent males. Furthermore, many of these studies collected their data online and a significant minority of studies examined various other aspects of video game addiction using non-self-report methodologies. These include studies using polysomnographic measures and visual and verbal memory tests (Dworak, Schierl, Bruns, and Struder, 2007), medical examinations including the patient's history, and physical, radiologic, intraoperative, and pathologic findings (Cultrara and Har-El, 2002), functional magnetic resonance imaging (Han, Hwang, and Renshaw, 2010; Hoeft, Watson, Kesler, Bettinger, and Reiss, 2008; Ko et al., 2009), electroencephalography (Thalemann, Wölfling, and Grüsser, 2007), and genotyping (Han et al., 2007).

Prevalence of Online Gaming Addiction

Estimated prevalence rates of problematic gaming range from 1.7% to over 10%. These studies also indicate that, in general, males are significantly more likely than females to report problems relating to their gaming. According to King et al. (2012), the differences in methods of assessing game-based problems may partly account for differences in prevalence rates. Furthermore, many studies fail to assess prior problems (i.e., lifetime prevalence). King et al. (2012) also noted that some studies do not consider subclinical cases (i.e., meeting some but not all criteria for problematic use), and the presence of co-morbid psychopathology is not routinely assessed.

There are some generalizations that can be made with regard to the demographic characteristics of online gamers and problem gamers. The literature, to date, suggests that adolescent males and young male adults appear to be at greater risk of experiencing problematic online gaming. However, the course and severity of these problems are not well known (King et al., 2012) and the finding that this group is more at risk may be a consequence of sampling bias and the fact that this group plays video games more frequently than other socio-demographic groups. It has also been suggested that university students may be vulnerable to developing problematic video gaming. Reasons for this include their flexible tuition and study hours, ready access to high-speed broadband on a 24/7 basis, and multiple stressors associated with adjusting to new social obligations and/ or living out-of-home for the first time (Young, 1998; King et al., 2012).

Negative Consequences of Excessive Online Gaming

Irrespective of whether problematic online gaming can be classed as an addiction, there are now a relatively large number of studies all indicating that excessive online gaming can lead to a wide variety of negative psycho-social consequences for a minority of affected individuals. These were recently summarized by Griffiths, Kuss, and King (2012) and included (i) sacrificing work, education, hobbies, socializing, time with partner/family, and sleep, (ii) increased stress, (iii) an absence of real life relationships, (iv) lower psychosocial well-being and loneliness, (v) poorer social skills, (vi) decreased academic achievement, (vii) increased inattention, (viii) aggressive/oppositional behavior and hostility, (ix) maladaptive coping, (x) decreases in verbal memory performance, (xi) maladaptive cognitions, and (xii) suicidal ideation. These potential psychosocial negative consequences clearly indicate that excessive online gaming is an issue irrespective of whether it is an addiction. It also suggests that more extensive recognition is needed of the wide range of potential negative and life-limiting consequences of excessive online gaming.

Factors Associated With Problematic Online Gaming

A number of studies have examined the role of different personality factors, comorbidity factors, and biological factors, and their association with online gaming addiction. In relation to personality traits, online gaming addiction has been shown to have association with neuroticism (Mehroof and Griffiths, 2010; Peters and Malesky, 2008), aggression and hostility (Caplan, Williams, and Yee, 2009; Chiu, Lee, and Huang, 2004; Kim, Namkoong, Ku, and Kim, 2008; Mehroof and Griffiths, 2010), avoidant and schizoid interpersonal tendencies (Allison, von Walde, Shockley, and Gabbard, 2006), loneliness and introversion (Caplan et al., 2009), social inhibition (Porter, Starcevic, Berle, and Fenech, 2010), boredom inclination (Chiu et al., 2004), sensation-seeking (Chiu et al., 2004; Mehroof and Griffiths, 2010), diminished agreeableness (Peters and Malesky, 2008), diminished self-control and narcissistic personality traits (Kim et al., 2008), low self-esteem (Ko, Yen, Chen, Chen, and Yen, 2005), state and trait anxiety (Mehroof and Griffiths, 2010), and low emotional intelligence (Parker, Taylor, Eastabrook, Schell, and Wood, 2008). It is hard to assess the etiological significance of these associations with gaming addiction as they may not be unique to the disorder. Further research is therefore needed.

Treatment of Online Game Addiction

Clinical interventions and treatment for problematic and/or addictive video game play vary considerably in the literature, with most of the very few published studies employing some type of cognitive-behavioral therapy (CBT), pharmacotherapy, and/or self-devised psychological interventions (Griffiths and Meredith, 2009; Han et al., 2009, 2010; King, Delfabbro, and Griffiths, 2010; King, Delfabbro, and Zajac, 2011; King et al., 2012). Currently, the evidence base on the treatment of problematic and/or addictive online gaming is limited. Furthermore, the lack of consistent approaches to treating problematic online gaming addiction makes it difficult to produce any definitive conclusions as to the efficacy of treatment, although at this stage CBT (as with the treatment efficacy of other addictions) appears to show good preliminary support (King et al., 2012). There remains a need for controlled, comparative studies of psychological and pharmacological treatments, administered individually and in combination with each other, to determine the optimal treatment approach.

The lack of comparative treatment studies might suggest that there is a general lack of demand for psychological services for problematic video game play and/or video game addiction (King et al., 2010). Adult gaming addicts may not seek treatment, or seek treatment at a later stage for other psychological problems (e.g., depression) that develop after experiencing the severe negative consequences of gaming. In South East Asia there appears to be significant demand for treatment for online-related problems including gaming addiction. The South Korean government has reportedly established a network of over 140 counseling centers for treatment of online addiction (Kim, 2008). In Western countries, gaming addiction clinics have also started to emerge in places such as Holland and the UK (Griffiths and Meredith, 2009; King et al., 2010; 2012). There are also treatment groups that are modeled on 12-step self-help treatment (e.g., Online Gamers Anonymous) (Griffiths and Meredith, 2009). However, little detail is known about the treatment protocols or their efficacy.

Conclusions

Based on the published empirical studies it appears that in extreme cases, excessive online gaming can have potentially damaging effects upon individuals who appear to display compulsive and/or addictive behavior similar to other more traditional addictions. However, the field has been hindered by the use of inconsistent and non-standardized criteria to assess and identify problematic and/or addictive video game use. Furthermore, most studies' recruitment methods have serious sampling biases with an over-reliance on self-selected samples.

On the positive side, there has been a diversification in the way data are collected including experiments, physiological investigations, secondary analysis of existing data (such as that collected from online forums), and behavioral tracking studies. There has also been increased research on adult (i.e., non-child and non-adolescent) samples reflecting the fact that the demographics of gaming have changed. Furthermore, there has been increasing sophistication in relation to issues concerning assessment and measurement of problematic and online gaming addiction. In the last few years, instruments have been developed that have more robust psychometric properties in terms of reliability and validity (e.g., Demetrovics et al., 2012).

There are too few clinical studies that describe the unique features and symptoms of online gaming addiction. Most of the studies tend to examine problematic online gaming from the perspective of the individual. However, there is a small body of research suggesting that the characteristics of the games themselves may have a role in the acquisition, development and maintenance of online gaming addiction. These studies have investigated the role of structural characteristics of video games in maintaining problem playing behavior (Wood, Griffiths, Chappell, and Davies, 2004; Westwood and Griffiths, 2010; King, Delfabbro, and Griffiths, 2011), but there is little empirical research that examines why some individuals may be protected from developing excessive playing habits, or simply mature out of their problem playing behavior.

References

Allison, S. E., von Wahlde, L., Shockley, T., and Gabbard, G. O. (2006). The development of the self in the era of the Internet and role-playing fantasy games. *American Journal of Psychiatry, 163*(3), 381–385.

Caplan, S. E., Williams, D., and Yee, N. (2009). Problematic Internet use and psychosocial well-being among MMO players. *Computers in Human Behavior, 25*(6), 1312–1319.

Charlton, J. P., and Danforth, I. D. W. (2007). Distinguishing addiction and high engagement in the context of online game playing. *Computers in Human Behavior, 23*(3), 1531–1548.

Chiu, S. I., Lee, J. Z., and Huang, D. H. (2004). Video game addiction in children and teenagers in Taiwan. *CyberPsychology and Behavior, 7*(5), 571–581.

Cultrara, A., and Har-El, G. (2002). Hyperactivity-induced suprahyoid muscular hypertrophy secondary to excessive video game play: A case report. *Journal of Oral and Maxillofacial Surgery, 60*(3), 326–327.

Demetrovics, Z., Urbán, R., Nagygyörgy, K., Farkas, J., Griffiths, M. D., Pápay, O., and Oláh, A. (2012). The development of the Problematic Online Gaming Questionnaire (POGQ). *PLoS one, 7*(5), e36417.

Dworak, M., Schierl, T., Bruns, T., and Struder, H. K. (2007). Impact of singular excessive computer game and television exposure on sleep patterns and memory performance of school-aged children. *Pediatrics, 120*(5), 978–985.

Festl, R., Scharkow, M., and Quandt, T. (2013). Problematic computer game use among adolescents, younger and older adults. *Addiction, 108*(3), 592–599.

Griffiths, M. D. (1997). Computer game playing in early adolescence. *Youth and Society, 29*(2), 223–237.

Griffiths, M. D. (2010). The role of context in online gaming excess and addiction: Some case study evidence. *International Journal of Mental Health and Addiction, 8*(1), 119–125.

Griffiths, M. D., and Davies, M. N. O. (2005). Does video game addiction exist? In J. Goldstein and J. Raessens (Eds.), *Handbook of computer game studies* (pp. 359–368). Boston: MIT Press.

Griffiths, M. D., and Hunt, N. (1998). Dependence on computer games by adolescents. *Psychological Reports*, 8(2), 475–480.

Griffiths, M. D., Kuss, D.J., and King, D.L. (2012). Video game addiction: Past, present and future. *Current Psychiatry Reviews*, 8(4), 308–318.

Griffiths, M. D., and Meredith, A. (2009). Videogame addiction and treatment. *Journal of Contemporary Psychotherapy*, 39(4), 47–53.

Han, D. H., Hwang, J. W., and Renshaw, P. F. (2010). Bupropion sustained release treatment decreases craving for video games and cue-induced brain activity in patients with Internet video game addiction. *Experimental and Clinical Psychopharmacology*, 18(4), 297–304.

Han, D. H., Lee, Y. S., Na, C., Ahn, J. Y., Chung, U. S., Daniels, M. A., et al. (2009). The effect of methylphenidate on Internet video game play in children with attention-deficit/hyperactivity disorder. *Comprehensive Psychiatry*, 50(3), 251–256.

Han, D. H., Lee, Y. S., Yang, K. C., Kim, E. Y., Lyoo, I. K., and Renshaw, P. F. (2007). Dopamine genes and reward dependence in adolescents with excessive Internet video game play. *Journal of Addiction Medicine,* 1(3), 133–138.

Hoeft, F., Watson, C. L., Kesler, S. R., Bettinger, K. E., and Reiss, A. L. (2008). Gender differences in the mesocorticolimbic system during computer game-play. *Journal of Psychiatric Research,* 42(4), 253–258.

Kim, E. J., Namkoong, K., Ku, T., and Kim, S. J. (2008). The relationship between online game addiction and aggression, self-control and narcissistic personality traits. *European Psychiatry,* 23(3), 212–218.

Kim, J. (2008). The effect of a R/T group counselling program on the Internet addiction level and self-esteem of Internet addiction university students. *International Journal of Reality Therapy,* 27(2), 4–12.

Kim, M. G., and Kim, J. (2010). Cross-validation of reliability, convergent and discriminant validity for the problematic online game use scale. *Computers in Human Behavior,* 26(3), 389–398.

King, D. L., Delfabbro, P. H., and Griffiths, M. D. (2010). Cognitive behavioural therapy for problematic video game players: Conceptual considerations and practice issues. *Journal of CyberTherapy and Rehabilitation,* 3(3), 261–273.

King, D. L., Delfabbro, P. H., and Griffiths, M. D. (2011). The role of structural characteristics in problematic video game play: An empirical study. *International Journal of Mental Health and Addiction,* 9(3), 320–333.

King, D. L., Delfabbro, P. H., and Griffiths, M. D. (2012). Clinical interventions for technology-based problems: Excessive Internet and video game use. *Journal of Cognitive Psychotherapy: An International Quarterly,* 26(1), 43–56.

King, D. L., Delfabbro, P. H., Griffiths, M. D., and Gradisar, M. (2011). Assessing clinical trials of Internet addiction treatment: A systematic review and CONSORT evaluation. *Clinical Psychology Review,* 31(7), 1110–1116.

King, D. L., Delfabbro, P. H., and Zajac, I. T. (2011). Preliminary validation of a new clinical tool for identifying problem video game playing. *International Journal of Mental Health and Addiction,* 9(1), 72–87.

Ko, C. H., Liu, G. C., Hsiao, S. M., Yen, J. Y., Yang, M. J., Lin, W. C., et al. (2009). Brain activities associated with gaming urge of online gaming addiction. *Journal of Psychiatric Research,* 43(7), 739–747.

Ko, C. H., Yen, J. Y., Chen, C. C., Chen, S. H., and Yen, C. F. (2005). Gender differences and related factors affecting online gaming addiction among Taiwanese adolescents. *Journal of Nervous and Mental Disease, 193*(4), 273–277.

Kuss, D. J., and Griffiths, M. D. (2012). Internet gaming addiction: A systematic review of empirical research. *International Journal of Mental Health and Addiction, 10*(2), 278–296.

Mehroof, M., and Griffiths, M. D. (2010). Online gaming addiction: The role of sensation seeking, self-control, neuroticism, aggression, state anxiety, and trait anxiety. *CyberPsychology and Behavior, 13*(3), 313–316.

Parker, J. D. A., Taylor, R. N., Eastabrook, J. M., Schell, S. L., and Wood, L. M. (2008). Problem gambling in adolescence: Relationships with Internet misuse, gaming abuse and emotional intelligence. *Personality and Individual Differences, 45*(2), 174–180.

Peters, C. S., and Malesky, L. A. (2008). Problematic usage among highly-engaged players of massively multiplayer online role playing games. *CyberPsychology and Behavior, 11*(4), 480–483.

Phillips, C. A., Rolls, S., Rouse, A., and Griffiths, M. D. (1995). Home video game playing in schoolchildren: A study of incidence and pattern of play. *Journal of Adolescence, 18*(6), 687–691.

Porter, G., Starcevic, V., Berle, D., and Fenech, P. (2010). Recognizing problem video game use. *The Australian and New Zealand Journal of Psychiatry, 44*(2), 120–128.

Ross, D. R., Finestone, D. H., and Lavin, G. K. (1982). Space Invaders obsession. *Journal of the American Medical Association, 248*(10), 1177.

Skoric, M. M., Teo, L. L. C., and Neo, R. L. (2009). Children and video games: Addiction, engagement, and scholastic achievement. *CyberPsychology and Behavior, 12*(5), 567–572.

Soper, W. B., and Miller, M. J. (1983). Junk time junkies: An emerging addiction among students. *School Counsellor, 31*(1), 40–43.

Thalemann, R., Wölfling, K., and Grüsser, S. M. (2007). Specific cue reactivity on computer game-related cues in excessive gamers. *Behavioral Neuroscience, 121*(3), 614–618.

Van Rooij, A. J., Schoenmakers, T. M., van de Eijnden, R., and van de Mheen, D. (2010). Compulsive Internet use: The role of online gaming and other Internet applications. *Journal of Adolescent Health, 47*(1), 51–57.

Westwood, D., and Griffiths, M. D. (2010). The role of structural characteristics in video game play motivation: A Q-Methodology Study. *Cyberpsychology, Behavior and Social Networking, 13*(5), 581–585.

Wood, R. T. A., Griffiths, M. D., Chappell, D., and Davies, M. N. O. (2004). The structural characteristics of video games: A psycho-structural analysis. *CyberPsychology and Behavior, 7*(1), 1–10.

Yellowlees, P. M., and Marks, S. (2007). Problematic Internet use or Internet addiction? *Computers in Human Behavior, 23*(3), 1447–1453.

Young, K. (1998). *Caught in the net*. Chichester: Wiley.

Games Cited

Blizzard Entertainment (2004), *World of Warcraft*, Vivendi Activision Blizzard.
Verant Interactive (1999), *EverQuest*, Sony Online Entertainment.

17 Living in a Virtual World?

An Excessive Gamer Typology

Emese Domahidi and Thorsten Quandt

Problematic Computer Game Use

The research on problematic game use is dominated by some central concepts, such as violence (e.g. Anderson, Gentile, and Buckley, 2007; Weber, Ritterfeld, and Mathiak, 2006) and addiction (e.g. Charlton and Danforth, 2007; Grüsser, Thalemann, and Griffiths, 2007; Lemmens, Valkenburg, and Peter, 2009). The focus of the analysis of the possible dangers of violent content is on first-person shooters (FPSs), which are suspected of promoting aggression and serving as blueprints for violence. The research on addiction, on the other hand, is dominated by a problematization of massively multiplayer online role-playing games (MMORPGs), such as *World of Warcraft* *(WoW)* (Blizzard Entertainment, 2004). If, and in which cases, the terms of addiction and dependency are applicable to the excessive use of computer games and its negative consequences is highly disputed in academia (Charlton and Danforth, 2007; Griffiths, 2008; Turner, 2008). This is primarily due to the fact that online addiction in general and (online) computer gaming addiction are not yet part of the standard diagnostic manuals[1] in medicine and psychology (at the time of writing). Only pathological gambling, which is listed in the DSM-IV as an impulse-control disorder, could provide some criteria that were applied to the problematic use of (online) computer games. Some authors adapted criteria of pathological gambling and developed, tested, and validated the first instruments to diagnose pathological (online) computer gaming (e.g. Grüsser et al., 2007; Kim, Kim, and Kim, 2008; Lemmens et al., 2009; Meyer, Janz, Zeng, and Pietrowsky, 2009). The items used in these instruments vary considerably in phrasing and quantity, depending on the target group for which the instrument was designed and validated. Those differences between instruments and questionnaires also influence the response to the question about the spread of pathological gaming and the prevalence rates in different countries (for an overview see Festl, Scharkow, and Quandt, 2013). Obviously, there is a strong positive correlation between addiction scale scores and time spent on games (Lemmens et al., 2009), but it seems evident that excessive gaming is not necessarily addiction. Spekman, Konijn, and Roelofsma (2012) conclude, "that gaming addiction clearly goes beyond excessive gaming".

Scholars have criticized that excessive gaming is often solely defined by gaming time (e.g. Griffiths, Davies, and Chappell, 2004) and obviously time-based definitions of excessive gamers vary greatly according to different studies. Griffiths et al. (2004) specify that players who play more than 80 hours a week are playing excessively. Hussain and Griffiths (2009) declare that 30 hours a week might be defined as excessive gaming, while Quandt, Festl, and Scharkow (2011) identify gamers who play more 21 hours a week on average as problematic users. Although the criteria for the identification of excessive use are controversial, there is ample evidence for problematic gaming habits among a minority of excessive gamers (e.g. Festl et al., 2013; Nomura and Goto, 2012; Hellström, Nilsson, Leppert, and Åslund, 2012), and that excessive use has more negative consequences than average use.

Griffiths (2010), for example, argues that excessive gaming needs to be distinguished from addictive gaming, based on the negative impacts on other areas of the gamers' lives rather than just on the amount of time spent playing. Ko, Yen, Chen, Chen, and Yen (2005) found gender-based differences between problematic gamers, and Hellström et al. (2012) emphasized that gaming motives are far more important than just the playing time when it comes to the negative consequences of gaming. The gaming patterns that excessive gamers display are often associated with problems such as narrowed-down leisure activities (e.g. Rehbein, Kleimann, and Mößle, 2010), lower self-esteem, lower satisfaction with everyday life (e.g. Ko et al., 2005), and the substitution of real-life relationships (e.g. Young, 2009). Negative consequences of excessive gaming have been repeatedly revealed by surveys, interviews with excessive gamers, and experimental studies.

The above-mentioned studies provide a good insight into the topic but often focus solely on addiction. Our current study therefore approaches the phenomenon of excessive gaming from a more general real-life (RL) perspective. By considering the subjective perspective of the interviewees and their context, we provide a deep insight into the lives of excessive gamers. In order to understand the excessive gaming better, we need to distinguish between different excessive user types and identify problematic use patterns related to the game, the life of the gamer, and the social surroundings.

Method

As the RL aspect of excessive gamers has not been at the center of research, a qualitative approach (see Denzin and Lincoln, 2011) and an explorative design (see Lindlof, 1995) are suitable for broadening the view and getting access to new aspects of the phenomenon. So our study is based on a micro-level analysis and examines the everyday experience of individual excessive users via semi-guided, biographically oriented interviews of one to two hours in length.

Following existing studies, we identified excessive gamers in the first step based on their gaming time, and therefore examine gamers who spend at least three hours a day (Quandt et al., 2011; Quandt and Wimmer, 2008) on games. Simultaneously, we want to differentiate between these players, and provide categories to distinguish between problematic and non-problematic excessive gamers. So we go beyond the time-based approach to identify problematic game use.

As we deliberately included many different cases in our study, our main research question was:

RQ 1:　Can we identify different types of excessive gamers?

With this attempt, we follow the approach of Bartle (1996), who differentiated four different types of playing multi-user dungeons (MUDs), according to the gamer's game or person orientation, and the wish to act or interact. Karlsen (2004) criticized Bartle by claiming that gamers, in fact, belong to different types at the same time. We acknowledge that the excessive gamers' types are ideal types. A person might belong to different types in different life situations or stages (see Domahidi and Quandt, 2010) and may also belong to in-between types. Still, we believe that an excessive gamers' typology helps us to differentiate this group and to see that gaming time is just one criterion for problematic game use. Even though we used an explorative design, our study has some clear focal points. As several scholars (e.g. Griffiths, 2010; Griffiths et al., 2004; Hellström et al., 2012) have pointed out, it is not enough to examine the time spent on gaming. Research literature (see above) has pointed to different areas that might be important: (1) the interaction within the game, (2) the everyday life of the gamer, and (3) the social environment. Our research was guided by three additional research questions:

RQ 2.1:　How do excessive gamers interact within the game?
RQ 2.2:　How do excessive gamers organize gaming and their everyday life?
RQ 2.3:　What are the reactions of, and interactions with, people within the social environment of excessive gamers?

The interview guidelines included different questions dealing with the socio-demographic information and the users' personal and professional background, the everyday life of the users, including their RL and virtual-life (VL) social environments, their general gaming preferences and experiences, as well as the perceived impacts of excessive gaming. The interviews were analyzed on the basis of a qualitative content analysis (Mayring, 2002) and by using ATLAS.ti for data analysis.

Sample

In the analysis, we used the selective sampling technique to meet our research objectives and therefore only examined gamers who spent at least three hours a day on gaming. All participants in the study are or were excessively playing games (defined on the basis of the time spent on gaming), but differed in social background, education, age, life, and work situation. Overall, we interviewed 41 players between the ages of 19 and 43. The average age of the interviewees was 27 years. The survey included 33 men and 8 women, accounting for the fact that there are still more male than female gamers in Germany. Fourteen of our interviewees were university students, some of them were working part time besides their studies, while two respondents were doing an apprenticeship. Sixteen other interviewees were employed in full-time jobs and two people had part-time jobs. One person was on an invalidity pension. The others were currently not employed. While we did not choose our respondents based on their genre preferences, we found that most of them played either MMORPGs or FPSs. The interview data indicate that *WoW* is a key game for excessive users, especially for the female respondents in our study. MMORPGs, such as *WoW*, are often popular among excessive gamers (Lenhart, Jones, and Macgill, 2008) because of the open environment where the gamers can develop their characters and start their adventures.

Results

To examine (1) the *interaction with the game*, we asked questions about the differences between the behavior in RL and VL. About half of our respondents pointed out that it is not even possible for them to act completely differently in their RL and VL, as they bring their personality to the game. The other half said that they act differently in RL and VL contexts, and enjoy being able to switch roles and have the possibility of experiencing new situations.

```
I mean, in the game everyone can be, even if he's just a
handyman in real life, a big boss. Or the other way round, a
big boss can be just a follower and doesn't have to be the guy
who always leads the way. [Interview transcript]
```

Additionally, we asked our interviewees how they would describe their social and communicative behavior in the game. Most of our respondents see themselves as "communicative" and "team players," with just some telling us that they played in an aggressive and more strategic way. The players who prefer aggressive and strategic gameplay concentrate on achievements, or even on disturbing other players in the game. No matter what the choice of playing style was, it became clear that time and attachment to the virtual personality played an important role.

The interview analysis regarding (2) the *integration of gaming into everyday life* shows that most of our respondents have a constant and pretty ordinary life. They work or go to university during the day. Besides that, they spend time with their friends and families, and they mainly play during weekends or at night. These respondents succeeded in embedding gaming into their everyday life, as the gaming happens in their spare time and usually does not substitute other activities. In sharp contrast to this group, one-third of the respondents have a daily routine dominated by and organized mainly around gaming. Grosso modo, these interviewees are either unemployed, or just in part-time employment, or they are students neglecting their studies. In general, they are without binding, "external" occupational obligations. These respondents often play during the daytime. It seems that their life is occupied by gaming, as the quote from one interviewee shows:

> Most of the time I get up around 11am and do my household chores. Around half past 12, when there is nothing else to do, I turn on the computer and play until around 3pm. Then it always depends on the shifts of my husband—when he has an early shift he gets home around 2pm and I pause gaming from half-past 2pm till 5pm so I can spend time with him. Then I continue gaming from 5pm till 11pm, 12pm, 1am, 2am. When he has a late shift it can happen that I don't pause gaming and play all day.

Most of the interviewees reported that they had hobbies besides gaming. The most frequently named leisure-time activities were sports, followed by meeting with friends, reading books, and listening to music. However, excessive gaming tends to conflict with other activities: Two-thirds of the interviewees admitted that gaming has at least some impact on their everyday life and routines. One-third even said gaming had a strong impact on their life, not only on their spare-time activities, but also on work or school. In general, we found that most of our interviewees embed gaming into their everyday life.

> Limiting myself works pretty well for me. It's like a pack of sweets that you stop eating before you feel sick. So, when I am playing, even if it's a lot of fun, I stop when I have to work the next day.

Gamers who belong to this group use their free time for gaming and have a highly structured life. Just a minority have a daily routine dominated by and organized mainly around gaming.

The social consequences of excessive gaming are discussed very often. Therefore, some interview questions focused on the personal relationships of gamers. The analysis of (3) *the social environment* is helpful for figuring out how people around the respondents deal with their gaming habits. Unsurprisingly, excessive gaming can be a problem for the social environment. Over half of the respondents told us that they had conflicts with their families once in a while because of their gaming habits. Some said they had no problems with their families mainly because, for example, the parents did not know exactly what was going on in their lives, and that they had become excessive users of video games. Most of our respondents told us about quarrels with their parents over gaming—even though all of them were adults. This is, in part, a generational problem, because the older generation is not experienced with video games, and might not accept gaming as a "normal" leisure activity. It could also be related to the feeling of responsibility of parents in light of the negative consequences of excessive gaming, even if the children are grown-up. Ten respondents noted that they had already experienced very negative reactions in their circle of friends. So the following quote illustrates that gamers are sometimes confronted with extreme reactions—up to and including the loss of their peers.

> At this time I completely isolated myself, all of my friends broke their ties to me, because every time they called I didn't have time or my reaction was stroppy because they just disrupted me.

But besides these negative experiences, the respondents also pointed out positive social experiences. Two-thirds of our respondents reported that somebody in their RL social environment also plays (sometimes also excessively). In these cases, the gamers tend to play together with their friends, relatives, or partners, and share the experience, strengthening the social contact by playing. Most of our respondents made friends in the virtual world as well. They tended to mix the "two spheres" of RL and VL by meeting friends from the game in their RL, too. As the following statement describes, these meetings can be game related, but also serve for other spare-time activities:

> We just met a couple of times, for fun, and went out to party, barbecue, normal stuff. We then didn't really talk about any game, very normal actually. We really grew together over time, I mean, when you play together with the people for two years, then you know these people quite well.

Apparently, excessive gaming can lead to long-term relationships in the game and even outside the game: The large majority of the gamers in our study tend to play in more or less stable VL groups, such as guilds or clans. We found two different approaches to these groups, though: For one group of our respondents, their guilds or clans seem to replace RL sports clubs. The other group perceives gaming more as being "just for fun," without the need to compete. People who regard their guilds as places to have fun put more value on chatting and other social aspects of group interactions.

Excessive Gamer Types

Despite some similarities in the biographies, our respondents differed substantially regarding their gaming preferences, the integration of gaming into their everyday life during phases of excessive gaming, and their social environment. On that basis, we could identify four general types of excessive gamers: active–integrated, sensation-seeking, meaning-seeking, and passive–secluded (for an overview see Table 17.1).

Table 17.1 Excessive Gamer Types

	Active-integrated	Sensation-seeking	Meaning-seeking	Passive-secluded
Interaction with the game				
Genre preferences	All genres	Mainly shooter/all genres	Mainly role-playing games	Mainly role-playing games
Way of playing	Competitive	Competitive	Social/team-play	Social/team-play/competitive
Integration of gaming into everyday life				
Life structure	Highly structured, self-monitoring	Highly structured, self-monitoring	No structure, loss of control	No structure, loss of control
Other activities	Low degree of substitution, utilization of otherwise unused spare time	Low degree of substitution, utilization mostly of otherwise unused spare time	Other activities and social contacts are in part replaced	Other activities and social contacts are replaced
Social environment				
Identification with virtual groups	low	low	high	medium
Social environment	RL meetings, expanded circle of friends	RL meetings, expanded circle of friends	Focus on online groups	Focus on online groups

The data indicate that the active–integrated excessive gamers are open-minded and generally very active in their leisure time. They have other spare-time activities besides gaming and often a large circle of friends. They enjoy the social side of gaming but they clearly distinguish between the importance of RL and game-related social contacts. Active–integrated gamers do not identify that much with their virtual groups and avatars. For them, online gaming is one spare-time activity among others, and very often not that different from sports or board games. A competitive orientation is important for these gamers. Hence, they participate in RL competitions, too.

The second group of excessive gamers—sensation-seeking—mostly prefer FPSs but play all genres. These gamers succeed in embedding gaming into their everyday lives. It seems as if they are mainly seeking a spare-time activity that they cannot find in RL. Even if gaming has a huge importance for them as a leisure-time activity, the identification with avatars and online groups is quite low. They also prefer playing competitively and have their social focus on RL contacts.

The third type of excessive gamers—meaning-seeking—mainly prefers role-playing games. These gamers show a high identification with the game and their online groups. They are not just looking for a spare-time activity, but also for social contacts, and roles to play that they cannot experience in RL. So they are very much focused on "their" online groups and on virtual worlds. They often have an RL environment that is disappointing for them. They therefore concentrate on their online teams and on social contacts in the game.

Finally, passive–secluded gamers tend to live more solitary lives and to act more cautiously when it comes to social contacts. In the interviews, they gave the impression of being socially anxious, and had notably fewer friends than the other interviewees. In general, they appeared to be more passive in their life in general. These gamers often focus solely on games as a resource for leisure-time activities and social contacts. Friends from VL contexts are very important and tend to replace RL contacts. Typical for these gamers is a deep immersion into the virtual world. Unsurprisingly, they showed clear signs of escapism. Very often the passive–secluded players tried to escape an RL that was meaningless for them, or was even regarded as being menacing or overwhelming. Most passive–secluded gamers show a very high identification with virtual groups and game characters, and much less with their "RL" surroundings.

Conclusion

As our study is a qualitative approach, we cannot generalize the particular patterns and types we found in our sample for all gamers, or even for other excessive gamers in other contexts. Nevertheless, the study shows that there are several forms of excessive gaming with different effects on different people. Some of our interviewees use gaming as an enrichment of their life, while others use it for compensating for problems or filling a void in their life. Even if there are numerous negative effects of excessive gaming, there are people who succeed in embedding gaming as their main hobby into their everyday life without experiencing major conflicts. However, there are others who do not succeed in doing so, which has severe effects on their everyday life and social environment. The two relatively more problematic excessive gamer types—meaning-seeking and passive–secluded—are at risk of such severe effects, because they prefer the game to their RL duties and social contacts. The game seems to be one aspect of this problematic behavior, but the actual causes might lie in RL and not in the virtual world.

Nevertheless, the study shows that a distinction between several groups of problematic users is essential for a better understanding of excessive gaming as a social phenomenon. Our study uncovers that there is no uniform effect of one specific game on everybody out there, and that some of the biographies under analysis clearly contradict the idea of excessive gaming being very similar to drug abuse and addiction. Accordingly, we need to reconsider some of the common ideas about excessive gaming. A solely gaming time-based definition of excessive gaming is not sufficient. Rather, it is more appropriate to distinguish frequent gamers based on their interaction with the game, the integration of the game into their everyday life, and the social environment of the gamers.

Note

1   Neither the ICD–10 (WHO 1993) nor the DSM-IV (APA 1994) include Internet or gaming addiction. Internet game addiction is expected to be included in the upcoming DSM V Section III, as a condition on which more research is still needed.

References

Anderson, C. A., Gentile, D. A., and Buckley, K. E. (2007). *Violent video game effects on children and adolescents*. New York City, New York: Oxford University Press.

Bartle, R. (1996). *Hearts, clubs, diamonds, spades – Players who suit MUDs*. Retrieved from http://www.mud.co.uk/richard/hcds.htm.

Charlton, J. P., and Danforth, I. D. W. (2007). Distinguishing addiction and high engagement in the context of online game playing. *Computers in Human Behavior, 23*(3), 1531–1548.

Denzin, N. K., and Lincoln, Y. S. (2011). Introduction: The discipline and practice of qualitative research. In N. K. Denzin and Y. S. Lincoln (Eds.), *The SAGE handbook of qualitative research* (pp. 1–19). Los Angeles, CA: Sage.

Domahidi, E., and Quandt, T. (2011, May). *"And all of a sudden, my life was gone": A biographical analysis of extreme gamers*, Paper presented at the 61st Annual International Communication Association Conference, Boston, MA.

Festl, R., Scharkow, M., and Quandt, T. (2013). Problematic computer game use among adolescents, younger and older adults. *Addiction, 108*(3), 592-599.

Griffiths, M. D. (2008). Videogame addiction: Further thoughts and observations. *International Journal of Mental Health and Addiction, 6*(2), 182–185.

Griffiths, M. D. (2010). The role of context in online gaming excess and addiction: Some case study evidence. *International Journal of Mental Health and Addiction, 8*(1), 119–125.

Griffiths, M. D., Davies, M. N. O., and Chappell, D. (2004). Online computer gaming: A comparison of adolescent and adult gamers. *Journal of Adolescence, 27*(1), 87–96.

Grüsser, S. M., Thalemann, R., and Griffiths, M. D. (2007). Excessive computer game playing: Evidence for addiction and aggression? *CyberPsychology and Behavior, 10*(2), 290–292.

Hellström, C., Nilsson, K. W., Leppert, J., and Åslund, C. (2012). Influences of motives to play and time spent gaming on the negative consequences of adolescent online computer gaming. *Computers in Human Behavior, 28*(4), 1379–1387.

Hussain, Z., and Griffiths, M. (2009). Excessive use of massively multi-player online role-playing games: A pilot study. *International Journal of Mental Health and Addiction, 7*(4), 563–571.

Karlsen, F. (2004). *Media complexity and diversity of use: Thoughts on a taxonomy of users of multiuser online games.* Proceedings of the Other Players conference; Center for Computer Games Research, IT University of Copenhagen, Denmark. Retrieved from https://files.itslearning.com/data/547/1523/2004%20 media%20complexity%20paper.pdf.

Kim, J., Kim, M., and Kim, E. J. (2008, May). Proceedings from the 58th Annual International Communication Association Conference: *Developing the problematic online game use (POGU) scale: Identifying underlying factors and testing convergent and discriminant validity.* Montreal, Canada.

Ko, C. H., Yen, J. Y., Chen, C. C., Chen, S. H., and Yen, C. F. (2005). Proposed diagnostic criteria of Internet addiction for adolescents. *The Journal of Nervous and Mental Disease, 193*(11), 728–733.

Lemmens, J. S., Valkenburg, P. M., and Peter, J. (2009). Development and validation of a game addiction scale for adolescents. *Media Psychology, 12*(1), 77–95.

Lenhart, A., Jones, S., and Macgill, A. R. (2008). *Adults and video games.* Pew Internet project data memo. Retrieved from http://pewinternet.org/~/media// Files/Reports/2008/PIP_Adult_gaming_memo.pdf.pdf.

Lindlof, T. R. (1995). *Qualitative communication research methods.* London, United Kingdom: Sage.

Mayring, P. (2002). Qualitative content analysis: Research instrument or mode of interpretation? In M. Kiegelmann (Ed.), *The role of the researcher in qualitative psychology* (pp. 139–148). Tübingen, Germany: Huber.

Meyer, F., Janz, C., Zeng, Y., and Pietrowsky, R. (2009, September). *The excessive online role-playing scale: A diagnostic instrument for the determination of clinically relevant usage of massively multiplayer online role-playing games.* Paper presented at the 6th Conference of the Media Psychology Division of the German Psychological Society, Duisburg, Germany. Abstract retrieved from http://www.piaorcs.uni-duesseldorf.de/25questions_results.pdf.

Nomura, T., and Goto, Y. (2012). *Exploring personality traits of excessive online game users in Japan.* Proceedings of the 10th Asia Pacific Conference on Computer Human Interaction, Matsue, Japan.

Quandt, T., Festl, R., and Scharkow, M. (2011). Digitales Spielen – Medienunterhaltung im Mainstream. GameStat 2011: Repräsentativbefragung zum Computer- und Konsolenspielen in Deutschland [Digital gaming – media entertainment in the mainstream. GameStat 2011: A representative survey on computer- and console-gaming in Germany]. *Media Perspektiven, 9,* 414–422.

Quandt, T., and Wimmer, J. (2008). *Online-Spieler in Deutschland 2007: Befunde einer repräsentativen Befragungsstudie* [Online gamers in Germany 2007: Findings from a representative survey study]. In T. Quandt, J. Wimmer, and J. Wolling (Eds.), *Die Computerspieler: Studien zur Nutzung von Computergames* [The computer gamers: Studies on the use of computer games] (pp. 169–192). Wiesbaden, Germany: VS Verlag.

Rehbein, F., Kleimann, M., and Mößle, T. (2010). Prevalence and risk factors of video game dependency in adolescence: Results of a German nationwide survey. *Cyberpsychology, Behavior, and Social Networking, 13*(3), 269–277.

Spekman, M. L. C., Konijn, E. A., and Roelofsma, P. H. M. P. (2012, May). *Excessive gaming: Healthy enthusiasm or pathological personality?* Paper presented at the 62nd Annual Conference of the International Communication Association, Phoenix, AZ.

Turner, N. E. (2008). A comment on "~Problems with the concept of video game 'addiction': Some case study examples". *International Journal of Mental Health and Addiction, 6*(2), 186–190.

Weber, R., Ritterfeld, U., and Mathiak, K. (2006). Does playing violent video games induce aggression? Empirical evidence of a functional magnetic resonance imaging study. *Media Psychology, 8*(1), 39–60.

Young, K. (2009). Understanding online gaming addiction and treatment issues for adolescents. *The American Journal of Family Therapy, 37*(5), 355–372.

Games Cited

Blizzard Entertainment (2004), *World of Warcraft*, Vivendi Activision Blizzard.

18 Friendship Quality Matters for Multiplayer Gamers

The Role of Online and Real-Life Friendship Quality in the Relationship Between Game Addiction and Psychological Well-Being in a Sample of Adolescent Online Gamers

Antonius J. van Rooij, Tim M. Schoenmakers, Regina J. J. M. van den Eijnden, Ad A. Vermulst, and Dike van de Mheen

Introduction[1]

Previous studies have demonstrated that a small group of online video game players has trouble controlling their gaming behavior (Chiu, Lee, and Huang, 2004; Gentile, 2009; Grüsser, Thalemann, and Griffiths, 2007; van Rooij, Schoenmakers, Vermulst, van den Eijnden, and van de Mheen, 2011). While these people show a loss of control over gaming that can result in considerable harm, there is an ongoing debate on the classification of this behavior as a new addiction; that is, "video game addiction" (VGA) (American Psychiatric Association, 2010; Wood, 2008).

Previous research has established criteria that conceptualize "behavioral addictions" (Griffiths, 2005). They have been modified to fit the specific nature of VGA (van Rooij, 2011; van Rooij, Schoenmakers, van den Eijnden, Vermulst, and van de Mheen, 2012). This leads to the operational definition of VGA as an addiction-like behavior, which includes experiencing (a) a loss of control over the behavior, (b) conflicts with the self and with others, (c) preoccupation with gaming, (d) the utilization of games for purposes of coping/mood modification, and (e) withdrawal symptoms (van Rooij, 2011; van Rooij et al., 2012). This definition places the behavior on a dimensional continuum (Helzer, van den Brink, and Guth, 2006) and does not refer to a "clinical" diagnosis.

Researchers consistently find relationships between measures of VGA and psychosocial problems, such as depressive mood, social anxiety, loneliness, and negative self-esteem (Ko, Yen, Chen, Chen, and Yen, 2005; Ng and Wiemer-Hastings, 2005; Rehbein, Psych, Kleimann, Mediasci, and Mößle, 2010; van Rooij et al., 2011; Wood, Gupta, Derevensky, and Griffiths, 2004). These findings make sense, as one would expect some degree of harm to be associated with an excessive behavior that interferes with healthy psychological and social functioning. Therefore, we hypothesize that a positive relationship exists between psychosocial problems and VGA (hypothesis 1).

Furthermore, accounts of VGA are often linked to multiplayer, "online" games (Council on Science and Public Health, 2007), and specifically to massively multiplayer online role-playing games or MMORPGs (Hussain and Griffiths, 2009; Rehbein et al., 2010). The social features of these types of online games have been associated with "problem video gaming" (King, Delfabbro, and Griffiths, 2010). For example, some of the more successful multiplayer online games have the unique feature of having an ultra-large budget (due to recurring monthly payments and popularity). This has enabled some publishers to create highly sophisticated reward structures in these games (i.e. in *World of Warcraft* [Blizzard Entertainment, 2004], *(WoW)*, coupled with a virtually endless supply of game content and deep social structures. As the gamers become more involved with their online gaming friends, peer pressure to play increases. From this, a high quality of online friendships (QOF) and the level of VGA are thought to have a positive relationship (hypothesis 2a).

However, online games include "highly socially interactive environments providing the opportunity to create strong friendships and emotional relationships" (Cole and Griffiths, 2007, p. 575). A positive effect of online gaming can be explained through the Self Determination Theory (SDT) (Ryan and Deci, 2000), which poses that relatedness is one of the three core components in any intrinsically motivated behavior, such as online video game gaming. Additionally, fulfillment of relatedness has been linked to improved well-being (Reis, Sheldon, Gable, Roscoe, and Ryan, 2000). The effect of social support on the alleviation of negative psychological symptoms was demonstrated within the popular online game WoW (Longman, O'Connor, and Obst, 2009). Thus, having high-quality, in-game, online friendships is thought to have positive effects on psychological well-being (hypothesis 3).

Seemingly paradoxical, this idea actually complements hypothesis 2a: While higher-quality online friendships are thought to be associated with higher levels of VGA (through mechanisms such as peer pressure), maintaining high-quality online friendships is hypothesized to reduce negative psychological symptoms (hypothesis 3). This positive effect is expected to be more pronounced at higher levels of VGA, where social support is more strongly needed. Therefore, the positive relationship between addiction level and psychosocial problems is expected to be attenuated by higher-quality online friendships and (vice versa) strengthened by lower-quality online friendships (hypothesis 4).

While the phenomenon of having exclusively online friendships might be new, real-world or "real-life" friendships are not. In fact, gamers are not the socially disconnected group of online dwellers that some have suspected: "Rather, they were more functional individuals who maintained contact with real-world friends and relatives in a more complex manner online"

(Hussain and Griffiths, 2008, p. 47). Firstly, similarly to online friendships, we expect quality of real-life friendship (QRF) to suffer under VGA and to be negatively associated with it (hypothesis 2b). Again, we expect those who maintain high-quality friendships in spite of the VGA to do better. In addition to fulfilling the relatedness need as posed by the SDT (Ryan and Deci, 2000), close real-life friendships have been associated with lower social anxiety (La Greca and Lopez, 1998), higher self-esteem, and better psychosocial adjustment (La Greca and Harrison, 2005). Thus, we hypothesize that maintaining good real-life friendships positively moderates the relationship between VGA and negative psychological symptoms (hypothesis 5).

Besides the explorative work describing a preference for online communication over real-life communication among heavy gamers (Hussain and Griffiths, 2008), no efforts have been made to examine the moderating role of online and real-life friendship quality in this relationship between VGA and psychosocial well-being. Nevertheless, it is clear that social relationships are an integral part of multiplayer online video games and need to be taken into account in the study of VGA. The current chapter therefore aims to test the five hypotheses in a large adolescent sample.

Method

Sample

This study uses the 2009 sample of the yearly "Monitor Study Internet and Youth." The sample includes ten Dutch secondary schools and contains information from 171 classes. The total sample response rate was 83%, resulting in 4074 completed questionnaires. After accounting for some missing values on demographic variables, an effective sample size of 4054 was established. Non-response is mainly attributable to entire classes dropping out due to internal scheduling problems: 12% of all classes did not return any questionnaires. The average response rate per class for the remaining classes was 92%. For more details see earlier publications (van Rooij, Schoenmakers, van den Eijnden, and van de Mheen, 2010; van Rooij et al., 2011).

A subsample (n = 1468) of online multiplayer gamers was identified as those who spend at least one hour per week on online multiplayer games with others (this category does not include casual browser games, such as Facebook games). This subsample is skewed with 81% boys (50% main sample) and a slightly lower age at 14.1 (main sample: 14.3). The majority of both the online gamers' subsample (58%) as well at the main sample (59%) are enrolled in higher (as opposed to lower) secondary education.

Measures

Psychosocial outcome measures. Measures were used to establish various aspects of psychological well-being, focusing on self-esteem, loneliness, depressive mood, and social anxiety. Firstly, Rosenberg's ten-item Negative

Self-Esteem Scale (Rosenberg, 1989) was used (Cronbach's α = .87). Answers are given on a four-point scale ranging from "does not fit me at all" to "fits me well." Example item: "At times I think I am no good at all." Secondly, the UCLA ten-item Loneliness Scale (Russell, Peplau, and Cutrona, 1980) was used with a five-point answer scale, ranging from "does not fit me at all" to "fits me completely" (Cronbach's α = .87). Example item: "I feel lonely." Thirdly, a Dutch translation of the six-item Depressive Mood List (Engels, Finkenauer, Meeus, and Deković, 2001; Kandel and Davies, 1982, 1986) was used, with a five-point answer scale ranging from "never" to "always" (Cronbach's α = .82). Example item: "I feel too tired to do anything." Finally, a ten-item Revised Social Anxiety Scale for Children (La Greca and Stone, 1993) was used (Cronbach's α = .89) with a five-point answer scale, ranging from "not at all" to "very much." Example item: "I am quiet when I'm in a group." The translations have demonstrated good reliability and have been used in earlier studies (Meerkerk, 2007; van den Eijnden, Meerkerk, Vermulst, Spijkerman, and Engels, 2008; van Rooij et al., 2011).

Video Game Addiction Test (VAT). The 14-item VAT scale was validated using the same sample that was used in the current study: The scale demonstrated a one-factor model fit, excellent reliability (Cronbach's α = .93), and good construct validity (van Rooij, 2011; van Rooij et al., 2012). The VAT has a strong relationship (r = .74) with a related scale; namely, with the Game Addiction Scale (Lemmens, Valkenburg, and Peter, 2009). Example item: "How often do you find it difficult to stop gaming?" Answer options range from "never" to "very often" on a five-point scale.

Quality of online and real-life friendship. To assess the quality of friendships, we used Buhrmester's relationship inventory (Furman and Buhrmester, 1985), which was previously used and translated into Dutch (Valkenburg and Peter, 2007). Valkenburg and Peter also created two eight-item versions of the questionnaire: one pertaining to exclusively online relationships ("think about exclusively online friends, who you do not see in real life") and one to real-life friendships ("think about your real-life friends, who you also encounter in real life"). While these scales comprise various elements (relationship satisfaction, approval, and support), they all load on a single factor (Selfhout, 2009, p. 245), and as such they are combined into a single measure for each version of the scale. Example item: "How often do you turn to these friends for support with personal problems?" (Valkenburg and Peter, 2007, pp. 1174–1175). In the current sample, both scales demonstrate excellent reliability (QRF: α = .90; QOF: α = .93).

Strategy of Analyses

The first three hypotheses are correlational in nature. Thus, SPSS 19 was utilized to establish descriptive statistics and zero-order correlations. In order to study the hypothesized moderating role of online (hypothesis 4) and real-life (hypothesis 5) friendship quality, we follow Hayes and Matthes (2009), who state that a moderating effect "reveals itself statistically as an interaction between the independent and moderator variables in a model of the outcome variable." Therefore, multiple linear regression models were used. Tested interactions were restricted to the directly hypothesized relationship between the VAT and the friendship scales, and the potential interaction between the two friendship quality scales themselves to avoid chance capitalization. After identification of an interaction through the regression models, the post-hoc procedure and SPSS macro developed by Hayes and Matthes was used to probe and plot the nature of the identified moderation effects (Hayes and Matthes, 2009). The conditional effect of the various predictors was established for various values of the moderator variable, using three groups: one SD above the mean (high), one SD below the mean (low), and the mean itself (Hayes and Matthes, 2009; Selfhout, et al., 2009).

Results

1 Zero-Order Correlations

Table 18.1 presents the correlations for the various psychosocial variables, the QOF, the QRF, and the VAT. In line with hypothesis 1, moderate positive correlations ($p < .001$) are found between VAT and the various psychosocial variables: depressive mood ($r = .38$), loneliness ($r = .33$), social anxiety ($r = .30$), and negative self-esteem ($r = .29$). In line with hypothesis 2, a positive relationship (hypothesis 2a) was found between QOF and VAT ($r = .18$, $p < .001$), and a negative relationship (hypothesis 2b) was found between VAT and QRF ($r = -.13$, $p < .001$). In contradiction with predictions from hypothesis 3, a positive relationship was found between QOF and three out of the four included psychosocial problems. Only loneliness is negatively related with QOF.

Table 18.1 Pearson Correlations for Psychosocial Measures, Friendship Quality, VGA, and Online Gameplay for a Sample of Online Game Players (N = 1468)

	1	2	3	4	5	6	7
1 Video Game Addiction Test	1.00						
2 Quality of Online Friendships	0.18***	1.00					
3 Quality of Real-Life Friendships	−0.13***	0.25***	1.00				
4 Depressive Mood List	0.38***	0.17***	−0.07*	1.00			
5 Loneliness Scale	0.33***	−0.03	−0.41***	0.41***	1.00		
6 Social Anxiety for Children	0.30***	0.11***	−0.16***	0.48***	0.49***	1.00	
7 Negative Self-Esteem Scale	0.29***	0.12***	−0.18***	0.51***	0.56***	0.48***	1.00

* $p < .05$, ** $p < .01$, *** $p < .001$

2 Three-Step Linear Regression Model

The model in Table 18.2 presents the coefficients for the full regression model (third step), which includes the interaction terms for QRF and VAT, QOF and VAT, and QOF and QRF. The model identifies several interaction terms (albeit minor ones). The interaction for depression is ignored, as the third step does not add significant explanatory value to the model, which means that three interaction terms are identified; namely, QRF*VAT and Loneliness ($\beta = -.07$, $p < .05$), QOF*VAT and Loneliness ($\beta = -.09$, $p < .01$), and QRF*VAT and Social Anxiety ($\beta = -.12$, $p < .01$). To facilitate interpretation of the interaction terms as indicators of possible moderation, the three interactions are explored further using graphs and statistical probing (see below, 3: "Moderation probing"). Besides these interaction terms, model results show a positive relationship between VAT and the various psychosocial outcome measures ($p < .001$): depression ($\beta = .36$), social anxiety ($\beta = .24$), negative self-esteem ($\beta = .29$), and loneliness ($\beta = .29$). Results also show that female online gamers tend to score higher on the various psychosocial outcome measures ($p < .001$, $\beta = .20$ and higher).

Table 18.2 Prediction of the Various Psychosocial Measures from the VAT Score and Friendship Quality for the Online Gamers' Sample

	Depression ($R^2=.24$, $p<.001$)		Loneliness ($R^2=.27$, $p<.001$)		Social anxiety ($R^2=.15$, $p<.001$)		Negative self-esteem ($R^2=.23$, $p<.001$)	
	β	ΔR^2	β	ΔR^2	β	ΔR^2	β	ΔR^2
(Constant)								
Gender (0/1=girl)	0.27***		0.18***		0.20***		0.28***	
Education level (0/1=high)	0.01		−0.07*		0.01		−0.10**	
Age	0.01		−0.01		0.00		−0.09**	
		0.06***		0.03***		0.03***		0.10***
VAT	0.36***		0.29***		0.24***		0.29***	
QOF	0.10**		0.02		0.08*		0.10**	
QRF	−0.07*		−0.33***		−0.12**		−0.19***	
		0.18***		0.24***		0.12***		0.13***
QRF * VAT	−0.07*		−0.07*		−0.12**		0.03	
QOF * VAT	−0.01		−0.09**		0.00		−0.02	
QOF * QRF	0.02		0.04		−0.01		0.04	
		0.00		0.02***		0.01**		0.00

Note: QRF = quality of real-life friendships, QOF = quality of online friendships, VAT = Video game addiction test.
* $p < .05$, ** $p < .01$, *** $p < .001$

3 Moderation Probing

Figures 18.1, 18.2, and 18.3 visualize the moderating effect of friendship quality (hypotheses 4 and 5). VAT scores were mean-centered during the analyses (mean = 1.6) but are reported as scale values (non-centered) in the figure. Figure 18.1 shows the moderating effect of the QOF for loneliness. For those with high online friendship quality, higher VAT predicts less loneliness ($b = .17$, $p < .001$), while for those with a low online friendship quality, higher VAT is related to more loneliness ($b = .28$, $p < .001$).

Figure 18.2 shows the moderating effect of the QRF for loneliness. For those with high real-life friendship quality, higher VAT predicts less loneliness ($b = .20$, $p < .001$), while for those with a low real-life friendship quality, higher VAT is related to more loneliness ($b = .26$, $p < .001$). The difference is less pronounced than for online friendships.

Figure 18.3 shows the moderating effect of the QRF for social anxiety. For those with high real-life friendship quality, higher VAT predicts less social anxiety ($b = .20$, $p < .001$), while for those with a low real-life friendship quality, higher VAT is related to more social anxiety ($b = .34$, $p < .001$).

Discussion

This chapter investigated the relationship between VGA and psychosocial well-being, focusing on the moderating role of online and real-life friendship quality in this relationship. Findings demonstrate a positive

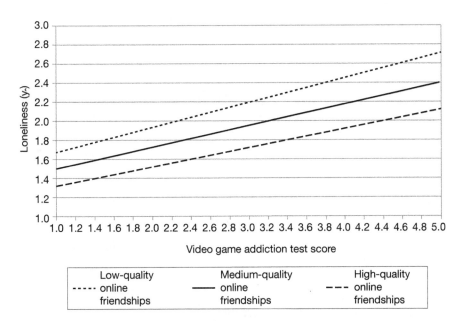

Figure 18.1 Conditional Effects of Online Friendship Quality on the Prediction of Loneliness by Video Game Addiction (VAT).

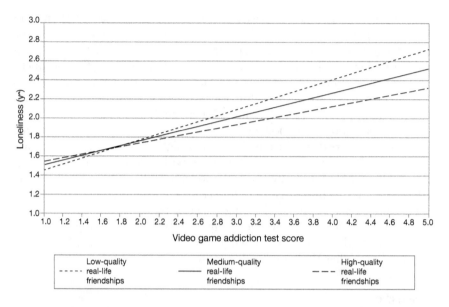

Figure 18.2 Conditional Effects of Real-Life Friendship Quality on the Prediction of Loneliness by VAT.

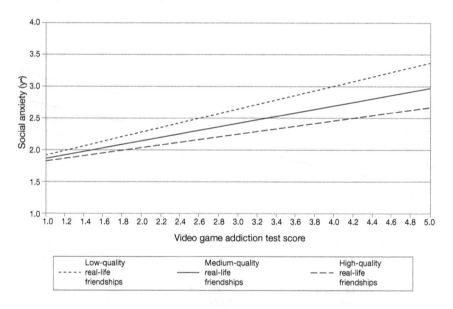

Figure 18.3 Conditional Effects of Real-Life Friendship Quality on the Prediction of Social Anxiety by VAT.

relationship between VGA and psychosocial problems, thus confirming hypothesis 1. Furthermore, results confirm higher VGA scores are associated with higher-quality online friendships (hypothesis 2a) and lower-quality real-life friendships (hypothesis 2b). An unexpected finding was the positive association between a higher QOF and psychosocial problems: social anxiety, negative self-esteem, and depressive mood (not loneliness). This finding contradicts hypothesis 3, but does not necessarily mean that online friendships are bad for you, as the finding describes an association, not a cause. A likely explanation for the finding is the fact that adolescents with heightened psychosocial problems tend to prefer online communication to face-to-face communication (Valkenburg and Peter, 2011).

Research shows that higher-quality online friendships are an integral part of the online game experience, and thus, are positively associated with VGA (King et al., 2010). However, we also argue that maintaining high-quality online (and real-life) friendships should be associated with better psychosocial health (Reis et al., 2000), due to the fulfillment of the need for relatedness (Ryan and Deci, 2000; Tamborini, Bowman, Eden, Grizzard, and Organ, 2010). This leads to two more hypotheses, which state that maintaining high-quality online (hypothesis 4) and real-life (hypothesis 5) friendships is expected to reduce negative psychological symptoms associated with higher VGA.

In line with hypotheses 4 and 5, the relationship between VGA and certain aspects of psychosocial well-being was found to be moderated by the quality of online and real-life friendships. Three specific instances of moderation were found. Gamers with low-quality online and real-life friendships are lonelier at higher levels of VGA, compared to gamers with (respectively) high-quality online and real-life friendships. Thirdly, gamers with a low QRF demonstrate more social anxiety at higher levels of game addiction, compared to gamers with a high quality of real-life friendships.

While the effect sizes involved are low, the findings are relevant, as they demonstrate that friendship quality can potentially alleviate the negative psychosocial symptoms of loneliness associated with higher levels of VGA—even if the friendships are virtual. With regard to social anxiety, it is possible that those with a higher level of game addiction, especially if they have low-quality real-life friendships, have less opportunity to practice real-life social skills, and this results in higher social anxiety (Beidel et al., 2007; Bonetti, Campbell, and Gilmore, 2010). On the other hand, the causality might be bi-directional or even reversed: Those with social anxiety could be more prone to have low-quality real-life friendships and escape into VGA. Given the cross-sectional nature of the current study, both explanations could be true.

The current study has several limitations. First, this study uses cross-sectional data, which means that all results should be interpreted as relationships between variables—and certainly not as "effects" or "causes." Given the scarcity of research in this area, although this study provides valuable insights, future research in this area would benefit from a longitudinal perspective. Second, the study necessarily uses self-report data, which carries the risk of various forms of bias, for example, social desirability bias (Podsakoff, MacKenzie, Lee, and Podsakoff, 2003). Third, the study shows weak relationships in terms of effect size. While the findings present a valuable contribution to existing knowledge, they should be interpreted in the light of their epidemiological nature. Care should be taken in extrapolating findings to therapeutic settings. Fourth, the study focuses on the quality of friendships in order to fit the theoretical expectations; however, quality of friendships is just one aspect of adolescent social life. One could expand on this topic by including, for example, the number of friends that each adolescent has (Valkenburg and Peter, 2007).

The current chapter explored the relationship between psychosocial problems and VGA, and the possible moderation of this relationship by the quality of online and real-life friendships. Clear relationships were found between psychosocial problems and VGA, and QOF and VGA. Furthermore, the study demonstrated three instances of moderation of this relationship by online friendship quality (for loneliness) and real-life friendship quality (for social anxiety and loneliness). In these cases, the relationship between game addiction and lower psychosocial health is found to be weaker for those with high-quality online and offline friendships. These findings demonstrate that online and real-life friendship quality play a role in the severity of problems associated with VGA.

Note

1   The current chapter describes an empirical study in the area of video game addiction, which is a rewritten and updated version of a chapter in the PhD thesis "Online video game addiction: Exploring a new phenomenon" (van Rooij, 2011).

References

American Psychiatric Association (Ed.). (2010). Substance-related disorders (Internet). *American Psychiatric Association – DSM–5 Development*.

Beidel, D., Turner, S., Young, B., Ammerman, R., Sallee, F., and Crosby, L. (2007). Psychopathology of adolescent social phobia. *Journal of Psychopathology and Behavioral Assessment, 29*(1), 46–53.

Bonetti, L., Campbell, M. A., and Gilmore, L. (2010). The relationship of loneliness and social anxiety with children's and adolescents' online communication. *Cyberpsychology, Behavior, and Social Networking, 13*(3), 279–285.

Chiu, S.-I., Lee, J.-Z., and Huang, D.-H. (2004). Video game addiction in children and teenagers in Taiwan. *CyberPsychology and Behavior, 7*(5), 571–581.

Cole, H., and Griffiths, M. D. (2007). Social interactions in massively multiplayer online role-playing gamers. *CyberPsychology and Behavior, 10*(4), 575–583.

Council on Science and Public Health (Ed.). (2007). *Emotional and behavioral effects, including addictive potential, of video games*. Chicago, IL: American Medical Association. Retrieved from http://www.ama-assn.org/resources/doc/csaph/csaph12a07-fulltext.pdf.

Engels, R. C. M. E., Finkenauer, C., Meeus, W. H. J., and Deković, M. (2001). Attachment and adolescents' emotional adjustment: The associations with social skills and relational competence. *Journal of Counseling Psychology*, 48(4), 428–439.

Furman, W., and Buhrmester, D. (1985). Children's perceptions of the qualities of sibling relationships. *Child Development*, 56, 448–461.

Gentile, D. A. (2009). Pathological video-game use among youth ages 8 to 18: A national study. *Psychological Science*, 20(5), 594–602.

Griffiths, M. D. (2005). A "components" model of addiction within a biopsychosocial framework. *Journal of Substance Use*, 10(4), 191–197.

Grüsser, S. M., Thalemann, R., and Griffiths, M. D. (2007). Excessive computer game playing: Evidence for addiction and aggression? *CyberPsychology and Behavior*, 10(2), 290–292.

Hayes, A. F., and Matthes, J. (2009). Computational procedures for probing interactions in OLS and logistic regression: SPSS and SAS implementations. *Behavior Research Methods*, 41(3), 924.

Helzer, J. E., van den Brink, W., and Guth, S. E. (2006). Should there be both categorical and dimensional criteria for the substance use disorders in DSM-V? *Addiction*, 101 Suppl , 17–22.

Hussain, Z., and Griffiths, M. D. (2008). Gender swapping and socializing in cyberspace: An exploratory study. *CyberPsychology and Behavior*, 11(1), 47–53.

Hussain, Z., and Griffiths, M. D. (2009). Excessive use of massively multi-player online role-playing games: A pilot study. *International Journal of Mental Health and Addiction*, 11(1), 47–53.

Kandel, D. B., and Davies, M. N. O. (1982). Epidemiology of depressive mood in adolescents: An empirical study. *Archives of General Psychiatry*, 39(10), 1205–1212.

Kandel, D. B., and Davies, M. N. O. (1986). Adult sequelae of adolescent depressive symptoms. *Archives of General Psychiatry*, 43(3), 255–262.

King, D. L., Delfabbro, P. H., and Griffiths, M. D. (2010). The role of structural characteristics in problematic video game play: An empirical study. *International Journal of Mental Health and Addiction*, 9(3), 320–333.

Ko, C.-H., Yen, J.-Y., Chen, C.-C., Chen, S.-H., and Yen, C.-F. (2005). Gender differences and related factors affecting online gaming addiction among Taiwanese adolescents. *The Journal of Nervous and Mental Disease*, 193(4), 273–277.

La Greca, A. M., and Harrison, H. M. (2005). Adolescent peer relations, friendships, and romantic relationships: Do they predict social anxiety and depression? *Journal of Clinical Child and Adolescent Psychology*, 34(1), 49–61.

La Greca, A. M., and Lopez, N. (1998). Social anxiety among adolescents: Linkages with peer relations and friendships. *Journal of Abnormal Child Psychology*, 26(2), 83–94–94.

La Greca, A. M., and Stone, W. L. (1993). Social anxiety scale for children—revised: Factor structure and concurrent validity. *Journal of Clinical Child Psychology*, 22(1), 17–27.

Lemmens, J. S., Valkenburg, P. M., and Peter, J. (2009). Development and validation of a game addiction scale for adolescents. *Media Psychology*, 12(1), 77–95.

Longman, H., O'Connor, E., and Obst, P. (2009). The effect of social support derived from *World of Warcraft* on negative psychological symptoms. *CyberPsychology and Behavior*, 12(5), 563–566.

Meerkerk, G.-J. (2007). *Pwned by the Internet. Explorative research into the causes and consequences of compulsive Internet use.* Doctoral Thesis, Erasmus University Rotterdam, The Netherlands. Retrieved from http://repub.eur.nl/res/pub/10511/.

Ng, B., and Wiemer-Hastings, P. (2005). Addiction to the Internet and online gaming. *CyberPsychology and Behavior, 8*(2), 110–114.

Podsakoff, P. M., MacKenzie, S. B., Lee, J. Y., and Podsakoff, N. P. (2003). Common method biases in behavioral research: A critical review of the literature and recommended remedies. *Journal of Applied Psychology, 88*(5), 879–903.

Rehbein, F., Psych, G., Kleimann, M., Mediasci, G., and Mößle, T. (2010). Prevalence and risk factors of video game dependency in adolescence: Results of a German nationwide survey. *Cyberpsychology, Behavior, and Social Networking, 13*(3), 269–277.

Reis, H. T., Sheldon, K. M., Gable, S. L., Roscoe, J., and Ryan, R. M. (2000). Daily well-being: The role of autonomy, competence, and relatedness. *Personality and Social Psychology Bulletin, 26*(4), 419–435.

Rosenberg, M. (1989). *Society and the adolescent self-image* (Revised ed.). Middletown: Wesleyan University Press.

Russell, D., Peplau, L. A., and Cutrona, C. E. (1980). The revised UCLA loneliness scale: Concurrent and discriminant validity evidence. *Journal of Personality and Social Psychology, 39*(3), 472–480.

Ryan, R. M., and Deci, E. L. (2000). Self-determination theory and the facilitation of intrinsic motivation, social development, and well-being. *The American Psychologist, 55*(1), 68–78.

Selfhout, M. H. W. (2009). *Me, myself, and you: Friendships in adolescence.* Utrecht, The Netherlands: Lambert Academic Publishing.

Selfhout, M. H. W., Branje, S. J. T., Delsing, M., Ter Bogt, T. F. M., and Meeus, W. H. J. (2009). Different types of Internet use, depression, and social anxiety: The role of perceived friendship quality. *Journal of Adolescence, 32*(4), 819–833.

Tamborini, R., Bowman, N. D., Eden, A., Grizzard, M., and Organ, A. (2010). Defining media enjoyment as the satisfaction of intrinsic needs. *Journal of Communication, 60*(4), 758–777.

Valkenburg, P. M., and Peter, J. (2007). Online communication and adolescent well-being: Testing the stimulation versus the displacement hypothesis. *Journal of Computer-Mediated Communication, 12*(4), 1169–1182.

Valkenburg, P. M., and Peter, J. (2011). Online communication among adolescents: An integrated model of its attraction, opportunities, and risks. *Journal of Adolescent Health, 48*(2), 121–127.

van den Eijnden, R. J. J. M., Meerkerk, G.-J., Vermulst, A. A., Spijkerman, R., and Engels, R. C. M. E. (2008). Online communication, compulsive Internet use, and psychosocial well-being among adolescents: A longitudinal study. *Developmental Psychology, 44*(3), 655–665.

van Rooij, A. J. (2011). *Online video game addiction. Exploring a new phenomenon.* PhD Thesis. Erasmus University Rotterdam, The Netherlands: Retrieved from http://repub.eur.nl/res/pub/23381/.

van Rooij, A. J., Schoenmakers, T. M., van den Eijnden, R. J. J. M., and van de Mheen, D. (2010). Compulsive Iinternet use: The role of online gaming and other Internet applications. *The Journal of Adolescent Health, 47*(1), 51–57.

van Rooij, A. J., Schoenmakers, T. M., van den Eijnden, R. J. J. M., Vermulst, A. A, and van de Mheen, D. (2012). Video game addiction test: Validity and psychometric characteristics. *Cyberpsychology, Behavior and Social Networking, 15*(9), 507–11.

van Rooij, A. J., Schoenmakers, T. M., Vermulst, A. A., van den Eijnden, R. J. J. M., and van de Mheen, D. (2011). Online video game addiction: Identification of addicted adolescent gamers. *Addiction, 106*(1), 205–212.

Wood, R. T. A. (2008). Problems with the concept of video game "addiction": Some case study examples. *International Journal of Mental Health and Addiction, 6*(2), 169–178.

Wood, R. T. A., Gupta, R., Derevensky, J. L., and Griffiths, M. D. (2004). Video game playing and gambling in adolescents: Common risk factors. *Journal of Child and Adolescent Substance Abuse, 14*(1), 77–100.

Games Cited

Blizzard Entertainment (2004), *World of Warcraft*, Vivendi Activision Blizzard.

19 Isolated Violence, Isolated Players, Isolated Aggression

The Social Realism of Experimental Research on Digital Games and Aggression

Malte Elson and Johannes Breuer

Introduction

The link between violent content in digital games and aggression is one of the most controversial topics in media effects research. Numerous studies have been conducted to answer the one decisive question: Does playing violent digital games result in socially inacceptable expressions of aggressive behavior? Despite the large body of cross-sectional correlational and experimental studies and meta-analyses that have been conducted to answer this question, the results diverge so much that the interpretation and contextualization of the effects' magnitude alone still causes heated and, at times, polemic debates among scholars (Grimes, Anderson, and Bergen, 2008). Particularly the real-life implications of the findings are heavily discussed (see Bushman, Rothstein, and Anderson, 2010 vs. Ferguson and Kilburn, 2010).

Several scholars have identified a number of problems that limit the validity of the findings in this area, such as unclear conceptual definitions of violence and/or aggression (Grimes et al., 2008), improper variable manipulation, operationalization, and control (Adachi and Willoughby, 2011a; Elson, Breuer, Van Looy, and Kneer, 2012), questionable measures of aggression (Ferguson, 2011), or a lack of ecological validity or observable real-world impact (Sherry, 2007; Ward, 2011). An additional limitation is the general neglect of the social dimension of gaming (Schmierbach, 2010; Southwell and Doyle, 2004; Williams, 2005). Most of the studies on digital games and aggression focus on the content of the games, while the other factors identified by Gentile (2011), such as game mechanics and the (social) context, have received very little attention.

Many of the experimental studies on the effects of digital games on aggression follow a certain pattern in their design: Participants either play a violent or a non-violent game. In almost all cases, these games are single-player games or the studies only use the single-player mode. After playing, the participants' level of aggression is measured via a behavioral test. In most of these studies, the researchers use two or more games that differ in the amount and/or type of violent content that they feature, such as *Grand Theft Auto: Vice City* (Rockstar North, 2002) and *Tetris*, for example (Cicchirillo and Chory-Assad, 2005). What is problematic in this approach, however, is that most games differ on more dimensions than just their graphical displays of violence. Other characteristics that can influence the player experience are, for example, game speed (Elson et al., 2012), difficulty, or competitiveness (Adachi and Willoughby, 2011b). In addition, games may be played alone, such as point-and-click adventure games, or together with other players, such as massively multiplayer online role-playing games (MMORPGs) or sports games. What further complicates this matter is that these characteristics are often confounded with violent content, as some genres, such as the notorious first-person shooters (FPSs), are usually faster-paced, feature more violent content, and are more likely to be played competitively and against other human players.

As the example shows, the nature of digital games as interactive and social media adds a whole new layer of potentially influential variables. The interactions with the game or other players and the outcomes of these can strongly affect the experience of a player and, thus, their cognitions, emotional state, and subsequent behavior. This covers all types of social behaviors, such as talking to others about the playing experience, or directing game-induced anger toward another person that may or may not have been part of the previous gaming experience.

Games as Social Media

Just like their non-digital counterparts, digital games are interactive and inherently social media. According to de Kort and IJsselsteijn (2008), the social context of digital game playing is one of the most important factors shaping the player experience, that is, at the same time, frequently neglected in user-experience research. Most of the stimulus material for research on digital games and aggression comes from the genre of the FPS, for example, *Counter-Strike: Source* (Valve Corporation, 2004), or fighting games, for example, the *Mortal Kombat* series. Although social interactions in these games are not as important as in the MMORPGs, such as *World of Warcraft* (Blizzard Entertainment, 2004), most of the recent and current FPSs support at least one multiplayer mode (nowadays very often online), and the popularity of fighting games has always been associated with the possibility of the co-located competitive play that they offer.

In a representative survey study, Quandt, Scharkow, and Festl (2010) found that 57% of German gamers frequently play with others in person, and 38% play with others online. Industry data from the USA indicate that co-located play is a common activity for 62% of gamers (Entertainment Software Association, 2012). Despite the popularity of playing with or against other players, the violent games in aggression research are usually presented in a single-player mode, which puts the generalizability to the users' actual experience of everyday digital game playing into question.

Playing together with or against others, be it mediated or co-located, alters the overall experience of a game, and is thus likely to affect some of the commonly measured outcome variables in aggression research. Gajadhar, de Kort, and IJsselsteijn (2008), for example, found that positive affect and feelings of competence were increased, and tension was decreased, when their participants played against human opponents. Ravaja et al. (2005) found that playing against a human opponent elicited more positive emotional responses, but also led to increases in spatial presence, engagement, self-reported physiological arousal, and anticipated threat. Except for anticipated threat, all effects were larger when playing against a friend rather than a stranger. A substantial body of research also indicates that playing a violent game cooperatively with others increases cooperative or helping behavior after play (Ewoldsen et al., 2012; Greitemeyer, Traut-Mattausch, and Osswald, 2012; Velez, Mahood, Ewoldsen, and Moyer-Gusé, in press). Ekman et al. (2012) even suggest that shared gaming experiences may lead to synchronization in physiological arousal among the players, making the emotional reactions to in-game events and to the actions of other players a highly complex, reciprocal process.

There can also be aversive effects with human co-players. Following the assumptions of the classical frustration–aggression hypothesis by Dollard et al. (1939), and its reformulation by Berkowitz (1989), the frustrations experienced by players can increase the inclination to act or respond aggressively after play. While in single-player games frustrations typically arise from a mismatch between the game's demands and the player's skills, in a multiplayer game, human co-players or competitors can be major sources of frustration (Schmierbach, 2010). As inferior co-players or superior opponents can reduce the experience of self-efficacy, they can, ultimately, also negatively affect feelings of success and enjoyment (Klimmt and Hartmann, 2006). Unfriendly verbal exchanges, such as trash-talking, can also be expected to increase the likelihood or intensity of aggressive behavior (Eastin, 2007). Despite its relevance for explaining aggressive behavior in general, frustration has been taken into account by only a few studies on the effects of digital games (e.g., Anderson and Carnagey, 2009; Schmierbach, 2010; Valadez and Ferguson, 2012). None of these studies, however, explicitly looked at frustration arising from the interaction with other players. A recent study by Shafer (2012) found that competition and unfavorable outcomes (i.e., losing) in multiplayer game modes can seriously reduce enjoyment and increase hostility. These results suggest that interactions with other players, and especially their outcomes, can indeed have strong effects on a player's emotional state, thoughts, and (immediate) behavior.

Aggression as Social Behavior

In studies on digital games and aggression, the most commonly used measure of aggressive behavior is the modified competitive reaction-time task (CRTT), originally published by Taylor (1967). In more recent versions of the test (e.g., Anderson and Dill, 2000), participants are told that they would play a reaction-time game on a computer against another participant (while actually everything is randomized and preset). Aggressive behavior is measured here by the intensity of a noise blast that the participants have to select as a punishment for a simulated opponent. While some authors testify for the construct validity of the CRTT (Anderson and Bushman, 1997; Anderson, Lindsay, and Bushman, 1999; Giancola and Zeichner, 1995), others have criticized the lack of standardization and convergent validity for the CRTT (Ferguson, 2011; Ferguson and Rueda, 2009; Tedeschi and Quigley, 1996). Most of the criticism the CRTT received can also be directed at the hot sauce paradigm (HSP) by Lieberman, Solomon, Greenberg, and McGregor (1999). In this test, participants are asked to add hot sauce to a soup (or another type of food) for a person who does not like spicy food. The amount of hot sauce chosen is used as a measure of aggression. Similar to the CRTT, the HSP has been used in various different ways and a thorough validation that scholars have called for (Ferguson and Rueda, 2009; Ritter and Eslea, 2005) has only just begun (Beier and Kutzner, 2012).

A shared problem with these tests is the absence of a real target for the aggressive behavior. In both the CRTT and HSP, the participants do not see the alleged targets of their aggression, and, hence, do not receive any direct feedback about their reaction. Berkowitz's (1989) advice on testing the frustration–aggression hypothesis is also true for media-effects research: Participants in laboratory studies should be provided with appropriate targets for their aggressive behavior. Aggressive behavior is always directed at something or somebody. The anonymous, invisible persons presented as targets in the CRTT and the HSP can hardly be deemed appropriate. As Dollard et al. (1939) suggested, the strongest aggressive reactions are most likely those directed toward the source of the experienced frustration. In the case of digital games, this would be the game itself, or human co-players, or opponents. The latter, again, emphasizes the need for multiplayer studies.

Another problem with these tests that reduces their (social) realism is that aggressive behavior is permitted or even explicitly encouraged by the design and the instructions. Although some versions of the modified CRTT provide the option of choosing a volume and duration of zero, the settings chosen by the simulated opponents are likely to function as provocations that evoke aggressive responses of retaliation. It is also not fully clear whether the tests really measure aggression, or other, possibly related, constructs such as *schadenfreude* (HSP) or the tendency to retaliate (CRTT). Results obtained with such tests—and especially their implications—have to be interpreted with caution, since the experimental situation makes the aggressive reactions shown more instrumental than hostile (participants are instructed to behave "aggressively"), and the aggressive behavior in these tests causes no physical harm and is not sanctioned (Ferguson and Rueda, 2009; Tedeschi and Quigley, 1996).

Where to Go From Here

The previous sections were meant to show that one major problem in research on digital games is the neglect of the social dimension of both gaming and aggression. To address this issue of a lack of social realism, there is a need for real multiplayer studies in this area. To begin with, games used in experimental research on aggression should be played the way they are typically played outside the lab. If a study uses a popular multiplayer FPS, participants should, ideally, play it in multiplayer modes against other human players and not against computer-controlled bots. The same is true for console sports games and all other games and genres that are played against human opponents for the most part. Studies with more than one player could not only help to increase the ecological validity, but also provide new possibilities for the measurement of aggression in experimental research. Additional participants or confederates who play with or against participants can be used as the target of aggression in the CRTT or the HSP. In addition, this would open up the option of having a real two-player version of the CRTT instead of a simulated interaction based on pre-defined patterns. Multiplayer studies also have the practical side effect of being able to gather data for multiple participants in one session.

Against the background of the growing popularity of multiplayer games and game modes, the application of the frustration–aggression hypothesis could be a fruitful approach for research on digital games (Eastin, 2007; Williams and Clippinger, 2002). In a study on the effects of technological advancement and violent content, Ivory and Kalyanaraman (2007) found frustration to be the only covariate that had an effect on their outcome measures of arousal, aggression, involvement, and presence. Accordingly, the authors suggest to include frustration as a control measure in future studies. Expanding on that idea, frustration can be treated as a dependent variable (i.e., as one outcome of a playing experience), an independent variable (e.g., as a cause of aggression), or as a mediator or moderator variable.

As these examples show, it is generally advisable to study the link between aggression and digital games with theoretical and methodological approaches that go beyond simple models of direct effects from one independent to one dependent variable. Especially the social context of the playing experience can be expected to be an important moderator variable. Hence, what applies to frustration is also valid for the interaction between players. Communication before, during, and after playing is likely to affect aggressive emotions, cognitions, and (re-)actions in both directions. Negative comments and insults might further increase aggression, while compliments or friendly small-talk could potentially ameliorate the effects of losing. On a comparative level, it would be interesting to see whether the effects of violent content, or winning and losing differ when a game is played alone, against a friend, or against a stranger. There is reason to believe that the effects of game content, mechanics, and social context are additive. Following this suggestion, the strongest effects on aggression could be expected for a highly competitive player who lost to a trash-talking stranger in a fast-paced, violent shooter game. In order to test these assumptions, future experimental studies on aggression and digital games should attempt to systematically vary features of the game and the social context, while rigorously controlling others. This would help to attribute any effects that are found to their actual causes. Multiplayer studies are an essential step in the process of increasing the social realism of experimental research on aggression. Instead of isolating violent content, players, and aggressive behavior, this would lead to a more holistic and ecologically valid understanding of the variables and processes involved in the complex relationship between the use of digital games and aggression.

References

Adachi, P. J. C., and Willoughby, T. (2011a). The effect of violent video games on aggression: Is it more than just the violence? *Aggression and Violent Behavior, 16*(1), 55–62.

Adachi, P. J. C., and Willoughby, T. (2011b). The effect of video game competition and violence on aggressive behavior: Which characteristic has the greatest influence? *Psychology of Violence, 1*(4), 259–274.

Anderson, C. A., and Bushman, B. J. (1997). External validity of "trivial" experiments: The case of laboratory aggression. *Review of General Psychology, 1*(1), 19–41.

Anderson, C. A., and Carnagey, N. L. (2009). Causal effects of violent sports video games on aggression: Is it competitiveness or violent content? *Journal of Experimental Social Psychology, 45*(4), 731–739.

Anderson, C. A., and Dill, K. E. (2000). Video games and aggressive thoughts, feelings, and behavior in the laboratory and in life. *Journal of Personality and Social Psychology, 78*(4), 772–790.

Anderson, C. A., Lindsay, J. J., and Bushman, B. J. (1999). Research in the psychological laboratory: Truth or triviality? *Current Directions in Psychological Science, 8*(1), 3–9.

Beier, R., and Kutzner, F. (2012). *Choose a juice! The effect of choice options and intention on aggression in a modified hot-sauce paradigm.* Paper presented at the 13th Annual Meeting of Society for Personality and Social Psychology, San Diego, CA.

Berkowitz, L. (1989). Frustration–aggression hypothesis: Examination and reformulation. *Psychological Bulletin, 106*(1), 59–73.

Bushman, B. J., Rothstein, H. R., and Anderson, C. A. (2010). Much ado about something: Violent video game effects and a school of red herring: Reply to Ferguson and Kilburn (2010). *Psychological Bulletin, 136*(2), 182–187.

Cicchirillo, V., and Chory-Assad, R. M. (2005). Effects of affective orientation and video game play on aggressive thoughts and behaviors. *Journal of Broadcasting and Electronic Media, 49*(4), 435–449.

de Kort, Y. A. W., and IJsselsteijn, W. A. (2008). People, places, and play: Player experience in a socio-spatial context. *Computers in Entertainment, 6*(2).

Dollard, J., Miller, N. E., Doob, L. W., Mowrer, O. H., and Sears, R. R. (1939). *Frustration and aggression.* New Haven, CT: Yale University Press.

Eastin, M. S. (2007). The influence of competitive and cooperative group game play on state hostility. *Human Communication Research, 33*(4), 450–466.

Ekman, I., Chanel, G., Järvelä, S., Kivikangas, J. M., Salminen, M., and Ravaja, N. (2012). Social interaction in games: Measuring physiological linkage and social presence. *Simulation and Gaming, 43*(3), 321–338.

Elson, M., Breuer, J., Van Looy, J., and Kneer, J. (2012). *Comparing apples and oranges? The effects of confounding factors in experimental research on digital games and aggression.* Paper presented at the 62nd Conference of the International Communication Association, Phoenix, AZ.

Entertainment Software Association. (2012). 2012 Sales, demographic and usage data: Essential facts about the computer and video game industry. Retrieved from http://www.theesa.com/facts/pdfs/ESA_EF_2012.pdf.

Ewoldsen, D. R., Eno, C. A., Okdie, B. M., Velez, J. A., Guadagno, R. E., and DeCoster, J. (2012). Effect of playing violent video games cooperatively or competitively on subsequent cooperative behavior. *Cyberpsychology, Behavior, and Social Networking, 15*(5), 277–80.

Ferguson, C. J. (2011). The wild west of assessment: Measuring aggression and violence in video games. In L. Annetta and S. C. Bronack (Eds.), *Serious educational game assessment* (pp. 43–56). Rotterdam: Sense.

Ferguson, C. J., and Kilburn, J. (2010). Much ado about nothing: The misestimation and overinterpretation of violent video game effects in Eastern and Western nations: Comment on Anderson et al. (2010). *Psychological Bulletin, 136*(2), 174–178.

Ferguson, C. J., and Rueda, S. M. (2009). Examining the validity of the modified Taylor competitive reaction time test of aggression. *Journal of Experimental Criminology, 5*(2), 121–137.

Gajadhar, B. J., de Kort, Y. A. W., and IJsselsteijn, W. A. (2008). Influence of social setting on player experience of digital games. Paper presented at the 26th Conference on Human Factors in Computing Systems, Florence, Italy.

Gentile, D. A. (2011). The multiple dimensions of video game effects. *Child Development Perspectives, 5*(2), 75–81.

Giancola, P. R., and Zeichner, A. (1995). Construct validity of a competitive reaction-time aggression paradigm. *Aggressive Behavior, 21*(3), 199–204.

Greitemeyer, T., Traut-Mattausch, E., and Osswald, S. (2012). How to ameliorate negative effects of violent video games on cooperation: Play it cooperatively in a team. *Computers in Human Behavior, 28*(4), 1465–1470.

Grimes, T., Anderson, J. A., and Bergen, L. A. (2008). *Media violence and aggression: Science and ideology.* Thousand Oaks, CA: Sage.

Ivory, J. D., and Kalyanaraman, S. (2007). The effects of technological advancement and violent content in video games on players' feelings of presence, involvement, physiological arousal, and aggression. *Journal of Communication, 57*(3), 532–555.

Klimmt, C., and Hartmann, T. (2006). Effectance, self-efficacy, and the motivation to play games. In P. Vorderer and J. Bryant (Eds.), *Playing video games: Motives, responses, and consequences* (pp. 153–168). Mahwah, NJ: Lawrence Erlbaum Associates.

Lieberman, J. D., Solomon, S., Greenberg, J., and McGregor, H. A. (1999). A hot new way to measure aggression: Hot sauce allocation. *Aggressive Behavior, 25*(5), 331–348.

Quandt, T., Scharkow, M., and Festl, R. (2010). Digitales Spielen als mediale Unterhaltung [Digital games as media entertainment]. *MediaPerspektiven, 11*, 515–522.

Ravaja, N., Saari, T., Turpeinen, M., Laarni, J., Salminen, M., and Kivikangas, J. M. (2005). Spatial presence and emotions during video game playing: Does it matter with whom you play? *Presence: Teleoperators and Virtual Environments*, 15(4), 381–392.

Ritter, D., and Eslea, M. (2005). Hot sauce, toy guns, and graffiti: A critical account of current laboratory aggression paradigms. *Aggressive Behavior*, 31(5), 407–419.

Schmierbach, M. (2010). "Killing spree": Exploring the connection between competitive game play and aggressive cognition. *Communication Research*, 37(2), 256–274.

Shafer, D. M. (2012). Causes of state hostility and enjoyment in player versus player and player versus environment video games. *Journal of Communication*, 62(4), 719–737.

Sherry, J. L. (2007). Violent video games and aggression: Why can't we find effects? In R. Preiss, B. Gayle, N. Burrell, M. Allen, and J. Bryant (Eds.), *Mass media effects research: Advances through meta-analysis* (pp. 245–262). Mahwah, NJ: Lawrence Erlbaum Associates.

Southwell, B. G., and Doyle, K. O. (2004). The good, the bad, or the ugly? A multi-level perspective on electronic game effects. *American Behavioral Scientist*, 48(4), 391–401.

Taylor, S. P. (1967). Aggressive behavior and physiological arousal as a function of provocation and the tendency to inhibit aggression. *Journal of Personality*, 35(2), 297–310.

Tedeschi, J. T., and Quigley, B. M. (1996). Limitations of laboratory paradigms for studying aggression. *Aggression and Violent Behavior*, 1(2), 163–177.

Valadez, J. J., and Ferguson, C. J. (2012). Just a game after all: Violent video game exposure and time spent playing effects on hostile feelings, depression, and visuospatial cognition. *Computers in Human Behavior*, 28(2), 608–616.

Velez, J. A., Mahood, C., Ewoldsen, D. R., and Moyer-Gusé, E. (in press). Ingroup versus outgroup conflict in the context of violent video game play: The effect of cooperation on increased helping and decreased aggression. *Communication Research*.

Ward, M. R. (2011). Video games and crime. *Contemporary Economic Policy*, 29(2), 261–273.

Williams, D. (2005). Bridging the methodological divide in game research. *Simulation and Gaming*, 36(4), 447–463.

Williams, R. B., and Clippinger, C. A. (2002). Aggression, competition and computer games: Computer and human opponents. *Computers in Human Behavior*, 18(5), 495–506.

Games Cited

Blizzard Entertainment (2004), *World of Warcraft*, Vivendi Activision Blizzard.

Rockstar North. (2002), *Grand Theft Auto: Vice City*. New York, NY: Rockstar Games.

Valve Corporation (2004), *Counter-Strike: Source*. Bellevue, WA: Valve Corporation.

20 Self-Discrepancy and MMORPGs

Testing the Moderating Effects of Avatar Identification and Pathological Gaming in *World of Warcraft*

Jan Van Looy, Cédric Courtois, and Melanie De Vocht

Introduction

In the past decade, the popularity of massively multiplayer online role-playing games (MMORPGs) has grown exponentially with *World of Warcraft* (WoW) (Blizzard Entertainment, 2004) as one of the leading titles (Williams, 2006). As with most MMORPGs, players first create a digital alter ego to engage in social game playing in an online multiplayer virtual world containing thousands of players concurrently. In the course of the game, players act and interact socially through these personal avatars that are chosen from a range of races and classes. An implicit goal of the game is to "level up" (increase the strength and abilities of) your character by collecting experience points and by acquiring rare and powerful items (Cole and Griffiths, 2007). This freedom to tailor and grow an avatar raises the question of whether players create their characters out of sheer fantasy or rather grasp the opportunity to carve out an idealized version of themselves to engage in multiplayer interaction and competition. In this article, we draw upon current theoretical insights (Klimmt, Hefner, and Vorderer, 2009) and previous empirical research regarding identification in digital games (Van Looy, Courtois, De Vocht, and De Marez, 2012). More specifically, we first explore the moderating effect of identifying with a game character on the degree of self-discrepancy. Second, we look into the effect of self-discrepancy on pathological gaming and analyze whether pathological gamers are more drawn toward the experience of reducing self-discrepancy than non-pathological gamers.

Identification and the Theory of Self-Discrepancy

Klimmt, Hefner, and Vorderer (2009) argue that in digital games, in contrast to traditional, non-interactive media, players do not merely observe the media environment, but are an active part of it. This facilitates an experiential merger of the player with their game avatar, which is referred to as a process of *monadic identification*. More specifically, this merger implies a temporary partial unification of a gamer's self-concept with the perceived attributes of the game protagonist.

According to Klimmt et al. (2009), the enjoyment of identification is rooted in the ability to experience a temporary reduction of self-discrepancy while playing a digital game. Self-Discrepancy Theory, which was developed by Higgins in the 1980s, is based upon the notion that individuals experience psychological distress when a psychological distance exists between their actual and their ideal self. Thus, it postulates that "we are motivated to reach a condition where our self-concept matches our personally relevant self-guides" (Higgins, 1987, p. 321). Digital games hold the potential to temporarily enable such a condition. This particularly holds up for game situations in which the avatar can be fully customized, as in MMORPGs such as *WoW*.

This idea has previously been explored empirically in Bessière, Seay, and Kiesler's (2007) groundbreaking ideal elf study. In their research, they gathered personality ratings of players' ideal self, actual self, and main *WoW* avatar. They found that for the personality traits of conscientiousness, extraversion, and neuroticism, the mean discrepancies between players' ideal self and the avatar are significantly smaller than those between the players' ideal and actual self. This implies that, for these traits, players perceive their *WoW* avatar as more ideal than their actual self. An obvious explanation for this would be that, in line with Klimmt et al.'s (2009) proposition, players use their avatar to reduce self-discrepancy while playing. The study fails to provide definitive evidence for this, however.

Whereas the relatively smaller distance between the avatar and ideal self indicates that the player sees their avatar as more ideal, it does not necessarily mean that the player meaningfully identifies with their avatar and that they use it to temporarily relieve self-discrepancy. In fact, there are several possible alternative explanations. First of all, players are able to choose from a wide variety of fantasy characters (e.g. wizards, elves, warriors) that all possess characteristics that to some extent can be deemed more ideal. Moreover, players may assemble an avatar with ideal characteristics to facilitate their game play rather than because they relate these characteristics to themselves. Consequently, a meaningful association, such as identification between *WoW* players and their avatars, is a prerequisite for supporting the self-discrepancy thesis. Hence, to test the self-discrepancy hypothesis further, we propose the following hypothesis:

H1: Players who identify more strongly will perceive their avatar as more ideal.

Pathological Gaming in MMORPGs

Several studies have indicated that playing MMORPGs consumes a considerable amount of time. For example, in a sample of over 5000 players, Yee (2006) found that almost 23 hours are spent playing per week. Even more remarkably, a small proportion of 8–9% play over 40 hours per week. Hsu, Wen, and Wu (2009) point out that the problematic use of MMORPGs by this small, yet substantial proportion of players has become an important issue for both policy makers and the research community. In their study, they explored factors explaining pathological use of MMORPGs. They identified personal factors (curiosity toward the game and acquisition of rewards), social factors (in-game group belonging and obligations toward this group), and the role-playing factor as significant predictors of pathological gaming. The last factor refers to the interconnection of a user with their role and the avatar through which the role is played. These results are in accordance with the findings of Ducheneaut, Yee, Nickell, and Moore (2006), who found peaks in playing time whenever a highly rewarding level was about to be reached. Moreover, the average playing time per level steeply increases throughout the game and the average playing time of players with avatars that have reached the top level significantly exceeds that of players with lower-level characters.

These findings indicate that the activity of advancing an avatar, making it as ideal as possible, requires a significant amount of time, and thus can be expected to be a factor in explaining pathological gaming. In fact, Bessière et al. (2007) found that WoW players with lower levels of psychological well-being (self-esteem and depression) rated their avatars as more ideal than those who reported higher scores. Moreover, research by Lemmens, Valkenburg, and Peter (2009) has revealed positive links between pathological gaming and loneliness and aggression, whereas social competence and life satisfaction are negatively associated. Furthermore, heavy online gamers reported higher levels of social anxiety and a lower quality of interpersonal relationships. Given these findings, we predict that players with high scores for pathological gaming perceive their avatars as more ideal than their actual selves. Therefore, we propose a second hypothesis:

H2:   Players who perceive their avatar as more ideal have a stronger tendency toward pathological gaming.

If evidence is found for this second hypothesis, the question arises as to whether the experience of a temporary reduction in self-discrepancy through gaming is a factor in explaining the process of pathological gaming. Perhaps players use their avatars to make up for their perceived shortcomings and to experience a more idealized self. However, as we have previously discussed, the assessment of self-discrepancy requires a direct measure of identification. Otherwise, other explanations cannot be ruled out, for example, that pathological *WoW* players are attracted by the game mechanics in which avatar advancement is an important factor. The increased investment in the avatar could then produce an idealized perception of this avatar without the player identifying with it, and thus without the mechanism of self-discrepancy reduction playing a role. Finally, previous research by Smahel, Blinka, and Ledabyl (2008) found a small correlation between ad hoc measures of identification and pathological gaming. Therefore, we propose the following hypothesis:

H3:   Players who see their avatar as more ideal and identify more strongly have a stronger tendency toward pathological gaming.

Methodology

Participants and Sampling Procedure

Between November 2009 and January 2010, *WoW* players were recruited via game-specific online forums and mailing lists to fill out an online survey. This led to a sample of 304 *WoW* players (84% male), with a mean age of 24.54 (SD = 7.36). On average, the respondents reported having played *WoW* for 15.33 hours (SD = 13.91) in the week preceding the completion of the survey. They also indicated that they had been a subscriber for over three years (M = 3.09, SD = 1.54).

Measures

Personality self. Personality was measured using the Big Five Inventory (BFI) (John and Srivastava, 1999), whereby the items were preceded by "I see myself as someone who is ... ," for example, "I see myself as someone who is inventive": conscientiousness (a = .81), agreeableness (a = .75), neuroticism (a = .78), openness (a = .80), and extraversion (a = .72).

Personality ideal self. To measure ideal self, the BFI was used, whereby the items were preceded by "If I could choose the way I was in real life, ideally I would like to be someone who ... ": conscientiousness (a = .77), agreeableness (a = .74), neuroticism (a = .80), openness (a = .79), and extraversion (a = .76).

Personality avatar. Character personality was measured by the BFI with each item being preceded by "I see my main character in *World of Warcraft* as someone who ... ": conscientiousness (a = .77), agreeableness (a = .84), neuroticism (a = .78), openness (a = .82), and extraversion (a = .79).

Avatar identification. Avatar identification was measured using Van Looy and colleagues' (2012) validated 18-item Avatar Identification Scale, which is a multifaceted subscale of their Player Identification Scale (a = .96), incorporating elements of wishful identification, perceived similarity, and embodied presence. A median split was used to divide the results into high and low avatar identification (Mdn = 2.14).

Pathological gaming. Pathological gaming was measured using Lemmens et al.'s (2009) validated 21-item Game Addiction Scale. The scale was slightly adapted, changing each "game" reference into *WoW* (a = .90). A median split was used to divide the results into high and low pathological gaming (Mdn = 2.00).

First, the respondents completed the BFI of the actual self, followed by the Avatar Identification Scale, the BFI of the ideal self, the pathological gaming scale, and finally the BFI of the avatar. As such, identification and pathological gaming also function as filler tasks to avoid recall effects of the repeated implementation of the BFI.

Results

To determine whether the players' main characters were rated as more ideal than their actual selves, we computed discrepancies by subtracting personality scores of 'Self' and 'Avatar' from the ideal self. Next, paired t-tests were performed for each discrepancy pair. Significant results were found for conscientiousness (paired $t(301) = 9.47$, $p < .001$), neuroticism (paired $t(301) = -9.82$, $p < .001$), openness (paired $t(301) = -8.57$, $p < .001$), and extraversion (paired $t(301) = 5.34$, $p < .001$). Except for openness, players rated their character as more ideal than their actual self on all personality dimensions. These results mirror the findings of Bessière et al. (2007), who explained the opposite effect of openness by pointing to the fact that "characters in *WoW* typically do not enact a creative role; they act at the behest of the player" (p. 532).

To test for the three proposed hypotheses, analysis of variance was used, employing the discrepancy scores as within-subjects variables. For each analysis, assumptions of ANOVA were checked. All assumptions, including equality of variances, are met, except for mild violations of univariate normality. ANOVA is known to be robust for non-normality, however, especially when applied to larger samples (Hair, Black, Babin, Anderson, and Tatham, 2006).

H1:   Players who identify more strongly will perceive their avatar as more ideal.

To test for this hypothesis, avatar identification was employed as a between-subjects variable and its effect on the difference in distance between actual and ideal self to avatar evaluated. Interaction effects are found with all discrepancy pairs that were found to be significant by Bessière et al. (2007): conscientiousness ($F(1, 302) = 4.01$, $p < .05$), neuroticism ($F(1, 302) = 7.83$, $p < .005$), openness ($F(1, 302) = 14.67$, $p < .001$), and extraversion ($F(1, 302) = 4.05$, $p < .05$). Figure 20.1 depicts the marginal means' plots of these four significant interactions. For each interaction, players with high avatar identification have a character that is closer to their ideal self than those who score low for avatar identification. Except for openness, the ideal

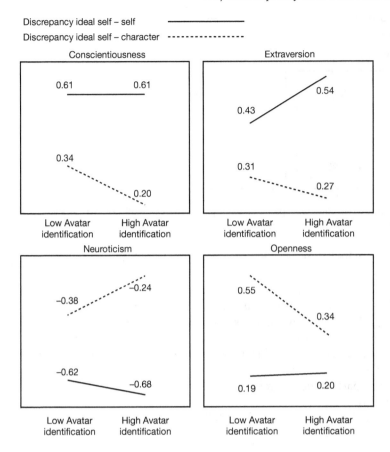

Figure 20.1 Marginal Means' Plots of Discrepancy*Identification.

self–avatar discrepancies are consistently smaller than the ideal self–actual self discrepancies. Thus, evidence is found for our first hypothesis.

H2: Players who perceive their avatar as more ideal have a stronger tendency toward pathological gaming.

To test this hypothesis, pathological gaming was used as a between-subjects variable and its effect on the difference in distance between actual and ideal self to avatar evaluated. Significant interaction effects were found for neuroticism ($F(1, 302) = 7.75$, $p < .05$), openness ($F(1, 302) = 6.96$, $p < .05$), and extraversion ($F(1, 302) = 4.85$, $p < .05$). Except for openness, the interactions depicted in Figure 20.2 show a pattern of a larger ideal self–actual self discrepancy, while the ideal self–avatar discrepancy is smaller.

H3: Players who see their avatar as more ideal and identify more strongly have a stronger tendency toward pathological gaming.

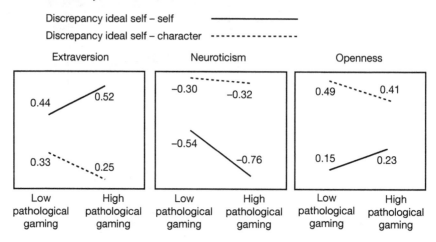

Figure 20.2 Marginal Means' Plots of Discrepancy*Pathological Gaming.

For this hypothesis, a three-way, mixed-model ANOVA was computed, combining the within-subjects discrepancy factor and between-subjects identification and pathological gaming factors. The results show a significant difference for neuroticism, whereas interaction effects are found for discrepancy*identification ($F(1, 300) = 4.22$, $p < .05$) and discrepancy*pathological gaming ($F(1, 300) = 4.06$, $p < .05$; Figure 20.3a). For openness, only the discrepancy*identification proves to be significant ($F(1, 300) = 10.28$, $p < .001$; Figure 20.3b). In the case of extraversion, the combination of interaction effects is not significant.

Discussion

Based on a substantially larger sample, the results of our research present an exact replication of Bessière and colleagues' (2007) findings. This indicates that WoW players perceive their avatars as more ideal than their actual selves on a majority of personality dimensions. As we have noted above, despite claims to the contrary, these findings do not provide final evidence for the self-discrepancy hypothesis, however. The fact that a player's avatar is more similar to their ideal than to their actual self does not necessarily mean that they use their avatar to alleviate psychological tension. In order to investigate this further, it was necessary to rule out the possibility that players do not meaningfully associate themselves with their avatar, and just see it as more ideal because the game depicts a more ideal world, or because creating a more ideal avatar is necessary for being successful in the game. This was explored by comparing discrepancies with avatar identification measurements, which showed that players who identify more strongly with their avatar perceive it as more ideal compared to their actual self. This shows that WoW players maintain a meaningful relationship with their

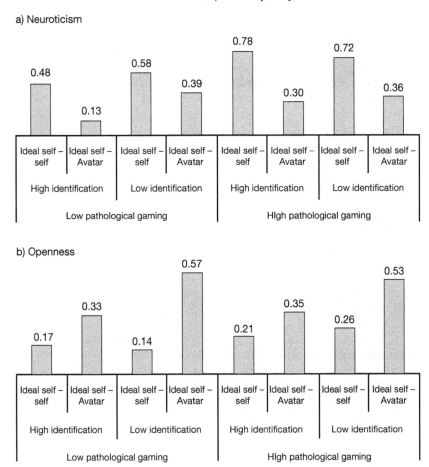

Figure 20.3 Marginal Means' Graphs of Discrepancy*Identification*Pathological
        Gaming.

avatar, which in turn provides further evidence for the self-discrepancy
hypothesis in relation to playing MMORPGs.

   Based on the idea that pathological gaming could be associated with
a stronger desire to reduce self-discrepancy and thus alleviate psychological tension, we compared pathological gaming scores and discrepancies. Results indicate that there is little difference in discrepancies between
players who report a high tendency toward pathological behavior versus
those who report a low one. Only for neuroticism did we find simultaneous
interactions between discrepancy, on the one hand, and identification and
pathological gaming on the other. This could imply that *WoW* players with
a tendency toward pathological gaming create and identify with avatars
that are more emotionally stable than their actual selves. In other words,
they create an avatar that is more ideal on the dimension of neuroticism

and then identify with it more strongly. For all other personality traits, however, there are no significant differences in discrepancies between more and less pathological gamers. This suggests that pathological gaming is not primarily motivated by the desire to alleviate psychological distress by reducing self-discrepancy. Rather, it is likely that self-discrepancy reduction is more generally related to game enjoyment. Further research is needed to verify this claim and to explore other aspects of game experience in relation to pathological gaming.

References

Bessière, K., Seay, A. F., and Kiesler, S. (2007). The ideal elf: Identity exploration in *World of Warcraft. CyberPsychology and Behavior, 10*(4), 530–535.

Cole, H., and Griffiths, M. D. (2007). Social interactions in massively multiplayer online role-playing gamers. *CyberPsychology and Behavior, 10*(4), 575–83.

Ducheneaut, N., Yee, N., Nickell, E., and Moore, R. J. (2006). Building an MMO with mass appeal. *Games and Culture, 1*(4), 281–317.

Hair, J. F., Black, W. C., Babin, B., Anderson, R. E., and Tatham, R. L. (2006). *Multivariate data analysis.* Upper Saddle River, NJ: Prentice Hall.

Higgins, E. T. (1987). Self-discrepancy: A theory relating self and affect. *Psychological Review, 94*(3), 319–40.

Hsu, S. H., Wen, M.-H., and Wu, M.-C. (2009). Exploring user experiences as predictors of MMORPG addiction. *Computers and Education, 53*(3), 990–999.

John, O. P., and Srivastava, S. (1999). The Big Five trait taxonomy: History, measurement, and theoretical perspectives. In L. A. Pervin and O. P. John (Eds.), *Handbook of personality: Theory and research* (Vol. 2, pp. 102–138). New York City, NY: Guilford Press.

Klimmt, C., Hefner, D., and Vorderer, P. (2009). The video game experience as "true" identification: A theory of enjoyable alterations of players' self-perception. *Communication Theory, 19*(4), 351–373.

Lemmens, J. S., Valkenburg, P. M., and Peter, J. (2009). Development and validation of a game addiction scale for adolescents. *Media Psychology, 12*(1), 77–95.

Smahel, D., Blinka, L., and Ledabyl, O. (2008). Playing MMORPGs: Connections between addiction and identifying with a character. *Cyberpsychology, Behavior, and Social Networking, 11*(6), 715–718.

Van Looy, J., Courtois, C., De Vocht, M., and De Marez, L. (2012). Player identification in online games: Validation of a scale for measuring identification in MMOGs. *Media Psychology, 15*(2), 197–225.

Williams, D. (2006). From tree house to barracks: The social life of guilds in *World of Warcraft. Games and Culture, 1*(4), 338–361.

Yee, N. (2006). The demographics, motivations, and derived experiences of users of massively multi-user online graphical environments. *Presence: Teleoperators and Virtual Environments, 15*(3), 309–329.

Games Cited

Blizzard Entertainment (2004), *World of Warcraft*, Vivendi Activision Blizzard.

Index

For Product Safety Concerns and Information please contact our EU
representative GPSR@taylorandfrancis.com
Taylor & Francis Verlag GmbH, Kaufingerstraße 24, 80331 München, Germany